Reasons or Results!

From Zero to Hero In 15 Months.

Making The Most of Shaklee's Fast-Track, First Year in Business, $100,000.00 Bonus Programs.

To Turn Your Financial Situation Around,

Permanently.

The Psychology of

Mastering Your Home-Based Business.

by

Sovereign M. Valentine

https://sovereign-valentine.mykajabi.com

Text Copyright© 2018
All Rights Reserved

About The Author

Sovereign Valentine has invested the last decades studying, experimenting and applying general business principles, as well as perfecting the business building principles contained herein.

After witnessing first-hand, the affects of growing up in poverty and the long-term consequences of living in poverty and avoidance of personal development, in his own family and circle of influence, as well as breaking free from poverty consciousness to surpass his upbringing, Sov has gone on to become one of the most accomplished personal trainers, speakers, published authors, entrepreneurs and helicopter pilots in the America.

Over the last few decades, Sov has studied the differences between the "haves" and "have-nots" narrowing the differences down to a few points and has dedicated a part of his life to teaching others how to build the lifestyle of their dreams, utilizing network-marketing as a means.

Through an intensive and extensive trial-and-error process and by consistently doing what was purported to work he found what really *does* work. He then goes about teaching the results with each new business partner and customer.

In Sov's words, *"There is no longer a mystery to earning massive income working from home. The science and art have been figured out...there are variations, but the fundamentals are time-tested and proven to work...it simply comes down to doing the correct things at the correct times and refining as you go...awareness! If you think you're an exception, you're not!"*

Sovereign's entrepreneurial spirit is rooted in a successful, fishing-worm business he started at age nine. With a sincere desire to be able to have his business with him wherever he goes using a laptop and cell phone, Sovereign's business experience is great and varied. From a combination of formal training and experimenting, he developed a system that absolutely works.

Sovereign says, *"If you aren't expanding your business partnerships and the resulting income by 1-2 people per month and taking full advantage of Shaklee's Fast-Track™ Program ($100,000.00 first-*

year bonuses) something is off. A properly designed and executed business plan will facilitate these numbers, (as well as improve overall lifestyle and time-freedom quotient) unless you aren't following through correctly."

In 1992, he became a Licensed Massage Therapist in Washington State. In 1994 he began doing small, informal nutrition presentations so that others could experience the profound impact that real nutrition has on the body. In 1996, he became a foot and hand reflexologist as well as an energetic healing master. In 1997, he became a certified hypno-therapist. In 1998, he began training others in hypnotherapy and in 1999 he became the first person ever at The Gabriel Institute to be certified as a Master Clinical Hypnotherapist. He went on to become certified in Fitness Training, Fitness Therapy, Sports Conditioning, Endurance Conditioning, a Specialist in Performance Nutrition as well as a Youth Conditioning Specialist, Golf Fitness Instructor, Senior Fitness Specialist and Community Emergency Response Team Member and Emergency First Responder.

Sovereign's thorough understanding of the systems of the body and how they relate to one another is reflected in his ability to fine tune his client's training and nutritional regimes for extra-ordinary *Results!* His published works include:

• *Reasons or Results* Performance Nutrition Training

• *Weighting To Wait,*

• *B.N.B.B.s:* 50-ish Reasons Why Actively and Purposely Withholding the B.N.B.B.s Is A Really Bad Idea,

• If I Were Her Trainer,

• Be Your Own Personal Trainer,

• *Reasons or Results!* Life-long Fat-loss System & 8 Week Fat-loss Journal

Available on Amazon and Amazon Kindle.

Foreword

The home-based business industry has evolved a lot over the last 60-years, but especially so in the last ten years, with all the advancements in the web and systems to utilize the internet to reach and meet people your local business could never even conceive of before this. There's never been a better, less expensive, easier and more efficient time to build a home-based business, than right now. These next ten years are going to make a lot of small-town Joe and Mary's multi-millionaires. There's never been a time like this before. All the pieces are in place for a person to go from unhappy, under-payed, over-worked and dis-satisfied employee to part-time, home-based, millionaire entrepreneur, who sets their own work schedule and has as much time with their family as they choose.

Generally speaking, the amount of information on small business and homebased business can be overwhelming…it's simply crazy. But accurate, success-based, proven strategies which produce healthy, consistent results that can be maintained over the long haul are simple in nature, but challenging to isolate, for the average citizen. Truthfully, the new person trying to figure out what is real, what is fake and what needs to be paid attention to is very challenging. More often than not, your average person who wants to work from home will try a few things, which prove fruitless, before finding the real deal which produces significant income and free time on 10-15 hours per week. That's because there are just as many people trying to rip people off with scams as there are genuine people-helping business people…*but we are here.* It just takes a little research and discovery to tell the real deal from the scams.

Much of what's out there is simply about spewing marketing and advertising claims for getting rich quick *(e.g. "…buy this, get rich")* and then saying, *"Here, give me your credit card number and I'll make you rich."*

The truth is that after having started and run all kinds of businesses for the last four decades, I definitely know real value versus scams & frauds, when I see them. Unfortunately, for newbies anxiously wanting to escape their own version of the rat-race, sometimes their enthusiasm overrides their ability to reason and months down the road, ten-of-thousands-of-dollars later, we hear back from people who didn't heed our advice and say, *"You were right…it wasn't what they said it was."*

The truth of the matter, after applying this kind of information for more than four decades, on both myself and with my clients, is that there truly are good business models designed to improve the lives of everyone they touch. This business model makes earning a good income and having time-freedom, faster and with less effort and cost, but they are few and far between and the general public simply can't tell a good business model from one that takes your money today and is out of business tomorrow. That's a part of what I do...assure quality and success through home-based, business development to show you how to increase income, increase your time-freedom and unplug from the rat-race, *whatever that means to you.*

In the United States right now, 42% of Americans will retire with less the ten-thousand dollars in their retirement account (3/7/18). At the same time, home-based business is providing secondary income, primary income and the freedom to come-and-go, as you please, to people willing to invest 10-15 hours, *per week,* doing specific actions, which we teach. Actions that are fun, simple and often exciting to do. The difference between having zero money at retirement or being strapped before the end of each month or having more than enough money, is based on what you do with those 10-15 per week, that most people use watching TV. The actions you apply or choose to skip are influenced by how you think about and perceive situations and experiences.

My experiences (having grown up in poverty, digging through the garbage for food, having lived in a Ford pickup for a time and other similar experiences) have shown that anyone with their mental and emotional capacity intact, has complete control to turn their financial situation around within a year and set themselves up to consistently improve their financial situation, from year to year.

When we hear the words scam, fraud and scheme, what they're talking about is either a program that insists you can get rich by giving someone your money or that you can get rich by doing nothing...neither of which work, but to make a scammer wealthy. Any time a program says, *"Just give us your money and you'll get rich,"* it most likely a scam. With any real business, if there isn't an investment of sweat-equity, skill-development, and personal-development along the way, the program simply isn't sustainable or ecological for all parties involved...as you develop as a person, so does your income and free-time. It's just that with so much information, most people don't know how to sort the chaff from the gold and the evaluation process can take a really long time if you don't have a way to narrow the field, based on others' successes. In my case, I was a natural business-person from a very early age, so what seems like work to many was fun and entertaining to me, resulting in a massive knowledge base of fact from fiction.

With home-based business, if the 10-15 hours per week you invest expanding your business isn't focused properly, on a focused set of proven actions, one person may earn no income while the other earns a hundred thousand dollars their first year…it comes down to being very specific in how you invest that 10-15 hours per week your first year…doing the money-making activities and skipping 'busy' work.

Secondly, any program that says you just give them your money and the business runs itself is a scam, playing off people's emotional hopes and fears. Having a home-based business requires 10-15 hours of solid, strategic action, *per week*. No one is going to take care of your money any better than you do, and giving it to someone else to get rich is recipe for disaster. *I have an acquaintance, In Seattle, who gave his $900,000.00 inheritance to a fraudster.*

The true secret is finding a business-trainer who has your overall health and wellness in mind (not just short-term results) [your financial health should be improving and you should be freeing-up your time, as the months roll by] and a business-trainer who has enough expertise to not only point you toward an amazingly effective program, but one who knows how to adjust the program to you for most effectiveness. Most business-trainers can run a business, but being able to teach others to do the same thing over and over is a unique skill-set, a lot of people lack. For most, if someone isn't producing the kind of income they want, the business trainer doesn't know what to tweak and adjust to get them back on track to reach their weekly, monthly and annual income goals. Helping you adjust course to get more efficiency out of your home-based business, so if its growth hits a plateau you know what to do next (accountability). This is the second part of what I do.

One of the things that makes me so effective as a home-based business trainer is that I've been doing this so long, that when a business partner isn't getting the results they want, I can narrow it down to which part of what they are doing or not doing to determine exactly what has to happen to take their success to the next levels.

There simply aren't any mysteries to earning a great income and having free time working from home anymore. A majority of entrepreneurs don't stick with the industry long enough to find out what *they didn't know...I have* and I teach others like you and me to apply it and succeed, especially during your first year in business, during the launch of your home-based business.

This book lays it out there in simple, concise form and states the basics from many angles and viewpoints, so there's no question what your focus and activity must be, as you progress through this book.

When you apply these tactics in the way I show you here, you and those who know you will likely be blown away by the *Results!* you are getting. This book is for people who want the results that speak for themselves…anyone can get some results in the short-run…almost every small business will produce some kind of results, in the short-run, but most get-rich-quick schemes, collapse within a short time and erode the confidence of would-be successes by undermining their faith in the potential to become financially successful by helping others gain value. We all have the neighbor, aunt or uncle who, *"…tried one of those things and it didn't work."*

In 2018, we have narrowed down the factors, which help assure home-based business success and which ones assure disappointment and lack of progress.

Any wealth-building program should leave you feeling lighter, clearer, relaxed, rejuvenated and more vital than when you started, as well as free of doubt that you can provide for you and your family's needs.

Apply this information and I predict you'll be so glad you did.

Read this book now; start turning your life around today and I look forward to seeing and hearing how good you feel about the *Results!* you are getting!

Once you've read the material, if you're the type to recognize what is real and not just the next fad and if you're willing to commit and follow through until the end, *I'll be there with you every step of your success.*

*The training guidelines contained herein, require in-person training, webinar training, zoom meeting trainings, phone trainings, text message exchanges, phone conversations and emails depending on your location relative to Sovereign Valentine's location.

**We successfully and effectively work with people in all 50 states and many countries outside the U.S., included as part of our team training.

Acknowledgments

I have not attempted to cite in the text all the authorities and sources in the preparation of this book. To do so would require more space than is available, in order to effectively serve you who apply this information. The list would include departments of the federal government, libraries, industrial institutions, web sources and many individuals as well as my personal experiences and those of my clients since the late 80's.

Inspiration was contributed by all those before me who succeeded as best they could with the information they had at the time, as well as all those after me who will improve upon this information to make the lives of others better. This book is a culmination of hundreds of books I read, thousands of hours of experimentation and thousands of hours of observing the why, how and where of my own and others' successes and failures.

A Word From The Author

Do it!

This is a *do it* book…read it, learn it…*do it.*

If you don't apply it as instructed, you'll miss out.

Reading this book provides the information, but is not the same as doing and does not imply any improvement in income, lifestyle or free-time without diligent application, mentoring, in-person and/or live training and feedback.

I work to make a living, but I live to see you get *Results!*

Sovereign Michael Valentine,

Montana, March 2018.

Disclaimer

This book is designed to provide information about the subject matter covered. It is produced and sold with the understanding that the publisher and author are not engaged in rendering certified or licensed financial advice, tax advice nor advice on the stock market. If you need immediate legal or financial help, go get it. It is not the purpose of this manual to reprint all the information that is otherwise available from other financial or business professionals, but to complement, amplify and supplement other texts. *From Zero To Hero In 15 Months,* is neither a cure-all nor a quick-fix for poor financial habits or money management problems. Anyone who commits to personal accountability for their financial wellness must expect to re-direct some time, energy and money without any guarantee for specific benefits within a fixed time frame. *This text is about how to most effectively invest 10-15 hours per week to improve your income from your home-based business and free up your time, over the course of one year. If you aren't willing to correctly invest 10-15 hours per week for at least one year, your expectations are not realistic.*

Every effort has been made to make this book as complete and accurate as possible. However, there may be mistakes both typographical and in content. Therefore, this book should be used as a general guide and not as the ultimate source of entrepreneurial practices.

The purpose of this book is to educate and inform. The very best results will come from participation. Neither the publisher nor the author shall have responsibility to any person or entity with respect to any loss or damage caused by or alleged to be caused directly or indirectly by the information contained in this book.

This book is not meant to replace the advice or treatments prescribed by your tax professional, attorney or accountant, but rather to accompany their advice. It is not meant to encourage financial advice, by the layperson. It is meant to inform you and open you to time-management choices that are available to those who seek a broader knowledge of how to increase their income working from home with a legitimate, legal, time-proven business model. Any application of the ideas set forth in this book is at the applicant's discretion and sole risk. If you are under a financial advisor's care for any reason, she or he can advise you *about information she or he is familiar with and which she or he has personally experienced.*

The information in this book is neither diagnostic nor prescriptive. It is informational only.

Neither the publisher nor the author of this book makes any warranties, expressed or implied regarding the currency, completeness or scientific accuracy or validity of this information nor does it warrant the fitness of the information for any particular purpose. It is intended to provide helpful and informative material on the subjects addressed in the publication. It is shared with the understanding that the publisher and author are not engaged in rendering specific, professional, financial-management, accounting nor tax services in this book. The publisher and author specifically disclaim all responsibility for any liability, loss or risk, personal or otherwise which is incurred as a consequence, directly or indirectly, from the use and application of any of the contents of this book. If you do not agree to this, you may return the book to the publisher at any time.

This book describes a legitimate, legal business model with 60-years success, which requires some time, energy and money to earn success. This is not an investment program nor a pyramid scheme nor a Ponzi scheme, where money is earned through interest paid on a savings or investment account, of any kid. Nor is it a get-rich-quick scheme.

Definitions:

There's a ton of terms that are unique to network-marketing, but you don't need to know all the terms to be successful, either as a Business-Expander or customer. I tend to not use the terms any more than I have to, to simplify communication. Where there aren't other terms, the following terms are used which are exclusive to network-marketing.

Sponsor: The person who helped you join and often the person responsible for your training. Your sponsor is a resource in order to be able to refer you to the information you need in varying circumstances, until you have a track record of answering the common questions, for your own business partners and customers. If your sponsor drops out or quits then you move up to the person they joined with.

Distributor, Business Builder and **Business-Expander** and are used interchangeably: This describes someone who is actively investing 10-15 hour per week locating business partners and customers who want, value and can afford to purchase their own products. Distributor is the original/old school name for a person pursuing their business launch, dating back to the 1960's, building and expansion of their own business. I personally coined the term "Business-Expander(s)" to emphasize the actions, processes and ease of "expanding" the customer base and locating qualified business partners, as opposed to "building", which to me implies struggle. Expansion, I think, implies an easy, simple-to-learn, do-able, copiable process that is easy to understand.

PayPlan: Description of the all the ways you get paid. There are at least seven (7) different forms/bonuses of pay in Shaklee. The way I look at it is, there's more money available then any other form of employment or business, as long as you consistently expand your business and you'll know about each one as you earn it. If you have specific questions I'm happy to answer them and there are brochures as well as videos available that go into more detail than most people want, describing the payplan. If I don't know the answer, I'll get them for you. The point is, you don't need to have an understanding of all the ways you get paid to receive those payments or expand you own business. I've seen people who turn-off potential business partners who go into such great detail about the payplan that no one can follow or keep up and assume they have to be an expert in the payplan in order to make money. Not true. Shaklee has a 60-year track record of monthly bonuses being paid, on time, to all their business-expanders. Shaklee's payplan pays the most of any company on the low end (for the beginner), the middle and on the high end for Masters. Many companies gyp (rip off) their new people or their advanced people, by skimming profits off. Shaklee pays it to the field with multiple forms of payments, rewards and incentives. With the *FastTrack*™ Program, a person can earn up to $100,000.00 their first 15 months in Shaklee, by meeting all the business partner and customer/product point requirements, which equates to about 15 business partners and 150 customers, in 15 and months (do-able), not to mention the trip and cars.

Rank: Descriptive name/label that corresponds to the number of business partners you have and/or the number of customers you have, all which related to how much product volume (product points) you average each month.

PV: Product volume or product points. How you bonus checks are calculated. Each product has a point equivalent. Add them up each month and that tells you how much PV you have.

Company Car: At each level of business development or rank, the Business-Expander qualifies for a higher level quality of car, every two years.

Free Travel: There are basically three different types of travel with Shaklee from more local/regional events and conventions to the annual, international, all-expense trips to exotic locations around the world.

There are a few other terms, but you don't need to know them to get started. As time goes on, little-by-little you'll learn more terms as you need to.

In order to appeal to the largest audience. *KEEP IT SIMPLE!*

Talk in terms people who aren't in the business can understand!

If people don't know what you're talking about, you risk losing them before they even begin!

You can do this.

It's simple.

It's do-able.

We'll be there with you every step of the way!

Big Picture

Scott Hamilton, Olympic Figure Skater says, *"We all have dreams and aspirations of doing something with our lives, whether its recognition or whatever and this is more about something that we give to ourselves...it's this aspiration, it's to do something with our skill-sets, with our natural calling, whatever that is and take it as far as you possibly can....this is to get people off the bench and to get them to, "...here are the steps that you can do better than you've ever done before." "...my first national event I came in dead-last...it was a habit...at nationals I would come in 9th...9th was my number...my first nationals, I fell five times in front of seventeen-thousand people....epic-fail. Honestly, I think it was everything...the way I trained, it was my intention, it was my focus, it was my everything...what I learned from that, it was so humiliating and painful,...kinda' dig deep...I'm made of better stuff than this and its up to me to change the way I train and change the way I can be and change the way that I live my life...I was a dedicated-loser for a long time. The last competition my mom saw me skate in I came in 9th, again...that was supposed to be my last competition...the idea was that I was this horrible loser that couldn't figure it out."*

"My mom died, and I went for a walk...I asked myself, "What are you going to do with all this grief?" What came to me was to honor her in everything I do. And so, it was a real wake-up call to show up with intention, show up with kinda' a long-play in mind... I don't care how well I do this year as long as its better than last year and the next and the next and the next and pretty soon, I was in a position where I never lost...winning the gold medal changed everything...it was like, "Here's how...and it was like...its pretty simple...find your passion, find your purpose."... "...it all begins with, "Wouldn't it be great...if I.."".

"I'll never play in the NBA, there's a lot of things I'm never going to do, but I found something my body, my mind, my heart can get behind...it was up to me to show up every day and just get better at it."

"Pick your wins. Winning can be just showing up that day, winning can be the first one in and the last one off. So, you build, like every win is

a brick in a foundation every little win you can accomplish furthers you to a bigger win and once you hit that bigger win, its like, "Whoa! There's all these other things I can now do, that I never thought of doing before! Honestly it changes EVERYTHING. We don't need to shield ourselves from failure because failure is honestly information, that's all it is. I fell an estimated 41,600 times, in my skating career, on the low end. I got up 41,600 times and that builds a muscle in our psyches, where yay, we fail, we get up, we fail, we get up. We're criticized, criticism can be debilitating...but then you think, "...is it fact? Or it opinion?" If its pinion, just delete, who cares?"

Scott won Gold at the 1981 World Figure Skating Championships, 1982 and 1983 U.S. and World Championships and won the gold medal at the 1984 World Championships and Winter Olympics. Scott's new book, *Finish First* is available now.

"It's always impossible, until its done."

Nelson Mandala

Table of Contents

About The Author	3
Foreword	5
Acknowledgements	10
A Word From The Author	11
Disclaimer	12
Definitions	15
Big Picture	18
Chapter One: A Business Of Products	25
Chapter Two: The Money Isn't In Convincing	47
Chapter Three: I Don't Concern Myself	57
Chapter Four: Be Clear On Leadership	64
Chapter Five: Other's Opinion Of You	77
Chapter Six: Projection	90
Chapter Seven: Attrition, Refining, And Screening	97
Chapter Eight: Average And Do-ers	117
Chapter Nine: Focus On The "Process"	125
Chapter Ten: Confidence And Competence	138
Chapter Eleven: Goal Setting	152
Chapter Twelve: Get 10 More	176
Chapter Thirteen: Clear About Your Goals	183
Chapter Fourteen: Unabashed And Unapologetic	187
Chapter Fifteen: Would You Eat Just One *M&Ms*™?	195
Chapter Sixteen: Momentum And Urgency	201

Chapter Seventeen: Let The Paint Dry	205
Chapter Eighteen: Be Respectful	216
Chapter Nineteen: You Cannot Possibly Run Out	227
Chapter Twenty: You Don't Need To Know It All, Part 1	235
Chapter Twenty-One: You Don't Need To Know It All, Part 2	246
Chapter Twenty-Two: Big Picture View	248
Chapter Twenty-Three: Becoming A Master	250
Chapter Twenty-Four: Rejection-Immune Master Locator	253
Chapter Twenty-Five: Making Full Use Of The Mind	257
Chapter Twenty-Six: What Do You Get	272
Chapter Twenty-Seven: Bakers Dozen; *The 13th Worm*	273
Final Words	277
Pre-Application Questionnaire	280
Appendix	282

The themes *repeated* throughout this book

are done so purposely and with great intent,

for the people who need them most,

and are by no stretch of the imagination a coincidence.

"Tell me something…imagine one year from now, all your financial concerns and basic needs are taken care of…you have no money worries…you don't have to work, or find a job per se. What are some things you have always dreamed of having or experiencing, unrelated to work of any kind, that you would buy, acquire or do?"

Chapter One

A Business *of* Products, *For* Products, *Because* of Products
...As A Result of Consistent and Wide-Ranging, Personal Product Usage

From being an entrepreneur, since I was a little kid, I can tell you that the most important part of being in business for yourself, regardless of what kind of business, is telling people [who you are (so they can locate you) and making sure they know what you do], offer or how you serve others (what you do). Also, technically defined as, *marketing:* telling people who you are; and what you do, so that they can [distinguish you from everyone and everything else out there]. This means getting people's attention, who [want or value what you offer] (locating the people who want what you have is relevant to them*/important to them) and have the means to acquire what you offer, for themselves. *grammatical brackets and parenthesis added to emphasis ultra-important words and ideas.*

**Relevant means importance *(to them/the customer).* In other words, if you offer dietary supplements, you're looking for people who want the benefits of your supplements (more energy, feel better, fat-loss, etc.)...*not people who don't want the benefits supplements or do not afford your products.* If you offer skin care products, you're looking for people who want the benefits of skin care products (youthfulness, look younger, firmness, etc.) and who choose to afford your products.

This means connecting what you offer with the people who want what you offer. That's the fastest way to build a customer base. The way(s) you do this are creative and endless, limited only by your imagination and persistence. When I refer to people being able to affording what you offer, I'm talking about people who [want what you offer]. The reason being that people do what they want...not what they need to do, should do or what is necessarily in their best interest. People do what they want to do. They put their money toward what they *want* to spend it on.

Lack of customer base simply means you haven't connected with people (who want the benefits of what you offer) to tell them who you are and what you do. Any time you want to grow your business, you simply find more people who want the benefits of what you offer…in other words, solve a problem that they know they have or help them discover a need they didn't know they had. In other words, a person might not know the reason they are frequently sick is because their immune system needs some nutritional support. Or, they might not know that there are skin care products that work way better than what they have been using. So, being in business for yourself means making people aware of who you are and how you can help them and create more value for them. Who you are and what you do.

The truth is that there are people out there looking for a person like you to help them. What separates the two of you is time and space. What connects you is getting your message out there, using the internet in ways that catches and holds their attention, until the two of you meet.

This topic being the first chapter is no mistake, either in placement within the book nor priority.

Beliefs:

Over the decades, I've found a big part of what separates the "haves" from the "have-nots" is each person's beliefs about what they are capable of, what they deserve, what they are worth, what they can have or cannot have and so on. Beliefs are funny phenomena because people can believe whatever they want and there is an area of the brain known as the Reticular Activating System (RAS), which the main purpose of this area of the brain is to prove that whatever a person chooses to believe, the RAS collects information, in that person's environment, to validate that those "beliefs" are real, for that person.

So, the person living in the trailer-court who believes life is hard and difficult and money is hard to get will be proven correct. The person who lives across the street who believes the world is full of opportunity, that there's plenty of money (you just have to choose a way to go about earning it) and that there's no limit to what you can achieve will also be proven correct. The person, like me who grew up in a trailer-court, but believes the world is their oyster and they will surpass their living conditions to go on to live an exceptional and abundant life, will also be proven correct. One study has shown that 90% of what a person believes they are capable of, isn't true, but rather simple ideas they were taught were true, and reinforced by those around them.

What permits or enables a person to go beyond their current situations/limitations is self-improvement, having good mentors and growing/expanding, as a person.

Selflessness-lose yourself to help others:

A common characteristic among successful people (people who see their income improving and their lifestyle improving) is the ability to make a living, while helping others improve their own life. This is how you make sustainable income and build a life full of purpose.

Without the products Dr. Shaklee invented and started taking and sharing with his patients in 1915, there likely would be no Shaklee Corporation. Through trial-and-error, attempting to get the medical community to look at the evidence of how much better people felt and looked when taking his *Vitalized Minerals* (the forerunner to *VitaLea*™ multi-vitamin (1915)), Dr. Shaklee and his brothers eventually founded Shaklee Corporation, in 1956...more than a 60-year track record of success!

Within a few months, Dr. Shaklee and his brothers had a hundred customers, via word-of-mouth. Dr. Shaklee wanted a company that would improve the lives of everyone it touched and rather than skimming off all the profits for himself, like the majority or companies do. He decided to utilize a business model where anyone who spread the word about Shaklee would get a big cut of the pie, based on the number of people who join and utilize the products...see and hear the pattern there?

Secondly, the legal definition of a valid network-marketing business/MLM company is one that offers *real products* that offer *real value* to those who purchase and use the products...meaning the customers/users lives are improved by consuming the products and services. Historically, companies that got in a lot of legal problems, were the ones who pretended to have products or pretended to have value-based products, but essentially charged people to join with the promise of making a bunch of money, simply for paying a fee and getting other people to pay a fee and get other people....also known as pyramid-schemes or

Ponzi-Schemes...meaning, money is going in and *some* people get paid *at first*, but eventually, when the number of people joining slows down, the system collapses and most people lose all the money they put in without any recourse. I personally know people who have been involved in pyramid and Ponzi schemes and they wanted me to put money in...which I did not, mainly on principle. I watched them get boxes of cash in the mail, but I still wouldn't get involved.

Ponzis and pyramids still exist today, and people join them all the time, thinking they'll make a bunch of money for no investment of energy/sweat equity. I've been offered to join them by family and friends and I politely declined and watched the drama play out. There are a lot of people who would rather risk losing all their money with the story they might get rich quick than invest their time and energy in a legitimate business...you'll encounter them on your own journey. There's no shortage of people who want to cut corners. The moral of the story is that people will avoid work, responsibility and accountability even if it means risking losing all their money...in other words, there's a high percentage of the population who won't invest in learning about legitimate forms of business, nor managing their own money, but who will dump their money in something illegal that is most assuredly going to collapse, before everyone gets their money back out. Someone will get hurt. It's one phenomena of human nature you'll likely encounter on your journey of launching, expanding and maintaining your own Shaklee business. There's always people who would rather run a scam than a legitimate, value-based business and seemingly no shortage of people who fantasize about earning millions of dollars, by creating no value to society. Ponzi's and pyramids are illegal, in every form in the United States, but they are around all the time, and easy to recognize.

There are some people who are so uncomfortable with financial wealth that they seem compelled to get rid of their money as quickly as possible, rather than learning to manage it. As I spoke about earlier, Rod inherited close to a million dollars and a con man convinced him it would be easier to give him the money and he would invest it in real estate for him. Rod inherited the money, was warned about the con artist, but he signed nine-hundred-thousand dollars over to the con man anyway and the con man began living high-on-the-hog. The last I heard the FBI was tracking him down, but he had already spent all the money.

Tonight, on the local news here in Montana, I heard that each year in the U.S. senior-citizens lose eighteen-billion dollars to scams letters they receive in the mail, promising a big check if they first submit a check for a processing fee, which is often nearly as much as the check promised to them, so its rational that there's a lot of skepticism out there for people who don't do their due diligence to find out what is real and what is a scam. That's something to keep in mind when talking to prospective business partners.

Another reason why the products in legitimate companies have to be value-based is that a lot of the pyramid-scheme type companies (that have come and gone) would "front-load" new distributors...in other words, require members to buy an amount of product, often thousands of dollars-worth, that they could neither sell, get rid of or use up. The term front-loading coincidentally mirrors what those new distributors experienced...the front of their garage loaded-up with products that they couldn't use or find anyone to buy...often, because they were way more expensive than what the very same products or equivalents would cost if you bought them at the store near your house (there's about a thousand of these types of companies that come and go each year, in the U.S. alone). These kinds of scams are notorious and every skeptic has a story of their aunt or uncle who has a garage full of product that they can't get rid of from a company that no longer exists. You'll hear these stories too, and it's good to know ahead of time that this happened to a lot of people in the 1970's and 1980's before the Federal Trade Commission started creating and enforcing laws about Ponzi and pyramid schemes, to protect the public. Eventually the Federal Trade Commission defined what makes a company real or a pyramid scheme or Ponzi scam, but most of the public hasn't taken the time to learn for themselves the differences.

Those kinds of scam companies open up, claim to be the next big thing, flood the market with their products and either can't keep up with demand, meaning their distribution channels suck or they start skimming money and stop paying the distributors and a couple people get chased out of town, after financially gutting the company. It happens over and over again because people don't do their due diligence to check a company out, and by the time the Federal Trade Commission or Attorney General's Office catches up with them, they're already out of business. It's similar to hiring a contractor to work on your house. I can't even count the number of people I've heard who pay a contractor to remodel their house or build their house only to have the contractor take the money and run. It happens with car mechanics too. It happens, in every industry and largely the burden is carried by legitimate companies that stick around and provide valid products, services and value for customers.

When I was researching helicopter flight schools, the same thing happened. In the Western U.S. there was a company named Silver State Helicopters that was doing a lot of open houses to recruit students into their helicopter school. They claimed to have a lot of helicopters to use at all their different schools, in different states. They had schools all over and held their open houses, offered financing and the ability to process military G.I. Bill school tuition.

I attended one of the open houses, near Everett, Washington, at Paine Field, with my girlfriend at the time. After a few minutes at the open house, I said, *"This is a scam...something is seriously off here."* We left. I had an uneasy feeling that the school was trying to pull-the-wool over potential students' eyes. To me, what they claimed in their ads and website didn't match up at all, in person. They did have a couple helicopters at the open house, but if they really had as many as they said, they would have had more...or at least I thought so.

Within months, online chatter and feedback was showing that students weren't able to get their flight time because there weren't enough helicopters. The owner had a few helicopters, but just moved them around for each open house...classic bait-and-switch. The school would essentially get students to sign over fifty-thousand dollars in tuition, then move onto signing the next student, and so on.

Ultimately, the owner took millions-of-dollars, of tuition and disappeared...the last I heard he was living in Nevada. The students were out their G.I. Bill money and no licenses or certifications to show for it with no hope of a refund. They would show up for class and the doors were locked, with no notice of why.

Every industry has hucksters who attempt to scam the public.

Another school I looked at was in a small town in Montana. Everything was legit about the school, it's just that it was so remote and the population is so low that even if I got my pilot's license there, there weren't enough students there to accumulate hours of flight to be able to earn commercial certification. With helicopters, it takes about 200 hours of instruction time to become a commercial pilot, but then you need another 800-1,000 hours of instructing others or flying tours or a combination, where you have enough hours to be insured by other commercial or federal agencies. The hours of the student or flight tour client counts toward your hours as a commercial pilot for experience. Both the student and pilot benefit from the flight time.

I looked at a school in Hawaii that seemed great and thorough and legit online, but when I went there in-person, they seemed to resent I showed up, as though I was the other pilots' competition…there wasn't a friendly, warm feeling like I wanted or expected.

Eventually, I found a school that had plenty of helicopters (largest fleet in the U.S.), the pilots seem to want to train other students, I could go at my own pace and they would not only prepare me for my commercial license, they were a very busy tour company and school, so that once I have my commercial license I could fly enough customers and students to get my 1,000 hours and move onto a commercial position of my liking and they had been in business for 25 years. In other words, not all helicopter schools are the same!

Now, how would it be if someone wanted to train others to fly helicopters if they didn't know how to fly helicopters themselves…if they weren't using the services or products of the helicopter industry?...How would that work?

Shaklee is a business of products. Using, experiencing and sharing/helping others get going on the products. If you don't use the products, experiment with them, find your favorites and tell others about them you're out of business, before you even start. That's the way any legitimate business is…if you don't understand the products, have firsthand experience with them you won't be able to establish a customer-base. First of all, that's what makes Shaklee a legal business entity. It's not the person you joined with responsibility to coax you into using products. Be curious about how the products will affect you…be curious about all the benefits you'll experience that you've been wanting, but didn't even know were possible. Shaklee products are unlike all others, both in concept and quality…but you can't tell until you use them consistently…put the supplements in your body, the skin-care products on your skin, use the household products around your house! Simple! It's your sponsor's job/priority (the person you joined with) to keep expanding their own business…to lead by example. It's not their job to tell you to use more products.

"No one is going to force success on you; you will find it to the degree you seek it." Tracy Monteforte

Secondly, if you use the products, consistently experiment with a wide range of the 300 or so products Shaklee has, find your favorites and keep track of all the ways your life is improved from the products, you'll be much less likely to be affected by others' negativity or skepticism, that you may be exposed to, during your launch and expanding journey. Critics and skeptics are everywhere in every industry. In other words, the products are so good for the body that once you use them consistently, your belief in your ability to build a business becomes unshakable. People who use the nutrition, skin care, personal care and household products have no doubt in their mind why and how *Shaklee is so different.*

As for the people who don't, well, I chalk that up as people who didn't believe they could succeed, from the beginning and how they unconsciously made sure that it didn't work out for them, was to refuse to use the products…they don't believe in their ability to be successful at anything. Without the products there is no business and if people don't find out with products they like the most (by using them and experimenting with them), then they're never really "in business"…they haven't invested in their own business! I've personally been using Shaklee since September 1993 and I was trying to find a Shaklee distributor since 1974, prior to that. At the time I'm writing this, I currently use a wide variety of different nutrition products…I love them.

One of the things you are expected to do in an ongoing basis is to try a wider variety of products…experiment with them. Find the ones you like the most. For decades there has been the concept of *"How changing brands can change your life".* The statistics show that people who are the most serious, focused and dedicated to building a large business organization use the greatest number of Shaklee products…they simply change brands, and whether all at once or gradually as they run out of store-bought products, convert their home over to buying from their own business. Again, makes sense, right? Why would anyone else buy products from you if you don't even buy and use your own products. In doing so, you build a base of Product Volume (PV), which is the basis of your own monthly bonus checks. The more you now about the products, the wider variety of people you can help, by offering solutions to problems they haven't found solutions to. *Makes sense, huh!*

It's an understatement to say that Shaklee products are very unique...*there's nothing that comes even close to them on the market*...you'll find this out in your own experiences.

Your responsibility:

It's your responsibility to get a starter package (a place to start), a selection of products that between you and the person who helped you join and the programs and information available from filling out your own the *HealthPrint*™ survey and from within the product catalog itself, pick out some products you will use to start developing experiences with the products, especially your first month, based on needs you have or problems you want help with. If you don't like the products (which I would find impossible, if you actually used them), then this isn't the business for you. If you're serious about building an organization, you'll need unshakable belief to put consistent effort into your business, not to mention a high energy level and that comes from daily use of the products. Generally, the more products a person uses, the faster and larger their group develops. How fast do you want your business to grow? In other words, the wider your experience base with the products, the higher your belief and the more momentum you gain in developing your group. Using the products isn't the only thing it takes to build your organization, but I'll cover that more in later chapters and go into detail. Using the products and experimenting [with the entire line] is the basis of your success.

There won't be anyone telling you to use products as time goes on. The person you joined with gets an email each time you place and order, as you will with your customers. From this information you can glean who is serious about building a solid base of personal experiences with the products and who isn't. The people who build highly profitable businesses are naturally curious and naturally look for ways to integrate the products into their life...they look for places to fit the products in...by doing so they have personal experiences with the products and they essentially become a product of the products. If you aren't placing orders for your personal use, you can't expect to build a business or experience benefits. You probably already know that each product has "Point-Values" (PV) attached to them, so the higher your points, the more your bonus check grows. That's one of about seven different ways you get paid in Shaklee. By using the products, you tend to think like a problem-solver and naturally learn to ask people to, *"... tell me more,"* about whatever problem they are having and politely offer to introduce them to some products that will help them feel better...that's the big-picture, general idea of how you develop a customer base, in any business. It's just that in Shaklee, a higher percentage of money goes to the people doing the work. There is some skill, etiquette and refinement involved in the process of expanding your customer-base, but nothing that every other Shaklee distributor hasn't learned in the last 60-years of Shaklee being in business.

Copy/model experts:

In 1991 I started attending massage school, in Seattle Washington at the Brian Utting School of Massage. At that time, it was the foremost school for clinical massage and preparing students to pass their state board exam, for a license as a health care provider in Washington State. In 1991-1992, this was a 700+ hour class that took place over twelve months. I was in school for three months, before I even told those closest to me about it. The reason being that I know those closest to us tend to try to talk us out of what we want to do, focus on the negative, focus on why it could never work, what all the problems are and so on. When I began attending massage school, I had never received a massage before. I knew I wanted to work with athletes and help people heal faster, but I had no experience with massage other than what I read from a book I bought at a local book store. But, like a lot of things, reading about it and actually learning a trade first-hand, from professionals in the field are two completely different things. I knew from prior experiences how much others can influence my choice to do something that I really wanted to do. I think it's true that if you want to do something and you're serious about it, don't go talking about to just anyone willy-nilly (protect your dreams)...people think that if you open up a topic that [they have permission to talk you *out of it*]. Unfortunately, even more people think that if they're talking about something [they are an expert on the topic]. Secondly, if you want to learn and master a topic, learn how to "do" it from people who are currently active and successful in that particular field or endeavor. Things change so fast nowadays, that what one person experienced a year ago isn't necessarily what your experience will be today...*especially if they didn't master the endeavor.*

Today, people tend to equate having some experience or "starting" something, without becoming successful at it as more important than following through and mastering it, *by injecting their opinion.* Everyone has a right to their opinion, but most opinions are based on half-effort versus all out, first-hand success, rather than facts. The reason being that most experts in a field are so busy doing what they are good at, that they don't have time to talk about it, unless they find someone truly committed to learning it themselves...remember, talking is not doing and talking is easier than doing...so, people talk like they're experts when they really don't have any first-hand experience...so, consider the source of others' opinions and know that many people are so afraid of their own failure that they unconsciously attempt to prevent others from taking risks and investing in their own dream and goals.

Stack the odds in your favor:

A good strategy is to make a commitment to yourself that you won't participate in idle chit-chat about *your decision* to build your Shaklee business, until you are properly trained, by the people you joined with. Speaking enthusiastically about the products and benefits of Shaklee are ultimately important down the road, as they are in any marketing or business-building vocation, but fair-warning, more people drop out of network-marketing their first week, as result of negativity from unnecessary, idle chit-chat from their casual circle of friends and family than people who become ultimately successful, because the decision to enroll, join, sign up and so forth does not imply you have the conversational skillset to defend your choice with those you would suppose would be the most supportive of your decision.

About 9 out of 10 people are surprised by the lack of morale-support they get from people around them for the decision to start their own business, regardless of the type of business, even though 69% of new small businesses are home-based businesses. In fact, there are almost **28 million small businesses** in the US and over 22 million are self-employed, with no additional payroll or employees (these are called non-employers). Approximately **543,000 new businesses** *get started* **each month!**

The type of person who sees the most success in the shortest period of time are the ones who make the decision to do so and don't discuss the decision itself with anyone else…the decision is already made, *by them*. In fact, the common factor for improving the quality of life and getting more out of life, comes down to the solid decision to do so. If casual acquaintances, family, friends, co-workers, etc., sense indecision, (even at an unconscious level), insecurity, lack of commitment or unsureness, most of the time they will attempt to talk you out of your decision. Hence, a definitive decision does not include casual chit-chat regarding the decision, itself.

A serious business person makes a decision, takes appropriate actions and then adjusts their course as they proceed to get the result they want from their business. A person who isn't decisive, but rather wishy-washy and hesitant are opening themselves up to being talked out of what they want to do. If you open up a conversation with idle chit-chat, you're inherently, but inadvertently inviting them to talk you out *the decision,* to do the business. REMEMBER: IF you talk about your business at all, its to do two things: 1) Tell people who you are, e.g. *("Hi, I'm Sov.")* and 2) Tell people what you do *("I help people lose weight.")*.

Any and all conversations from that point are built on the foundation of who you are and what you do…*not whether or not you're going to do it* or whether it's the right decision *for you.*

If you haven't joined yet, you're in the decision mode. Once you join, you're in the [business expansion mode], from that point forward. A "Business-Expander" and that's how you should look at yourself. A Business-Expander.

Get trained properly by watching others demonstrate proper form:

Until you have a success of gaining at least 10 customers, you really aren't prepared to respond adequately to people whom you think will support you, but who actually are so insecure that they can't be morally supportive in spirit or word. If you don't heed this warning, you may very well become a statistical drop out…if you choose to open yourself up to mass negativity, before you have adequate, first-hand experience and success at establishing your own customer-base, there's nothing your mentor/coach can do to help you with those people. If you randomly talk to people before you're trained, it's unlikely you'll be able to gain the where-with-all to regain focus and expand your business correctly. Most people aren't prepared for being talked out of or discouraged from their goals and dreams. The hesitancy that comes from lack of training (confidence and competence) comes across as hesitancy "about" your decision to expand your own business, but people interpret it as hesitancy as to whether you're going to build your business, or not. If you open up the conversation, you have invited to be talked out of your decision. I can't even count how many times I've seen people aspiring to improve their lives, their income level and quality of life, but then they open up idle chit-chat and allow others to talk them out of their dreams, over a cup of coffee. Sad. Years down the road, once they look back and reflect on what happened, they realize that had they been solid in their decision and simply focused on getting trained properly, they would have been living a whole different life a year from the launch of their business.

What's it take to succeed?

You have to have personal and professional success with the products before you can survive the potential onslaught of comments that insist the business model doesn't work…even though Shaklee has been in business for over 60-years and distributes hundreds of millions of dollars-worth of product each year and millions-of-dollars-worth of monthly bonus checks, every month. People who lean on negativity or have a negativity-bias don't care about the facts. And it goes that way with *every industry*. When I was in massage school, people I told about massage school insisted massage was only used for prostitution and couldn't be convinced otherwise. I even had people who said that once I was more "experienced", I wouldn't be as uptight about professionalism. When I went to hypnosis school, people insisted hypnosis was the work of the devil. But, you know what? *Hint, hint*…no matter what industry I was in and no matter how many people gave their unsolicited negative opinions, and no matter how misinformed or misconstrued the publics' opinion, I never have had any trouble finding clients or customers, in any of those fields. The point being that no matter what field you're in, you can find the people who want to pay you for your time, products, services [if you're willing to ignore the people who aren't your potential customers]. Then, from your satisfied customers (the ones who heed your suggestions) come referrals to more customers.

Hint, hint, I've even fine-tuned this process with my potential Shaklee supplement customers by bringing up the "idea" of nutrition. People who are so malnourished that nutrition doesn't make any sense to them, or they mainly intend to argue, debate or negate the need for dietary supplements never earn my offer...I don't permit that negativity in my circle and screen it out before it has a chance to rear its head. If people are sincere but irritable, I simply refer them to one of my books on Amazon where they can get the full story, without me needing to be exposed to negativity. I've eliminated the phenomena of rejection. If they're still interested, I offer a free consultation to anyone who purchases and reads one of my books. The qualifier is that they read the whole book before the consultation and this effectively screens out the people who intend to use it as a platform for debate.

My stance is, *"Here's who I am, here's what I offer...if you want to be shown exactly what to do to feel better, I'm happy to help."* I've been a personal trainer for 30 years, so I know what I'm capable of, I know where my expertise is, in the market-place and I know what are profitable habits...convincing people who don't believe in nutrition to use the best supplements money can buy, is outside my job description and pay scale...there's simply too many people looking for praying for what I offer than I don't have the time to convince people to believe differently, for their own good. There's already more business than I can keep up with myself...hence, finding and training new business partners to help with all the business, who are friendly, open-minded, positive and looking forward to a bright future is a better use of my time than trying to convince people who don't want the benefits I offer. Makes sense, huh!

Consider the source of "opinions":

If you were going to learn to fly helicopters, become a doctor or become a lawyer or a plumber, would you ask people in your area of expertise and interest or do you ask people who don't know anything about the trade you're interested in? If you really wanted to be a doctor, would you let people talk you out of it? If you wanted to be a plumber would you let others talk you out of it, just because you're familiar with them? Would you let a doctor train you to be a plumber? If you wanted to be a doctor, would you get trained by a plumber? Shaklee is the same way, in that it's requires a very specific skill-set. Some people are naturally good at the skill-set...sometimes they bring the skill-set from other arenas. Some people refine their skill-set after joining Shaklee, during the business-expansion mode of their business. Some require building the skills from the ground up, by "modeling" the "successful" behaviors and habits of the person they joined with.

It doesn't matter if you grew up with the particular skill-set network-marketing requires or you learn by modeling and copying the person you joined with, anyone *can* be successful in Shaklee. The basic requirement is knowing exactly, in great detail, what it is you want to get out of your business (your vision), then go to work, monitor the results you get or lack of results you initially get and then refine and fine-tune your approaches until you're in a habitual-routine, which enables consistent and predictable results…meaning, e.g. for every 10 people you talk to, one will be interested in looking at some more information, or something like this. Meaning, for an average amount of energy invested, you get an average return on your investment. As time goes on, that number might be four or five out of every 10, as it is for every business, a.k.a. market-share.

"Shhh, it's a secret."

No matter what the business or endeavor, no one gets a 100% return on their time and energy investment, *in the beginning*. But, if you stick with it and see it through, build a group of purposefully trained business-expanders and customers, you'll get more than you invested. Baseball players don't hit a homerun every time. Basketball players don't slam dunk or hit three-pointers every time. Football players don't get a touch down on every play. Golfers don't get a hole-in-one every time. Nothing works this way. BUT, the athletes who stand out have something in common…they all started out as a beginner who didn't know anything, but they consistently worked harder and smarter to refine their skills day after day, until exceptional performance is their average behavior.

In business, I've never heard of anyone succeeding every time. Have you? Is there anyone who succeeds at anything, every time? The idea is to learn the fundamentals correctly, develop a routine you can live with, monitor the results (to make sure it works) and then do it consistently enough to build the momentum, so that with each little success, your confidence and competence improves, which carries over to the next opportunity…the more confident you are, the more competent you become and the more competent you are, the more confident you become. The more confident you are, the higher your energy and the more relaxed you are with the process and in turn the easier the process becomes…again, you become a living example of the lifestyle you're promoting. Success becomes more success and its based in getting products for yourself, getting some to provide samples to people, in-person (don't send out samples, necessarily), and expanding your base of experiences with the products.

Sometimes new business-expanders are so excited about all the new opportunities they can't imagine that anyone wouldn't want to be involved. This came as a shock to me, too. Truth be told, and I'll cover this in greater detail in later chapters, but you could have the last drink of water on Earth and some people would turn you down. You could have a medicine that would save a person's life and they'll refuse to accept it. You can have nutrition products that will certainly make a person feel better, look better and prolong their quality of life and they'll behave as if you have ulterior motives. People will ask you specifically for help, then refuse your suggestions (there's an adjective for this, I won't share, here)…physicians experience this day-in and day-out, as long as they are in practice. Physicians have at least 20 years of education, often more, and people go to see them every day and don't take their suggestions. "Knowing" stuff doesn't equate to a higher income or improved lifestyle, nor a guarantee of success every time.

As a personal trainer, with 30 years professional experience and ten different certifications, I know, as well as any personal trainer, that people will talk for an hour about how they want to lose weight, write a check for five-thousand dollars for personal training and then not show up for their personal training sessions…eventually showing up to complain about how the personal training, *"…isn't working"*.

This is a phenomena of human nature, that is an extensive study in itself…far outside the scope of our work in Shaklee. Knowing the facts, nuances and tendencies of human nature can help prepare you for the truth and prevent shock when people exhibit such behaviors, but ultimately, we're looking for people who are [ready for better things in life, *right now…today]*. And that can be one of the hardest, most difficult concepts to clear up in your head, as a beginning Business-Expander. One of the things that makes this business different is that we use the products, become a product of the products, lead by example by demonstrating what we expect and help the people we can, *today. What matters most to success is what's doing today.*

Weekly, monthly, quarterly and annual bonus checks (your income) are dependent on the work you did leading up to last month. If our time isn't productive in the present, then the checks next month won't be up to snuff…how you help assure your income increases is by helping others get started. If we spend time convincing, persuading or being attached to which people join, then momentum generally comes to a halt when a person we expected to appreciate what we offer declines or doesn't follow through or simply won't return a call…*a defeatist mindset*…(doing what doesn't work and then complaining it didn't work!). That happened in everything from business to education, to clubs and organizations. It happens everywhere. But, the bright side is that it doesn't need to affect you reaching all your financial and lifestyle goals.

Think of it this way, if you attempt to drag a person to get started, you'll end up dragging them any time their motivation lags or things didn't go how they preferred…you inadvertently given them the wrong impression. And if you are spending your time dragging people, you'll use at least four times the energy that you would to simply train self-motivated people as well as miss out on the self-motivated, self-driven people who will duplicate themselves. You'll know which category of people you're working with, by how you feel when you've been around them. Self-motivated, self-driven visionaries leave people feeling empowered and energized…*clean, clear and refreshed feeling*…it's like an internal compass…a sense of healthy energy.

People who lack drive, motivation and clarity of vision or even confusion and conflicted leave people feeling tired and drained…it takes energy to be around them…mainly because any emotional-energy you put into them doesn't get used to create "more" of anything, but rather to co-miserate about what isn't going right, what's wrong with their life, how they don't have enough money, how they lack energy, who did them wrong, who let them down, who disappointed them and on and on…all of which you have solutions for, but like all change, it has to come from within the person themselves…a desire for something different, a desire to have more time-freedom, greater income, better health and so on combined with a willingness to do something different to get different outcomes!

Truth be told, there's a percentage of the population who wants and values what you offer, but that means investing time in locating and training the people who want what you offer, do what you do and repeat the process. Anything less, you'll be spinning you wheels, getting frustrated and wondering, *"What's off?"*…this is a sign about where and how you're investing your energy. Essentially, this is a business of using the products, locating the people who want a better life, training them to use the products and locating the people who want the same kinds of things…that's it. Very simple. It's been that way for more than 60-years!

This is not to say at all, divorcing your friends and family! Love them and pray for them! This *is* to say that during your working hours (those hours you said, from the beginning that you could invest creating additional income, each week)…those 10-15 hours are used to sort through the people who initially show interest and find the ones who will take your example *and run with it, while you continue to expand your own business.*

When you help people join who are naturally motivated, self-driven and inspiring to others, they'll likely bring in people of the same caliber. When things don't go as well as they hoped, they pull themselves up by the bootstraps, get their head back in the game and rise above the clouds of drama with renewed creativity…that's what high-achievers and successful people in any field do.

Think of it this way, statistically you get a certain amount of emotional-energy and time each day. The point of network-marketing is to duplicate effective and efficient "systems". If you try to do someone a favor by doing the work *for* them, they perceive that's how you build a business and they go about attempting to drag other people across the finish line…the system breaks down and ends right there because it's too much of an energy consumer…no return on the investment…it's not sustainable. AND, anyone can change their outlook on life at any time and become a self-motivated, self-driven person. It's up to them to get clear about what they want, are willing to work for (the way you are) and would prefer to have rather than wasting their energy on recycling how they feel about what they don't like about life…it's just that it's *their choice!* Their decision! No amount of convincing, persuading or fact-throwing will change a person's current situation, (remember the RAS screens for information that supports beliefs, even when the beliefs are not based on fact!), when they are bent on focusing on the negative or focusing on what didn't go well in the past…it's an inside job…people change themselves when they want to and decide to.

You don't gain any kind of wealth by going into debt and emotional-energy is no different. Because it can take 15-48 months to get your business built to the level you envision (depending how you use your time and how many people you talk to each week), investing emotionally in people who don't invest in their own welfare is a certain strategy for depletion and deficit and emotional bankruptcy…you can't afford the luxury of investing your positivity, in negativity.

Psychology experts have defined what's known as the six-stages of behavioral change. Essentially, it's a map that shows the six basic stages people go through to change their behavior to get different outcomes in life…different living conditions. The first step is a decision to change. It doesn't matter if its health related, career, relationship or recreation. In order to get a different result, you have to do different behaviors, habits and thought processes to improve your life…this comes as news to many people. Many people who aren't happy with their lives are attempting to improve their lives using the same strategy that got them where they didn't like being! -Attempting to stay the same, but get a different outcome!

Whether a person is going to a doctor for help, a therapist, or attempting to stop smoking or start exercising the person has to do the first step, which is to "decide" to change. With the clear, definitive decision their actions won't change and neither will their life.

The six stages go like this: precontemplation, contemplation, preparation for action, action, maintenance and termination (reaching the goal).

Before a person decides to change, they are in "pre-contemplation". At this stage a person may or may not be aware they have a problem and/or have no thought of changing in order to get a different result in life…often they think life "happens to them", or on accident, versus how much they can influence the outcomes they experience in life...essentially, they are dis-empowered by wasting energy and experience a phenomena referred to as "learned-helplessness", where they believe that no matter what they do, nothing will improve. These people often believe that success is luck, outside their control and haven't connected that a lot of success is the result of different habits. This describes a lot of my family and circle of influence, where I grew up, in the trailer-court.

From precontemplation to contemplation, the individual begins thinking about changing a certain behavior, to get a different outcome. Once a person realizes they have some influence, they begin to think about possibilities and entertain new ways of proceeding. They begin to realize there is a difference in daily habits between people who enjoy their lives and look forward to their future versus people who are chronically depressed, negative and blaming the world for their situations.

During preparation, the individual begins his plans for change, and during the action stage the individual begins to exhibit new behavior consistently. It's not uncommon that people think that because they have an idea that they have a "good idea" or that their thoughts are real. Critical thinking, or the ability to think about your own thoughts and analyze them is a higher level of functioning. One of the qualities considered unique to humans is the ability to think about their own thoughts, versus having thoughts and believing they are real regardless how irrational they are. This process is referred to as sentience: *the ability to think about your own thoughts.* A percentage of the population believes that if they have a thought and speak it aloud, that makes it real. They think if they keep repeating the idea that it will make it more real. How to know if a strategy is valid/real or not is to put it into action and monitor whether it brings the intended results or not. Often, doing the same thing over and over but expecting a different result is described as a definition of insanity. But, people still do it. They aren't happy with the results they're getting, but they keep doing what isn't working...often, they even attempt to get others to join in!

An individual finally enters the maintenance stage once they exhibit the new behavior consistently for over six months. Termination refers to having reached the goal.

To understand this human phenomena more thoroughly, you can Google: "Transtheoretical" or "stages of change model", but it's not necessary to grasp the main points of this book.

The whole point is that you don't have any control over how a person receives your message, how they interpret your message or even if they get what you're talking about…the point is you're simply the messenger…share the message…Dr. Shaklee referred to this as, *"…seeing the people"*. The business-expanders who make the process look effortless, eloquent and simple live by this model…they know its their job to share the message and be unattached to who joins them. That way they aren't wasting energy on people who aren't ready, aren't looking or aren't interested! Neither are they taking energy away from those who are ready, are looking and are interested!

Just keep a friendship bridge built, if possible, stay in touch and whenever their priorities change they know where to find you. At that time, if they're willing to do what you do, the success is there for them, too. More than likely, as you continue to use the products, you'll look so much different, they'll ask you why you look so much better…*get it now?* Touching base every few months is plenty.

What most new business-expanders don't realize is that there are so many people who are looking for a person like you, who offers what you have, that to spend time with people who don't want or value what you offer is a complete waste of time…you don't get your time back, If someone doesn't value what you have, move on! *Fast!*

Once you tell or share or expose a person to the primary benefits of what you're offering, in a focused, direct way, say "More energy" for nutrition, "More money" for the business, "Younger looking skin" for the skin care, etc., etc., then it's up to them to come to you. They don't forget what you offered. If they don't respond, keep moving until you locate the people who are looking for what you're offering…stay in motion…*move fast.*

Case example:

Years ago, a single mother, who was barely scraping by on $300 per month, as a waitress, found a card on the ground beside her car. The card read something like *"Golden Opportunity"*. The mom contacted the person on the card and partnered with them, launching her own home-based business with the intent to supplement her income.

By watching the person who helped her join expanding her business, the mom caught on to what needed to be done. One of her early assignments was to make a dream board…all the things she ever wanted to have, become or experience.

She went about spending 10-15 hours per week to launch her business, locating other people, just like her who were looking for their own version of a golden opportunity. Years later, when moving, she found her dream board stuffed away in the closet. She had achieved everything on her dream board, not to mention her dream home, but vacation homes as well and a five-figure monthly income.

Chapter Two

The Money Isn't In Convincing, Debating or Arguing...

Personally, I first tried Shaklee products around 1974, when I was about six years old. I'm not positive who brought the samples of the energy bars to our door, but I think it was one of my cousins.

My mom gave me half of one of the bars and even though I was a little kid, I knew I loved the flavor and I got some energy from it...*I felt better*. I wanted more, but my mom said we couldn't afford them. Needless to say, we always had donuts, cookies, chips, and all kinds of sugary junk food around the house, but that's beside the point and what I mean by the fact that you can offer exactly what a person needs and they still won't buy it from you.

With me, I had a lot of health problems from a very early age. Digestive problems, bloody-noses, fatigue, chronic colds and flu, and ultimately terrible, hay-fever type allergies that plagued me, until I was in my twenties. I remember lying over the edge of my bed, as a toddler crying and asking my mom why I was always sick. I'd get a bad bug, be sick as all heck, be well for a few days and then get sick again. This went on for a couple decades. My junior high years of school I missed more than 40 days of school each year. I had about every digestive problem a person can have, from the top to the bottom. Frequent heartburn that left me gasping, to stomach aches, pains, cramping and so on went on until my early twenties. If I ate tomato products my face would itch for days. If I ate chocolate my nose would bleed like a faucet. All my pillows were stained from nose bleeds, during the night. If I was outside in the cooler weather of Western Washington, my hands would turn blue and I'd get sick again. I was a mess. That went on into my twenties.

I had tried to find a Shaklee Distributor, since that first time I tried a Shaklee food bar. There was a girl in my class from elementary school, all the way through high school who brought those bars with her every day, but she wouldn't tell me where she got them and my mom wouldn't contact her mom. By age 12, I started experimenting with my own nutrition habits, in hopes of feeling better and becoming more healthy, but this was long before the internet and no one else in my family had an interest in improved health.

It wasn't until 1993, when I had moved out on my own and my girlfriend at the time brought home a packet of information from work, that I finally found a Shaklee Distributor. My girlfriend was a dental assistant and one of the patients was a nurse who was also a Shaklee Distributor. Within a month, I was signed up and finally getting the nutrition my body had been wanting for more than twenty years. That Shaklee person didn't know any of my health problems and simply told me to use the Energizing Soy Protein™ and VitaLea™ for thirty days and if I didn't feel better in some way, I could have all my money back. Now, mind you, I had been using some kind of supplements since I was a little kid. Along with all the other problems, I was so anemic during my physical to enter kindergarten I was prescribed iron to get my red blood cell count up. Apparently, the combination of digestion problems, picky eating and constant bleeding caused my red blood cell count to be deficient, leading to anemia and a fatigue. After that, my mom had me on Flintstones™, and as teenager I started experimenting with all kinds of supplements in hopes of feeling better. I wanted to feel how I felt from eating that, half of a Shaklee bar at age six. I think my body knew I needed extra nutrition.

After about three days on the Shaklee protein and multivitamin, I could feel the difference. It felt like I had been plugged-in for the first time in my life.

Within a few weeks, I mentioned to my Shaklee lady that I had a lot of digestive problem and she suggested the alfalfa tablets. Oh, my goodness…relief like I had never had. I had been consuming bottles of Pepto-Bismal™ and Tums™ since I was a kid with very little consistent relief. I started taking a few alfalfa with each meal and all the heartburn and indigestion went away! I couldn't believe it.

I told the nurse about my allergies and she made some other suggestions. At one point, I attended a class, held at a local elementary school class room, that was taught by a lady who was a pharmacist and naturopathic physician. She wasn't in Shaklee and I think it was like five-bucks to attend the class. One of my worst symptoms was itchy eyes that had about driven me crazy, since I was eight or nine years old. I remember the very first day, I ever had hay fever. I had it every year from May to

October until I was about 24 years old. Anyway, the pharmacist told me that my eyes were itching, likely because of a shortage of Vitamin A, or the safe type called Beta Carotene. I had been taking a couple capsules of 10,000 units each day, but she said since my eyes had been itching for so many years, I needed to build it up, first.

Mind you, I had been taking higher and higher doses of allergy medications, anti-histamines, decongestants, stimulants and so on for more than a decade. I can't even count how much I spent on allergy medications over a 16-year period. She suggested that I needed 30-40 times that amount of Beta Carotene, for a couple days, to get it built up in my system before I could reasonably expect any relief. I know that a lot of people would consider that a crazy amount, but I was desperate. I had been suffering for 16 years with eyes that itched so bad I felt like I was going crazy and the red membranes of my eyes would swell up over the colored iris part of my eyes, for days on end.

I went home after the class and the next day I took 40 capsules of Beta Carotene. I knew that Beta Carotene was non-toxic and the body just uses what it needs and discard the rest. So, the risk of harm was not likely, and couldn't come close to the harm the drugs were potentially doing. The second day I took another 40 capsules…guess, what…*no more itchy eyes.*

After 16 years of suffering, my eyes stopped itching. The itching just shut off like a light switch. After that, I took a lower amount, but the itchiness never returned. I could not believe it. Nowadays, there are some TV commercials that hint about the importance of good fats or essential fatty-acids and the importance of them for people with eyes that itch, due to dryness.

These are just two examples of the 20 or 30 amazing benefits I've gotten from Shaklee. I write about the benefits I've gotten in my books and blogging and videos and such, but I consider the allergy relief and digestion relief the two greatest benefits I received, because I suffered for so, long before I found Shaklee again. As a side note, I used to itch all over my body, inside and out during hay fever season. Literally, the inside of my body itched for months at a time and I couldn't scratch the itch. By consistently using Shaklee, all the terrible hay fever and allergies and associated symptoms went away. No longer did eating tomatoes cause me to itch. I can eat all the chocolate I want and my nose doesn't bleed. In fact, I don't remember the last nose bleed I had.

Hernias:

Around 2005 I needed to have a hernia surgery. By the time I went on for surgery both sides had torn, so I had double-hernia surgery. All leading up to the surgery the doctors and nurses said I would be down and out, for five weeks, minimum. I heard them, but told myself, *"We'll see"*. During the weeks leading up to surgery I did extra cardiovascular exercise on a stationary bike, drank extra Physique™ (Shaklee's recovery drink), and visualized my body healing, very fast.

Even when I first woke up, the hospital recovery room, from general-anesthesia, the nurse said it would take me five weeks, before I could start working again. At the time, I was lifting a lot of weight at my job on a daily basis. I had a vertical incision about eight inches long, below my belly button. It was covered in tape after the surgery and they told me to leave it on there, so I could shower without it getting wet or infected.

About five days after my surgery, I went back to the surgeon who had tried to talk me out of surgery, prior to me going in for surgery. He had seen people who had complications from the surgery and didn't want me to have it, unless the hernias were bothering me, which they were.

I went in his exam room, I lifted my shirt up and loosened my pants and he pulled the tape off the incision site and my doctor literally jumped. He couldn't believe how fast and how well the incision had healed. He said, *"Well! I guess this was a good decision for you!"* and promptly left his exam room. Five days later, I was back at work, lifting like I had all along. I was still a little sore on the inside, but I was back to work within ten days of surgery. My employer couldn't believe it, since many other people had the same surgery and were off work for weeks. I had to get a special note from my doctor saying I was fine to return to work, before they would believe me.

To me, Physique™ made all the difference in the world, as far as how quickly and thoroughly my body healed. Granted, I was taking two to three full servings each day leading up to and after the surgery. The worst side effect I had was some car-sickness on the way home from the hospital and the pain medications made me feel kinda' loopy, when I was on them.

In the big picture, while the rest of my family continued down the road of symptoms, followed with prescriptions, followed by more prescriptions and so on, my health has continued to get better and better year after year. In my family, diabetes, heart *dis*-ease and all the common killers run rampant, yet I'm healthy and fit. At 49, I've never needed eyeglasses or contacts, my hearing has improved with time, I exercise several hours a week…and all those chronic colds and flus? I don't remember the last one I had. My hands turning blue followed by a bug? Doesn't happen anymore. If anything, my hands turn red when they get cold.

Surprising to me was that ever since I was a little kid, every time I got a cold or flu my throat would get so sore I couldn't talk. I had troubles with my tonsils the whole time. Once I started taking the Shaklee zinc tablets and even letting them dissolve in my mouth, a sore throat that was unbearable would simply go away…*within minutes*. One of the things that set Shaklee's zinc apart, for me, is that it doesn't have sugar in it. For me, anything with sugar added made my throat hurt and swell more. My tonsils? No more problems with them and they had previously been chronically inflamed.

I had been working out for years before I found Shaklee the second time, in 1993. I'm used to trying supplements that don't deliver what they promise, taste terrible and often caused more digestive problems. When I started using Shaklee Performance™, I noticed the difference right away. At the point that I usually started to feel tired, my muscles didn't fatigue, but rather continued to "fire". I couldn't believe the difference. It really does what it was promised to do.

The list of things that improved with my health, as result of Shaklee is long and this doesn't begin to cover it. Needless to say, I'm a product of the products. Nothing anyone can say can convince me that all supplements are the same, since I used so many between the time I had that first energy bar in 1974 and I found Shaklee again in 1993. People can't convince me that food is enough, because I had been improving my diet since I was 12 years old. Food wasn't enough. To me, being on medications is often a sign that the body is breaking down, as a result of lack of nutrition density, from food alone. That is my experience. Others' opinions are just that…their opinions…in fact, in my family I had a lot of peer-pressure to not take supplements and continue eating sugary junk food. Some family members tried to convince me that my taking supplements and eating healthier was a sign that I thought I was better than them. And these things described here, are just from nutrition…they don't even take all the other product lines into account, they all work as good and are all mutually as safe. Always safe, always effective.

Some people might say I'm crazy for supplementing my diet with Shaklee, but again, I was sick for 24 years before I started seeing serious improvement, from using Shaklee and this was 12 years after I started improving my diet at age 12, despite peer-pressure to the contrary and a couple decades of taking OTC's and prescriptions that never got to the root of the problems…to me, *that's crazy.* To me, being sick all the time and missing out on life, suffering with all kinds of symptoms seems extreme to me. Some people seem tolerant of being sick…I'm not. Often, the people who say, *"…all supplements are the same,"* really haven't tried good supplements, so they have an opinion that is just that…an opinion.

For me, I've been using Shaklee's Energizing Soy Protein™ for going on 25 years. I've found that there's a massive difference in Shaklee's soy and all the others. In fact, about 94% of the soy on the market is genetically modified. Shaklee's is one of the rare ones that isn't GMO, is grown organically, without pesticides and so on. Yet, the public, in order to make themselves feel better lumps all soy in together. I've even had guys tell me that soy makes men feminine, but I think after 25 years I think me and my wife would notice if it was making me feminine. I think my beard shows the opposite effect. So, for me, I don't waste time trying to convince someone who is convinced of rumors. That's not the business that I'm in. If someone lacks the ability to analyze hype and fake advertising there's nothing I can do for them. I write extensively about fitness and nutrition and I don't like to tell part of a story unless I can tell the whole story. If people really want to know my professional opinion, they can read one of my books on Amazon, then we can talk.

There are Shaklee products that I tried, that I didn't feel I needed to take, but wanted to learn about them first-hand. For example, with Shaklee's herbal line. I don't have liver problems, but there's one that historically is proven to regenerate the liver without doing harm. I got three-months-worth, took it every day so I had personal experience with it. I did the same thing with the saw palmetto supplement that people often take for prostate problems. I don't have prostate problems, but I took it for three months, to have personal experience with it. From a true, science-based approach, people who take Shaklee consistently have better health, better lab results and DNA that is younger than their age as well as younger than people who don't take Shaklee.

If you really look at, research and analyze *The Landmark Studies* (both I & II), of long-term users of Shaklee, you'll see yourself the difference in health between people who take Shaklee and the ones who use other supplements or none at all…it's all right there and matches my *experiences.*

It's not realistic to think everyone will appreciate Shaklee or take the supplements, but the good news is that you don't need everyone in order to build a massive business…only a small percentage of the people you actually talk to is enough to improve your financial success and time-freedom.

The benefits you *experience*, from all the product lines, will be yours, too…no one can take those away from you or convince you didn't *experience* the benefits you did. Don't be turned-off by others' opinion of products they don't know anything about. Put them in your body, let nature take over. *Find out for yourself.* Satisfy your curiosity. I've been experimenting with nutrition for close to forty years and I still hear people repeating stuff that was considered old-science or outdated, in the 1970's. People believe what they want to believe, regardless of facts and I personally don't spend any of my time associating with people who insist on being negative or spreading rumors. Life is too short.

In summary, there's more information about nutrition available than you can ever use. To get the most out of Shaklee products, put them in your body and let nature take over…that's it…it's that simple. Its better to know where to get information about the products than to take all your time learning every detail and still not have a business. Its better to refer people to the source of the information than to be the expert, because being a nutrition expert takes too long and isn't copiable, in a timely fashion. Be an expert in your own product usage. Money is made by locating and training new business partners/expanders and establishing product consumers. That's where the majority of your time has to be invested.

People who focus on product details can build a consumer base, but they won't have the same kind of time-freedom nor the income that duplicating yourself 12-15 times, each year, brings.

Instead, have your potential customers fill out the *HealthPrint*™ questionnaire and let them choose what products they want. *THAT* is duplicable. If everyone had to become a nutrition expert to build a successful business in a timely fashion, no one would make it through the learning curve. Anyone can have someone fill out the *HealthPrint*™ questionnaire. Its that simple.

The money is in identifying people's needs, telling the stories of you're an others' experiences with the products, having potential customers fill out the *HealthPrint*™ questionnaire, offer them the money-back guarantee, help them get their first order, then follow up with them to make sure they got their order and everything is going good for them (that they know how to use the products).

This is one basis of building your customer base.

No such things as bad publicity:

One of the phenomena that occurs with inexperienced business people or anyone who starts marketing a product or service, without having a lot of prior successes, its that they are shocked and surprised by others' negativity and attitude toward their intentions to build a business, either on a new, novel idea or a business that has been around for more than 60-years (Shaklee).

Outside of network-marketing, we're used to disputing, arguing, dispelling, dramatizing, etc., when people gossip or make express opinions about us or our intentions…we defend ourselves! We have the luxury of wasting time, participating in conversations that are lose-lose propositions. Meaning, someone is going to walk away feeling bad. In those contexts, we can do that since our circle of influence is limited to the people we choose to be around most of the time. When people have irrational opinions or ideas, we simply avoid them or shut them down.

But, in network-marketing, there's a likelihood for people to have their opinions/make up opinions, whether they acknowledge the facts or not (people believe what makes them comfortable, based on the beliefs they choose to nurture, not necessarily what's real). It's not at all uncommon for people who choose to not pursue a career in network-marketing, or even use the products to proactively attempt to discourage and sabotage those of us who are going about creating the lifestyle of our dream…*its just a phenomena of human nature.*

Honestly, about 5,500 people join network-marketing as business-expanders EVERY DAY. The difference between the successful ones and the unsuccessful ones are the quality of training they get and whether they follow through on what they have been taught…*not whether the system works or not.* Just like exercise, weight loss, 12-step programs, medicine, career and everything else in life! It works when you work it! A person who starts anything, only to procrastinate, skip vital steps and ignore warnings will most likely sabotage their own efforts, then discourage others from following through to justify their own apathy. If they didn't follow-though and someone they know did and became wildly successful, what would that say about them?

But, the difference is that if we're expanding correctly, we're coming into contact with so many more people on a daily basis (either in-person, online, via phone, etc.) that its impossible to engage every person who has a negative opinion or idea about us or our intentions. It's impossible to silence every person who attempts to directly or passively interfere with our business expansion and expand the business at the same time…its one or the other. There isn't enough time and energy to do both and ultimately, it doesn't matter what anyone says about us, if we practice the fundamentals, we'll reach our goals. The more people you talk to and the faster you work through those people the faster your business gains momentum and grows, regardless of all the nonsense or negativity others try to cultivate. The majority of the population would rather choose to put their energy into attempting to control others' opinion than investing in their own future. This is a primary reason for people dropping out within their first month…their energy is on trying to control people who don't want or value what they offer, versus simply doing the actions to expand their business. Business expansion takes way less energy than managing negative opinions and attracts more positive energy to you, increases success and motivation and drive. Worrying about or addressing others' opinions uses a lot of emotional-energy and attracts more negativity, while depleting motivation, drive and vision to you (like begets like). The model is to simply "do you" and let others "do themselves" but don't engage, with them. If they don't value or want what you offer, they simply are not on, our radar. In other words, *"Let me help you or you help me, otherwise, let's get out of each-others' way."*

This kind of business requires such a specialized focus of attention that any actions or behaviors, which don't bring a return of positive emotional payoff, will likely do more harm than good. As with close relationships, trying to figure out why people do what they do, believe the way they do or behave the way they do is a rabbit hole…a waste of time that takes energy but doesn't return any energy. The key is to develop your inner circle of people whom you absolutely trust to hold a positive image, in mind, of you succeeding, and achieving all your goals and you do they same for them, so that you have at least one area of your life that possesses unconditional moral support.

Case example:

Bob was a very successful engineer for one of the top automotive producers in America. But the further he got along in his career and the more seniority he got, the more benefits his employer took away.

Bob was asked by an acquaintance if he was, *"…happy with everything or if he was keeping his options open?"* Bob said he was, "*…keeping his options open*," looked at a video and partnered with the people who helped him join. He and his wife started using the products, loved them and invested about 10-15 hours per week, locating people like themselves, who were doing well financially, but could see that the trend was that their benefits were decreasing and job demands increasing.

Over the years, Bob and his wife and family have travelled the world, first-class, every year and driven a new, top of the line car every two years, paid for by the company. Not only did their health improve and stress levels decrease, they helped hundreds of other people improve their health and wellness along the way and their retirement is a world of luxury compared to what it had been had he waited to be laid off by the auto manufacturer.

Chapter Three

I Don't Concern Myself
With People Who Don't Want Fishing Worms

When I was a little kid, of eight or nine-years old, I launched a fishing-worm business. My family lived in a trailer-court in Duvall, Washington. We lived next to a road that lead up to Lake Margaret, a well-known, summertime, trout-fishing lake. We lived in sheer poverty, a family of four living on about a grand, per month. Some people were worse off than us, but I felt poor. For a period from about 1975 until 1985, we spent a significant portion of our time dumpster-diving, for food and recyclables. With a route of about 25 dumpsters, we had a system down, which resulted in increasing our income, by about $500/month, cashing-in what other people threw away. I can truly say that I know what a difference $500 in income can make. It's the difference between night and day.

My sister was a baby-sitter in our neighborhood and I would generally hang out with the kids she was baby-sitting, watch TV, play outside and everything. One night she was baby-sitting a few doors over and it was pouring down rain and dark outside. I was running back to our house in the pouring rain, when I saw something on the sidewalk. It was visible in the reflection of the street light and reflection from the water on the sidewalk…it was a huge night-crawler worm…nearly a foot long. I had never seen a worm that big. I didn't even know they existed! I ran in the house and grabbed a flashlight and on the way back to the first worm, saw another…and another…and another. Some of them, as soon as the light hit them, they would retract back, into the ground, in a flash.

I wanted to collect some for fishing, so I grabbed a bucket and picked up the ones that were all the way out of the ground…the easy pickers. Then I went to the flower-beds where there were worms lying on the surface of the landscape bark and those were fairly easy to grab, too. I guess the worms come out of the ground because if they don't do so, they drown underground, during rain storms and it was pouring, that night.

Then, I walked out onto the big, lush green lawn. I noticed that if the light touched them and I held it there, they pulled back into the ground faster than I could grab them. But, if I saw them in the peripheral light, then moved the light away real quick, they didn't move. Being partially in the ground, I would grab the end that was out of the ground. If I pulled on them, they broke in half and the part in the ground was gone. They didn't necessarily die if they broke, but I didn't want them to break. So, if once I got a hold of a worm that was partially in the ground, I would just hold on, pause and the worm would tighten, but not get away…eventually it would get fatigued and just slide right out of the hole in the ground.

That first night in the rain, I picked hundreds of worms. My dad said I should put a sign out by the road to advertise worms for sale and I did! A hand-painted piece of wood about eight inches square, a white background with black letters. We nailed it to a power-pole, right in front of the trailer-court and it had an arrow pointing toward our trailer.

It said, *"Worms…$1/doz."*

I didn't have nice containers to put them in like the Coast-to-Coast hardware store down the street had in their fridge, but they didn't have huge nightcrawlers hand-picked like mine were. I rummaged through my grandma's garage and found her stash of empty cottage-cheese and yogurt containers. The quart and pint size ones. When people knocked on the door, I'd take them out to my 5-gallon bucket and pick out thirteen worms. I always gave people an extra one. It seemed like every time I was just about out of worms it would rain and I'd be out there with a flashlight picking worms, replenishing my inventory, with the neighbors watching me out their windows. It was fun. I'd throw in some dirt and grass and poke some holes in the lid, for air to get in.

Word spread on the lake and people were telling other fisherman where they got their night-crawlers. People often bought two dozen and I even had fisherman bring back the ones they didn't use and give them back to me because they appreciated the quality of the worms so much.

Eventually, after watching me sell so many worms and buying so much fishing tackle with my earnings, the next-door neighbor boy decided to start his own worm business, to do the same thing. He basically copied everything I did, except that he didn't take care of the worms, between sales. He would throw them in a bucket and just leave them. When he came out to get some of his worms they were all dead and rotten. He wouldn't change the dirt, wouldn't keep them cool, wouldn't keep them in the shade. His worms died and he gave up. I even saw people who stopped because of the sign, but knocked on his door first, asking for directions and he would take them out to his own worm bucket.

At the same time, I was mowing the man's yard across the street from us. Leo was paying me $7.50 each time I mowed his yard, during the summer months. The neighbor kids saw this and went over, in between my mowing times, hoping Leo would pay them to mow his yard. He declined…I mowed it exactly how he liked it.

There were a few times, we would get home to a note on the door of someone wanting worms, but we weren't there. So, my dad made me a box, from scrap wood pallets, which sat on the railing of our porch, that was big enough to hold about a dozen cups and we would put an ice-pack in the box, so fisherman could use the honor system, when we weren't there. This worked really well. During the summer time, when the Lower Snoqualmie River was at its lowest, I'd pick worms at night, package them up and fill the box, then head out fishing for the day about a half-mile away, down the hill from us. I had a favorite spot below the bridge, where the Woodinville-Duvall Road, enters the town of Duvall. The previous bridge was demolished and left in the river. When the water got low enough I would wade out waste deep to concrete section of the bridge, climb up on it and have a great fishing platform in the middle of the river. If it was a hot day, I'd alternate jumping in the river and drying off in the sun on the huge concrete block. It was pure bliss, in the summer time. I would usually bring leftovers or cheese and crackers as a snack, midway through the day. I caught some really nice cutthroat trout there. Regardless of whether I caught anything, it was very peaceful, getting away from th trailer-court.

The downside was that my dad was at home, sitting in his big recliner watching people come up to the door, take some worms and leave me some money. He, like the neighbor boy, watched this over and over. It started to burn in him…my dad wanted that money for himself. He had tried picking worms with me, but he was so unhealthy his hands would get so cold he couldn't feel the worms or he would get impatient and a lot of his worms were broken in half. It started to burn in him so bad that he started badgering me to give him the business. Mind you, I was about 10 years old at this point. I shrugged it off at first, I had helped him with collecting cardboard, bottles, cans, copper wire and anything we could recycle, since before I was in kindergarten. He kept after me and finally I was so sick of him complaining that all I did was fish and I shouldn't have a business if I wasn't going to stay at home, I just told him to take it.

My dad couldn't collect worms like I did, so he took to running a sprinkler on the lawn to soak the ground. Then he made an electric rod, which was essentially an iron rod, about a quarter-of-an-inch, in diameter, bent to ninety-degrees, at one end like a make-shift handle. Then he attached an electrical cord to the metal handle and wrapped it in black electrical tape. He would plug it in and stick it in the ground to send electricity into the wet ground. The worms would come out of the ground, attempting to escape the shock and he would pick them up. The worms were usually very small and scrawny. And, about half of them didn't live after being electrocuted.

People who don't have lives, people who don't have much going on, will often criticize those who do. Or, they'll criticize/discourage those working to improve their life, rather than simply improving their own life. Misery loves company. Learn to recognize miserable people who insist to stay that way, from a mile-away.

The fisherman didn't like the worms he picked, they were more like the small ones they could get at the hardware store and my dad raised the prices to $1.50 per dozen. Eventually, he realized he was killing more worms than he was getting, so he started buying them in bulk from a worm-farmer in Yakima, Washington, having them sent over on a Greyhound Bus. He had to drive 50 miles roundtrip, into Seattle, to pick them up at the bus station. Then he ran into the problem of containers. He wanted the containers to look like the styro-foam ones, at the hardware store, so he started buying the cups in bulk too. You can probably tell what was happening here. He saw a business that was working great, took it over, changed everything about it and ended up spending most of the money he made on expenses and disappointing the fisherman, buying the worms from me. Pretty soon, people went back to buying worms at the hardware store.

In retrospect, sometimes, I wish I hadn't given into my dad. But, the issue is much more complex. He was a deeply troubled man with more problems that you could shake a stick at. He was so deeply confused, conflicted and abusive it was just easier to walk away, than have yet another thing to fight about. Living with my father was hell for me and my siblings. Through all the abuse and craziness, I developed a deep curiosity about people, their motivations, goal achievement and psychology in general. The learning was bigger than the lesson.

Here's some of what that nine-year old boy learned from his business venture, that carries over to a lot of business.

Location, location, location:

I didn't like living in the trainer-court. Trailer-courts are very depressing to me. But, we lived on the road that lead to a lake…the road the fisherman used to get to the lake! The location made all the difference in the world, since it was right on their way. It was convenient for the customers. Makes, sense, huh!

Keep it simple:

It didn't occur to me that my worm containers weren't new or fancy, after all, the fishermen just threw them away when they were done with them. Sometimes they brought them back and we reused them. I wasn't trying to copy the hardware store, I focused on good, big, healthy worms. A good product. That's it!

Keep expenses down:

Kind of the same as keeping it simple, I didn't need to pay for containers…I wanted to use the money to buy my own fishing lures. I still have my boyhood collection of lures.

People will envy you:

I've found that a percentage of the population subscribe to the idea of earning what they have and encouraging other they can do the same. Another percentage wants what they see others have, but instead of earning it or making their own, they resent your success and want to take it away from you. The third category of people won't do what it takes to earn what you earn, nor do they leave you alone, but rather they just interfere in others' business for the sake of their satisfaction…if you won't give them what you earned, they'll attempt to interfere in your business, just out of principle...they don't come up with or act on their own original ideas. These kinds of personalities exist in all business.

Be clear about what you want out of it:

For me, having spending money to buy *Hot Wheels*™ cars and fishing tackle was where I was from ages 8-12. I watched the sales papers and filled by tackle box with lures, most of which I still have and use today. I couldn't wait for the Sunday sales ads to come out, so I could see what fishing lures were on sale at Ernst Hardware and Payless Drug Stores. When I had enough tackle and I didn't want to fight with my dad over why he didn't like I was earning money, while I was fishing, I walked away and he ran the business into the ground.

What do they value?

One of the obvious keys is that I was selling worms to people who wanted to buy worms. I was offering a solution to getting fish in the boat. Those customers recognized that they wanted to fish and worms would help them catch fish...I offered bigger worms for less money than the hardware store that was a half-mile away. I identified what they wanted...how would it have worked if I put a sign out for toothpaste or shoes or blankets? Remember that when you approach people. Sell worms to fisherman. More on this in later chapters.

Good idea:

Anyone can recognize a good idea when they see one, but few people consistently work to bring the idea into reality. If your actions take away value from others, or doesn't add value to others, people won't do business with you even if its convenient to do so. Ideas have been referred to as *"a dime a dozen"*. But without consistent work and care and maintenance of your business, all your worms will die. Collecting worms...or having good products is part of the battle...if you don't follow through, it doesn't matter how good the products were, to begin with.

Not everyone would be a good match for selling worms:

I enjoyed every part of the worm business. Sometimes, while picking worms, I would have to go in and stand by the heat of the woodstove to warm up, then go back out again, to continue. Not everyone would be cut out for working in the rain, picking worms, getting cold and muddy, nor pick the worms out of the bucket when the fishermen arrived. There's a lot of things that would gross out a lot of people. Not everyone is cut out for the worm business. There were people close by who wanted the money from selling worms, but didn't take as good of care for the worms, and they would die before they could be sold. Think about it. For me, I connected picking worms to buying fishing tackle, spending time on the river away from the trailer-court, and yes, collecting *Hot Wheels*™ cars.

Most importantly:

The most important key that carries over to Shaklee is that I took and found pleasure *in the process* itself. It was fun. It was work, but I made the work fun. It was related to adventure. It never occurred to me to count the number of people who drove by on the same road but didn't buy worms. The people that didn't buy worms either didn't want, need or appreciate my worms. Not every fisherman bought my worms, I don't think I would have had enough to supply *every fisherman*. Some fisherman got their own worms the same ways I did. Some didn't know bigger worms work better. Hundreds of cars passed by the trailer-court, every day. The only ones I paid attention to, were the ones who stopped in, knocked on the door or helped themselves when I wasn't home. People who weren't interested in fishing probably never even noticed the sign. A couple times people took worms without paying. Other times, people left more money than the price I charged.

If I were ever to live on a road that lead to a fishing lake, I'd do the same thing and sell worms again, just for the fun of it.

Sell worms to fishermen. Fishermen are happy about going fishing.

Chapter Four

Be Clear On Leadership

One of the major interrupters to successful expansion of your business (the next step after joining and making the decision to launch), is that you have to be decisive about your "identity as a leader". You can't be in a psychological and emotional state of wanting the main benefits of the business (more money and more free time) and also the state of telling yourself, *"I'll see how this goes...I'll see what others' response to me is."* No, that is interpreted (by others) as "indecision" at an unconscious level. Indecision is responded to as though you are a follower, unsure, indecisive and hesitant of yourself. In every interaction, there is a leader and a follower. Having your own Shaklee business is the decision and behavior of a leader...*you're creating something for yourself, leading by example.* But, if you communicate indecision, hesitancy and un-sure-ed-ness, then you are saying with your words that you're the leader, but your body language is that of follower. Other people respond to body language, not words. They listen to words, but joining you or not is based on body language, not what you say. Followers look to leaders for guidance. So, if you're saying with your words that you're a leader, but your body language (reflection of inner-beliefs) says you're looking to others for their approval and opinion, the incongruency stimulates them to give their opinion [about your decision to have your own business] instead of responding to what benefits you're offering. Meaning, because they sense hesitancy and insecurity, the prospective business partner or customer will respond as though their opinion, criticism and approval is what you're looking for...they give their negative opinion and then they withhold approval.

The secure, confident, self-assured person who has congruently decided to expand their business, regardless of others' opinion or approval exhibits body-language that demonstrates that the 'decision' to build a business is already made...its in the past...you're the leader, in this context. Now, the only discussion is whether or not the other person wants, values and will afford the products and services you are offering, in the here and now.

The person, who is saying, *"I'll build my business, if I get others' approval,"* is demonstrating two separate identities, that are not compatible. If you care about others' opinion, you haven't made a congruent decision, no matter what the context is. If you care about others' opinion, you have joined under to agreement to behave as a leader, but then go about behaving as a *follower*. And if you care about others' opinion, you aren't offering products and services…you're unconsciously offering permission for others to provide you with their opinion [about your decision] to expand your business. The decision [to] launch and build, was made when you filled out the form and got your starter package of products. If you behave as though there is still a question, it confuses people a though you have a hat that says, *"Leader,"* but your body language says, *"Follower"*. In these cases, the indecisiveness and incongruity stimulates others to lead *you*, rather than follow you and that means leading you away from your goals, by giving their opinion versus simply saying, *"Yes,"* or *"No,"* to the benefits you offer. [Any discussion other than, *"Yes"* or *"No"*, indicates you gave body language cues that indicate you are wishy-washy, on your decision [to expand your business].

A reason being that in most industries, being a leader is an "earned" position. In network-marketing, being a leader is about simply [deciding] to be a leader in order to double, triple, quadruple, etc., your productive time to increase your income and increase your free time. Just because you decided to go for it doesn't mean you have the skill-set, inner-belief or congruency needed to accomplish the thing. The decision is an idea, not the actual action to get the thing done. Then, when you get negative feedback, opinion or approval it interferes in your being able to do the actions of the person with the identity as potential business-expander….it stimulates the "old you". The previous you. The prospective business partners and customers mis-interpret you talking to them as a cue for them to remind you who you *used to be*.

Until you let go of seeking others' approval AND locate those who want, value and afford what you are offering, results will be very inconsistent. You have to decide to offer the benefits, no matter others' responses to locate those who want, value and afford what you offer in order to locate the cream-of-the-crop. In other words, whatever you're using to stir the milk is going to get some milk on it. You can't stir the milk, but not get milk on their stirrer itself. Its one or the other. If you try to stir the milk without getting milk on the stirrer, you're effectively trying to have two identities…you aren't owning your identity, as a Shaklee business-expander.

Every single business has a means/ways to expand business/increase the customer base. Grocery has cashiers and stockers. My worm business had me. McDonald's has cashiers and hamburger-makers. No matter what the business, if the person doesn't do their job, the business collapses. If I was afraid to touch worms, no business. If a stocker doesn't stock groceries, no grocery business. If a Shaklee business-expander doesn't offer more money, free time and product benefits, no business. So, it's real-simple. [Ignoring others' opinion or lack of approval makes you the leader.]

If you acknowledge or pay attention to others' opinion, [as though your decision isn't congruent and already been made] or you're still considering whether to follow through or not, you're now the follower.

Problems occur/people fail as business-expanders and miss out on income and free time/become attrition statistics, when they join (fill out the application and get their first order), but, then [behave] as though the decision is still up for discussion. If it's still up for discussion, you are in a passive, emotional state, not in charge of your own business (mind your own business). To launch and expand your business successfully, you have to be calmly assertive …dominant…a leader. Not dominating others, but dominating your mental and emotional state to steward (care for) you own business. In the beginning, your business is vulnerable, since you don't have a track-record of expansion, confidence and competence. Vulnerable, since you might believe in others' criticism, opinion and approval more than you believe in your ability to create and attain all the goals you have picked for yourself. Whatever you believe more will influence your behaviors, for better or worse. If you believe in your goals and dreams, you'll do the actions to reach them. If you believe more in others' opinion of your decision to attain your goals, you simply won't take the proper actions (consistently enough/10-15 hours/week)…you'll attrition out and say the system doesn't work. Another statistic.

[The reason being, that when we hear something someone says that we don't like or that disagrees with us, we either move away from people saying those things and move toward the action to reach our goals (confidence, competence, strong-beliefs), or we move away by stopping the actions which stimulated others to think they had a right/permission to give their opinion about us and stop doing the business expansion actions, which stimulated people to think they had a right to give their opinion to us (low confidence, low competence, weak personality/beliefs).]

Using the products and watching/listening to the people who helped us join successfully [demonstrate] expansion of their business, effectively builds confidence, competence and strong beliefs, until the new business-expander accumulates their own experiences to do the same.

Once you see the way to successfully build and expand, without concern for others' opinion, you can let go/release and focus on locating those who want, value and afford the products and services you offer. It makes the expansion process very simple. Once you rely on your belief in the benefits of the products and business, both you and others' evidence, your belief will exceed others' skepticism and you will have mastered the processes. Until you develop your own belief, you'll rely on the person you joined with and those they introduce you to.

You lead others:

Around 1997, an acquaintance of mine knew I was into Shaklee and knew I had been a horse veterinary assistant, in the late-eighties/early-nineties. She joined an MLM company that distributed health magnet products. Meaning clothes and such that contained magnets that were purported to improve health. I was in Shaklee at the time and building my customer base (albeit, not very effectively, since I lacked confidence) and she knew that. But, with that in mind, she set out that I would "work for her" and she joined the other MLM thinking she would do better to join them, convince me to join her and I would be in her downline. You'll likely run into this, too. People who have sabotage strategies going on will over-look the value of the solid training program you offer, ignore the value of your leadership and conclude that being "above" you will make them more money…missing the importance of leadership…*jumping to the conclusion that where they are placed makes the difference.*

I had another friend around the same time, who insisted she could train me to be more successful in Shaklee and she would join me, if I put her *above me*…meaning, I would train her, in the business, but she would benefit from the growth of my business. Needless to say, this doesn't exist, or work, but she insisted and even tried to convince me she was a highly-trained sales trainer, even though she had no experience in network-marketing. She did join, but when what she insisted would work didn't work at all. She not only was unsuccessful and quit, she went about trying to interfere and sabotage my efforts. Needless to say, she's not in my life any more.

Anyway, so this other lady joins the magnet MLM thinking she could get me to join her to sell product for her, while she sat back and counted her cash. Her whole focus and business plan was to get me into her group and have me moving products for her. So, the company had magnetic horse blankets that retailed for $1,200.00 each.

She thought that, since I had been a horse vet-tech for a few years, that this would be the slam-dunk way to get me to walk away from my company and join hers. I would just sell these $1,200.00 horse blankets to all my "connections" and she would be set. She had figured out how many I would sell for her, so she could reach her goals.

In my mind, I thought it was cute, that she would think I would be interested in those blankets. I didn't have a horse and never have owned a horse. She was attempting to sell worms to a non-fisherman.

Long story short, I explained to her that if she was serious, I could help her develop a plan to approach serious horse owners, who have hundreds-of-thousands-of-dollars invested in their race horses. In my mind, it's that category of people, who would spend that kind of money on those blankets...people who had spent hundreds-of-thousands-of-dollars, on the breeding fees alone, in hopes of getting a winning horse...gambling really. A lot of your average horse owners don't have money for veterinary care, let alone an extra $1,200. for a blanket. I explained her target market is the super-wealthy people who can drop that kind of money and still buy hay and grain for their horses. A lot of the horses I had helped with as a vet-tech were literally these quality of horses. I remember one time a mare gave birth to its foal and someone stole the foal before the owners could even see it. I had seen horses that were intentionally killed, so the owners could collect the insurance money, only to reinvest it in another breeding fee.

So, my suggestion to help her develop a solid plan, that would still create value for her and get her on her way, fell on deaf ears. Her thought process of building her business didn't extend beyond getting one person (me), whom she hadn't been very nice to prior, to sell horse blankets for her.

The morale of the story here is that you won't likely build significant income from your closest connections, nor the people who you might think. The people who first come to mind won't necessarily want, value or afford what you're proposing. You can know a person that joins every business that comes along, gambles their money away, gets involved in every scheme that shows up and when you offer them something of real value they aren't interested. There's a couple potential reasons for this.

First, is that they are really running a poverty-based program in their mind and since they don't believe they'll really ever be successful, they waste time, energy and money on things that relieve stress and distract in the moment, but most likely won't work out, to prove they're right that it can't be done…their main value is being "right", so they prove they are right by collecting experiences that prove it can't be done. Would you rather be right and unsuccessful or learn some new stuff and be ultra-successful? These kinds of people and personalities are outside the scope of the people you locate to expand your business…they simply don't qualify or fit the scope of our practice.

A second phenomena, is when people want to be the one that "found it". If they didn't find it first, they won't join you because instead of valuing your experience and lineage of expertise as a leader, who can expand their business, the want to be "above" you, because they think that will mean something to their bonus check. These types of people and personality do not value training, coaching nor mentorships. They aren't capable or interested in learning something new and valuable, let alone humbling themselves, to ask for help. It doesn't work that way and there's nothing you or I can do to help them unless they join you and learn to help others join them. That's how it works. No one has advantage over another, since the rubber meets the road for the people who honestly invest the right kind of energy, into expanding their own business. We'll help them join, to provide guidance and set an example of how to expand their business. The ones who do the same things will grow their own business. Unfortunately, it never pays to train someone, *before* they have joined you.

If they can't see or value the benefits you're offering, they inevitably miss out on your training. Until someone joins you, conversations should be based on "benefits" to [them]. Training is reserved for those who commit by joining you and meeting your requirements. Meaning, if a person won't join you unless you cover everything in the training, first, well that would be the same as being trained for a job that you haven't been hired for. Not happening.

A big part of your bonus check is based on leadership. As your business partners move up in rank, some incentives are based on this process. If they are above you, you would miss out on a lot of money, every month. That's part of why your training through demonstration has to be rock solid. For them to think that you'll train them, but they'll benefit financially from *you* being their leader, well, that's a person who has deservability issues and wants something for nothing…a handout and lacks the ability to recognize value. They're confused about how money is created…*through creating value [for others]*. Comments about "placement" in the group comes from an erroneous belief that you make money by taking it from others…the same thing my dad thought about the worm business…that if he controlled the business structure, he would get the same amount of money that I did from selling worms. In other words, its ot reasonable, be trained by a person, and then expect you'll earn money off the efforts of the person who trained you!

The big-picture, morale-of-the-story here is that you have a system that works and you're locating people who want to join you and get the same benefits. People with low self-esteem may have a false sense of flattery and think that since you asked them to join you, that they are going to call the shots and structure *your* business the way *they* want to. But, the good news it's that you're tipped off right away when people attempt these types of ploys…the reason being when you see these types of behaviors, where they indicate lack of belief in themselves and low self-esteem, it indicates what is up ahead if they did join you. If they're trying to cut corners and take short-cuts from the beginning, it will end up becoming a confusing and time-wasting endeavor, with those particular people. They have to be willing to follow what you were trained to do, which is hopefully, what was modelled by the person you joined with. If they can't follow, then they won't be able to lead when the time comes, it just doesn't work that way. The person who is learning this month will be leading their first business partners (with the help of the person who helped them join) next month. In these cases, keep the focus on locating new customers, as its unlikely they'll have enough confidence and self-esteem to identify you as a leader and follow you, but regardless, if they use the products they'll get great results.

If someone isn't familiar with the business-model, then they won't recognize a system that has been working for more than 60-years...the facts won't matter to them. And if they don't understand the business, they don't have any business trying to change the system. If someone who doesn't understand the business goes about trying to change the system, without first being successful, they'll just turn it into everything else that hasn't worked and that they haven't followed-through on in the past. Don't let people take away the power of your business by changing what works, but they have no personal-experience with.

Sometimes, the people who won't join you, will approach you at a later date wanting you to be in their organization (above you), *with a different company.* Again, the *"I found it"* or "Where you're placed" mindset...again, they missed the point that their success is dependent on a long history of success with a reputable company with a long history of success as well as a lineage of successful leadership...*not being above you.* [Remember, a thousand companies start up and go away every year]. Shaklee has 60-years of success, an un-beatable pay-plan and distribution/logistics system for 300 products, that are proven to work in a consistent, predictable manner. People who these points are lost on, incorrectly think that by joining a new company is a "better" idea and advantageous...what it really means is that those newer companies are headed for growing-pains that most companies never survive. Shaklee, on the other hand, has a decades-long track record of stability...something that can't be replicated by a new company. Newer is not better.

Additionally, Shaklee goes to such extreme lengths to assure the purest raw materials (supply chain) and quality control that is unseen by any other company, that it would cost hundreds-of-millions-of-dollars, just to start a company...in other words, no one else could or would afford to start the same quality of company, nowadays. When most companies are cutting corners on quality, without customers knowing it, and skimming the profits off, Shaklee was paying their distributors more than other companies and re-investing profits in research, development, quality control, science and new cutting-edge products. Some companies don't expand their product line, build business based on one, hyped-up product and if there is a problem with that product or the supply chain for that product, they're effectively out of business, over-night. With 300 different products, stability is inherently built *into* Shaklee, the business model is inherently more stabile.

Just like with personal training or helicopter instructions or any other learning experience, the beginner is there to learn, *until they master the fundamentals.* If the proper order of leader and follower isn't in the right order, everyone will be frustrated and disappointed because it isn't working. I've had personal training clients who think that since they are paying me, they "own" me and they are going to tell me how they're going to work out and what they'll do…then they complain and tell everyone it didn't work…[and you definitely never get referrals from people who won't accept your demonstration of proper instruction, because they don't get results by repeating what has never worked for them before].

The people who do what you properly demonstrate will insist you won't believe all the good that came from what you taught them, while the ones who won't do what they're shown will insist it doesn't work, even though Shaklee had paid millions in bonuses over the 60-years.

Even though you may have just launched your business, you're the leader of everyone who joins with you. You lead them, not follow them. Training begins when they join you, not before. While others are considering joining you, focus on benefits [to them].

For beginner business-expanders, it can take a few people to locate your first, strong business partners. How many? It depends on the quality of the people you're talking to. If its people like the ones who I was surrounded by in the trailer-court, it could take a few more. New business-expanders are often perplexed that people who are living in poverty aren't excited about a way to improve their living conditions. New business-expanders are also surprised at how easy it is to work with people who already have a great income, but want more control of their time and tax benefits of having a home-based business (being able to write-off expenses, on your taxes, that you would normally incur, anyway).

I think this is related to the idea that the higher up the socio-economic ladder prospective business partners are, the more they appreciate something that can improve their income and time-freedom! They recognize value! *Hint, hint.* New business-expanders tend to grow faster by approaching financially well-to-do people, even if they are outside their comfort zone, than by approaching people close to them, who they may feel more familiar with, yet lack the means to buy their own products and invest in their own business. It doesn't matter how comfortable you are approaching someone if they don't value what you offer or lack the means to afford what you offer. When you focus on approaching the people who have requested information about building their own home-based business and they set aside and prioritize the means to do so, your business can take off the first month.

If on the other hand, a new business-expander who insists on trying to convince people to want what they offer or "afford" what they offer, they're likely barking up the wrong tree and very often linger too long trying to get people who will never take action, to do so. *Move fast.*

Case example:

About a mile up Cherry Valley Road, past the trailer-court, in Duvall which I grew up in and where I had my worm business is today, what is known as a game farm, which the road passes right through. A place where Chinese, Ring-necked Pheasants are raised and released for hunting. On the right side of the road, facing to foothills of the Cascade Mountain Range is what's left of a big old barn, the foundation of an old cabin and some huge pens that the pheasants are raised in, prior to release. As a kid, I remember many times when pheasants, once released would make their way back up the slopes of the grassy, Lower Snoqualmie River Valley, to our yard!

But let's go back three or four decades, for the sake of the story. What's now a game reserve, was in the 1950's and 1960's a grass farm, which my father was the manager of. The remains of that cabin was the house my dad and two sisters lived in. You see, in that valley, the floor of the valley completely floods in several feet of water, two to three times a year. The water gets especially high when the snow is melting off and the tide is high in Puget Sound pushes the water far, back up into the valley. This makes for a unique situation, where the soil is incredibly fertile. Not only do you have soil and silt being delivered to the farmland throughout the year, water is constantly draining off the foothills from the top end. This made for anything grown there to be highly nutritious.

Back in the 50's, (long before I was born) my dad was the manager of that grass-dehydration farm, which was used to make nutritional supplements by a California-based company, he had never heard of. The hundreds of acres were cultivated for this nutritious grass, then dehydrated in the barn, essentially dried, then concentrated and packaged as a finished product, the early forerunners of nutritional supplements.

In fact, the supplements were modeled after one of the healthiest societies known on the planet…the ancient civilization known as the Hunza people. Remote and high in the mountains of Pakistan, is a mountainous valley in the Gilgit-Baltistan region of Pakistan. The *Hunza* is situated in the extreme northern part of Pakistan, bordering with the Wakhan Corridor of Afghanistan and the Xinjiang region of China. The Hunza are known for living super clean, healthy, disease-free lives. Much of the basis of their health is related to the consumption of the glacial runoff…*the water known as glacial-milk.* Research showed that the highly concentrated minerals, in this water they drink contributes to their long, healthy lives and prevention of *dis*-ease.

Now, back to Duvall. Some people realized that the soil in the floor of the valley in Duvall was very similar in nutritional content to the soil where the Hunza exist. There were a couple books written about the Hunza, in the 1960's, decades after the Hunza were 'discovered'. I have a copy of *Hunza Health Secrets,* on my bookshelf, today.

But in real time, my dad was farming, harvesting and storing the raw materials, running the dehydrator for the raw materials, but he wasn't able to make a living for him and his two teenage daughters…he was scraping by. His days full of work, but the income was miniscule. These are my two oldest sisters. My dad prayed and prayed that somehow, he would find a way to keep doing what he was doing, he loved it, but it wasn't enough income, to take care of his family, his first wife having died of asthma attack, years before.

Marvin moved on, his daughters grew up, got married and their own families going. Jump ahead about 20 years and my dad, my mom and myself are digging through a garbage bin behind a 7/11 store, on 148th Avenue in Redmond, Washington. Just one of our many bins on our daily route. I remember it was sunny but cool, it had just stopped raining.

A man in a business suit walks up and starts talking to my parents. I was about nine years old at the time. About the same time, I was selling worms and should have been in school that day.

The man was talking to my parents about how they could keep doing what they were doing, but that he could show them how to increase their income dramatically, on a part-time basis. After all, they most certainly were motivated and wanted to make money, right?

So, I remember the man coming over to our trailer in the trailer-court, a few days later. He wanted my parents to have me leave the room, but since it was about business and making money I insisted on being in the room. The man got out a big tablet on a tripod easel and began to draw pictures and talk.

Everything he said made complete sense to me. I could see how we wouldn't have to dig through the garbage for food and recyclables anymore. I was so excited. My parents sat there silently. The man left some samples of the product he had for my parents to use and they simply left them sitting where they were. My parents never touched them. I asked my mom, *"Aren't we going to use them?!"* My mom replied, *"No"*.

The samples sat by the door, until the man came back by and picked them up. We went back to digging through the garbage and did so for the next six or so years, until my dad died.

The crux or twist of the story, was that years later I found out that the company that owned the grass-dehydration farm, in their struggles to get their products to consumers, began marketing their products through network-marketing. It went on to become a global business, in the hundreds-of-millions in sales, each year. The man that started talking to my parents that day as we were digging through the garbage, was representative for that nutritional supplement company! My dad had prayed for a way to make more money from the nutritional-grass and it basically landed in his lap, but he didn't recognize it and his inner-conflict about money, sales and providing for his family, prevented him from taking advantage of the opportunity he, himself had prayed for, decades earlier. I found this out by doing research on the web. When my father died, he was a very ill, financially-broke, broken man. The whole time I as growing up, our yard overlooked that farm and I hunted there, many times.

Chapter Five

Others' Opinion Of You Doesn't Count

"We prefer not to get criticized, of course, but in many ways we're our own worst critic." Christopher Wray, FBI Director

"Criticism is something you can easily avoid by saying nothing, doing nothing, being nothing" -Aristotle

"Until one is committed, there is hesitancy, the chance to draw back, always ineffectiveness. Concerning all acts of initiative (and creation), there is one elementary truth the ignorance of which kills countless ideas and splendid plans: that the moment one definitely commits oneself, the providence moves too."-Goethe

New business-expanders tend to confuse 'approval by others' with likelihood of success in the business (this definitely described me in the beginning). The truth is, you're not trying to impress the people who aren't interested, nor value, nor choose not to afford what you have to offer. Your income and the time-freedom you'll gain by expanding your business, is in no way tied to nor attached to what other people think of you or their opinion of you or that you have chosen to expand your own business.

If 99% of the population disagrees with you, or your business, you'll still be able to build a massive income on a couple hours of work each day (10-15 hours per week). In my 'opinion', I've found that there are those people with such a deep-seated lack of understanding, desire or personality to improve or expand that they (at this time), cannot be taught or shown anything that is different from what they know or believe/makes them feel the most comfortable (right now). It doesn't mean they'll never be ready (remember the rule that the average sale requires seven exposures to a product or idea), it just means that until a person accepts or adopts an idea, they're very likely to criticize and discourage an idea that later they'll insist they valued all along and maybe even that it was their idea!

If you place a high priority on others' approval of you, especially family, friends, co-workers, classmates, acquaintances, etc., you'll likely never be successful in any business, let alone this one. People who start a business and become successful, do it despite others' opinions. Like a lot of others' businesses, the creative ideas you get are [for you and you only]...they aren't to be talked about, but rather acted on and followed-through on....that implies that you don't talk about your plans until you complete them and measure the results yourself. One of the unique things about network-marketing is that the approaches used most successfully, are [not] designed to get "everyone" to join, but rather to "screen" the masses for approximately 15 leaders each year, with some similar values as yourself and some satisfied consumers, of the products, as well.

What that time-frame implies is that much of the time, you're locating, talking to, approaching, ultimately "screening" many people to weed out the people who are not natural leaders and sales people or who don't have the income they need to buy products for themselves, for samples and for incidental expenses of launching a small business...or people who just lack the vision, belief and drive to create something out of nothing....or to screen out the people who rely on others' approval to act on their own good ideas. The people who won't do a thing unless they get the 'approval of their circle of influence' will have neither financial freedom nor time-freedom...they're effectively trapped by public approval. People who are satisfied with the 'perceived' safety and comfort of having a job, are not likely going to give good advice to someone who wants the freedom to earn as much as they want, have complete time-freedom and prefer freedom over the perceived security of a job. [If someone values perceived security of employment, their advice is all going got be biased toward advising us to do the same.]

I know a lot of people who are satisfied earning fifteen-hundred dollars per month and don't aspire to do any more than that. I've heard people say, *"I wouldn't know what to do with more than $1,500.00 per month."* That lets us know they lack imagination and will never have the drive to earn more than they know what to do with. What they don't know or don't want to face is that regardless how long they have been in their job, the thousands of people who are downsized and laid-off everyday never see it coming and expect everything to remain the same...which I can promise you, it never does.

This is a business that is built by *approving of yourself,* and by measuring your success in the business...in other words, approval comes after the fact, from your professional-peers...if you need others' approval to start and maintain momentum, you simply have it backwards and won't likely succeed...that goes for every business: If you need others' approval to move forward, you won't likely move forward on anything. It's very common for successful network-marketers to build up multi-million-dollar businesses, with thousands of customers and business partners, and the people who wouldn't participate or approve during the launch of the business [insist it won't work, even when it *is* built]...that's because other people's approval or disapproval is a mirror of how they feel about *themselves,* not about you, your potential for success or the viability of network-marketing. They'll insist it's, you, but its them!

People tend to "project" onto others what they truly think of themselves, their own insecurity or what they are avoiding or unconsciously fearful of. If they don't believe they are capable of succeeding, it shows up through doubt and criticism of you (those around them). The truth of this lies in the fact that people who believe in themselves encourage people who are trying new things and attempting to improve themselves or their situation. Knowing this, it's quite revealing what it means when you encounter or approach people, whether about earning more money or the benefits of the products. You'll quickly learn that others negative opinion of you or their disapproval means nothing, holds no value and is not an indicator of your potential. Like flying through clouds. Or above clouds. Your approach is to screen and attract 15 leaders each year...most people are not part of your inner-circle/leadership team. So, you have to be able to recognize the difference between clouds and clear blue sky, mud puddles and warm tropical water, organically-grown vegetables or conventionally-farmed vegetables, a car that won't make the trip vs a brand-new car, etc., *we're talking about 'sorting'.*

No such thing as bad publicity:

Outside of network-marketing, we're used to disputing, arguing, dispelling, dramatizing, etc., when people gossip or make opinions about us and so forth. We can do that since our circle of influence is limited to the people we choose to be around the most. If someone has irrational opinions or ideas, we just avoid them or shut them down.

But in network-marketing, there's a preponderancy for people to have opinions/make up opinions whether they have the facts or not.

Usually, the less a person knows or has experience, they more insistent they are that they know better…have you recognized that many people think because they have a thought and they can verbalize it, that the thought is therefore real. It's not at all uncommon for people who choose not to be involved in network-marketing to attempt to discourage or prevent those of us creating our own success even as we are having success, personally! Everyone has an opinion! **Often the people most attached to their own 'opinion' are the people with the least life experiences! Having an opinion makes people feel secure!**

BUT, the difference is that if we're building correctly we're coming into contact with so many more people that it's impossible to silence all the people who will try to interfere in your own progress…there's absolutely no way to control what everyone says about your decision to build your own network-marketing business. It's one or the other. The more people you talk to the faster your business grows, but the more people will have "opinions" about your choice. You should be working fast enough that you're accumulating a group and building your inner-circle which overrides/outweighs any negativity you cross paths with, rather than encountering negativity and then shutting down emotionally. The majority of the population would choose to put their energy into "popular opinion control" than just focusing on building their business (chasing their tail). That's one reason why more people quit or attrition-out, than become insanely successful…their focus is in the wrong direction, from the get-go and they simply burn out.

As with relationships, trying to figure out why people behave or treat you how they do is a waste of time. Develop your inner circle. *Your posse.* Your own support-circle. And it doesn't matter if it's with people you just met or people you've known as long as you mutually and unconditionally support one another in your endeavors. Trust and loyalty.

There will be people who simply can't focus on solutions, can't focus on things turning out good. They can't get their mind above current conditions. They insist things can't get better. They'll treat you like you used to be, dismiss what you're currently working to improve yourself on and insist on holding you in the light that is the most convenient for them. Withholding encouragement, refusing to cooperate in positive things, especially when they would benefit in the ways they insisted they wanted to benefit, while continuing to be stuck in lives they aren't happy with.

You can't make a person be happy, healthy or fun. Speaking globally/generally, whatever attitude a person is exhibiting right in front of you is the attitude they want to exhibit (believe what you see)...just because they verbally insist they want more out of life, doesn't mean they really will do the actions to get there.

How to know for sure is whether they back up what they say with the behaviors which earn the new level of success they insist they want. A personal might want to 'feel' that a prospective team mate has so much 'potential'. But until they match your 'feeling' with their own investment of time, energy and money (the same things they are using to maintain whatever life they currently are maintaining) [either passively or purposely] they aren't who your feeling is saying they are...they're a projection of imagination until they step up, and commit to investing the same time, energy and money that they are using [or inhibiting for that matter...yes, people do inhibit their own successes] for the current life they are living, regardless how much they say they want more of something or a different life completely. Either outcome is just a few decisions away. Even when people aren't happy with their life, it's the habits of daily living that keep that particular life maintained, stuck or seeming more real than any other. You can have a person who refuses to invest a couple or few-hundred-dollars to launch their business, but they spend hundreds of dollars on coffees and clothes to wear to their job...think about it. Even the lowest paying jobs have dress requirements. A person who won't invest in themselves or wants someone else to cover their expenses, simply isn't being reasonable. If a person wants to earn a great income, working part-time, from home, but doesn't want to invest any money to do so, they're placing unreasonable pressure on you attempting to make that happen for them. It simply isn't reasonable, nut they may be so far behind in understanding that it's impossible to communicate this to them

Where managing your mental, emotional and psychological energy comes into play is that if you're using your energy to convince others of anything (through words) you won't likely make it to the next level of your success or self-development. If your emotions rise when people tell you they'll expand a business, but drops off when you find they don't follow through, you'll be wasting your energy and inadvertently exhaust yourself. You want your emotional highs to be based on actual success...measured by people doing the actions of [using the product and finding more people who want the benefits]. Those are the only two things you get paid on, which are both based on controlling your own behaviors...the number of people you talk to and the number of people who follow through.

Meaning, the difference between a person who is positive, solution-oriented, the cup-is-refillable and a person who says they want what you're offering, yet is negative, has a problem for every solution and the glass is half-empty, is so radically different and refreshing that after the first one you'll never forget or mistake one for the other again.

Newbies tend to think that if someone doesn't respond or follow through or realize how amazing Shaklee is that they haven't done their part, so they keep taking another run at them, thinking it's a weakness of communication...it's not, as long as you have [shown them the benefits to them] right from the get-go. If they know the benefits and they aren't taking action, move on. It has to do with recognizing some people have the raw material to be amazing because they are so clean and non-sabotaging to themselves, while others get in their own way every step of the way. That *IS* to say that as a person moves up the ranks, a part of it is releasing, letting go and getting out of their own way more and more efficiently/effectively as time goes on. Meaning they have come to realize which parts of their personality and identity work in their favor of their dream-board being realized in this lifetime, while others may hold onto parts of themselves which get in the way of them moving forward, yet they still won't let those ineffective personality traits go in order to get what they insist they want...think of pruning a fruit tree to produce higher quality, tastier, more valuable fruit vs a tree full of wormy apples that the local deer population will enjoy. *"The apple don't fall far from the tree."*

Emotional-stability being one of the greatest attributes you will cultivate in yourself. Meaning, being able to remain solution-oriented, mentally and emotionally above current conditions, unaffected by "the facts" and remaining rooted in the vision and emotions associated with having accomplished your goal-board aspirations...*seeing and feeling them as already done.*

In employment, people afford themselves the luxury of moodiness, brooding, dumping, complaining, irreconcilability, etc., etc. But in entrepreneurship, you're the person steering your own boat. And in network-marketing (a sub-specialty of entrepreneurship), your (both conscious and unconscious) attitudes, beliefs, values, steer your ship (your frontline/first-level, effectively being your passengers) and take along passengers as well as setting the example for how well they set role modeling and what attitudes they pass on to the passengers, on their own ships. Like-begets-like. So, if you're not liking the results people are getting once the training starts, look at what you know you believe as well as what you don't know you believe. The ones that control your life the most are the ones you aren't aware of, since you can't address and improve what you don't know is affecting you! [Each level of success represents letting go of more that which is in your way and inhibiting your success]. If it were as simple as "Simon-says" or copy-cat. everyone would be successful in Shaklee and business, in general. Where a copiable-system breaks down is where a person's unconscious beliefs and values conflict or bump up against what is proven by someone else to work! *"Oh, I could never work on a Wednesday afternoon!"*

Exercise to hear inner/unconscious beliefs and values:

And how you find out the boundaries of your own self-imposed limitations and beliefs is to listen in on the inner voice that pops up in response to success principles that are beyond where you currently are. e.g. Statement: *"You can be a millionaire."* Inner Response: *"No I can't"* or *"That's right."*

Either in first person (I) or in third person (You), make statements about abundance, wealth, and time-freedom and listen in to discover what your inner voice responds with. Here's some examples:

Statement: *"You can have all the toys you want."*

Negative or limiting/conflicting belief: *"No, I can't be greedy."*

Positive or productive belief: *"There's plenty to go around."*

Statement: *"You can travel the world and have money left over."*

Negative or limiting/conflicting belief: *"Travel costs too much and is a waste of money."*

Positive or productive belief: *"I can pay for my travel through my business activities."*

Statement: *"You can earn a lot more money, now."*

Negative or limiting/conflicting belief: *"Everyone in my family is always poor."*

Positive or productive belief: *"I can learn new skills."*

Statement: *"You can build your business faster than anyone else ever has."*

Negative or limiting/conflicting belief: *"It's too hard."*

Positive or productive belief: *"Anyone who has ever broken a record is the first person to reach that level of achievement."*

Statement: *"There's plenty of money in the world for me."*

Negative or limiting/conflicting belief: *"There isn't enough."*

Positive or productive belief: *"There is enough, and I'll find it and earn it."*

The point is that most people have conflicting beliefs that are existing unconsciously (outside their own awareness), which affect outward performance. You can assume this may be the case, if you have trouble breaking through to new levels of performance and/or make gains, but then subsequently regress back to previous levels. This exists in all areas of life: career, family, relationships, income, recreation, fitness, health and so on.

One place its common to notice incongruity/imbalance, in beliefs and values, is when you hear yourself or someone saying conflicting things. If someone says, *"...you can launch your business to 3,000 PV points, in one month,"* that's reasonable and congruent. But, if they then add in that, *"... it's very hard and you shouldn't expect to be too successful at first,"* it's not only incongruent, but points out their limiting/conflicting beliefs which are in conflict with the first idea...you can't have it both ways and expect to maintain progress. Does that make sense?

One study has shown that about 90% of what people believe about their capabilities aren't real. They believe it, but it isn't fact. Yet, their beliefs control their behaviors. Beliefs determine experience.

Another place it shows up is when people who consistently start new things, but don't follow through begin attempting to get others to take advice from them, or someone who is known to start things but not follow through and in attempt to turn-over-a-new-leaf, launch their business but their family and friends won't provide morale support insisting, *"...this will be like all the other times."* (Hence, the importance of building your new circle of influence. If your family and friends lack faith in you, you can't wait for them to come along or trust you, you have to build your circle of influence outside your previous circle of influence. Once you're successful they'll see you have changed, but trying to improve their attitudes, before you have achieved it, is insanity.)

In the process of expanding your business, it's tempting to want others "approval" in your decision to build your business. When we don't get that approval, its commonly referred to as "rejection"/emotional hurt(s) or disappointment. More often than not, it's not actually "rejection", but simply that people don't know we have something they want or will benefit from. It's our job to present it in a way that they can see what we're offering is important to them. At the same time, some studies have shown that "perceived rejection"/lack of approval activates the same parts of the brain as physical pain. That's why it's important to "frame "or see others' responses as part of the "process" but not the closing scene.

Across all industries, statistically, most true "sales" require, on average, seven (7) contacts with the person about the product or service being offered before a sale is made. If we touch base once, the person misses the point and we don't approach them again it means we didn't follow through. That would be like shooting a basketball, missing the basket and assuming you could never get good at making baskets. Meaning, a conclusion was formed before there was enough evidence to say either way. If everyone did this in every endeavor, nothing would get done!

Newer business-expanders tend to default to old programming, as if disappointment in the moment indicates they won't be successful or reach their goals on time. This simply isn't true. As long as you continue moving forward and don't linger with people who don't want, value or don't afford what you offer, you'll still hit your goals.

The person who tries once, insists they didn't like the feeling of not reaching their goal *the first time*, concludes its not possible and refuses to get more training or model someone successful, in their field (the refining process), will end up on the sideline criticizing those who did follow through, possibly wishing for the rest of their life that they had followed through for the rewards. If you hit a hole-in-one, the first time it just means you didn't know what to do…you didn't get in your own way! You can quit or you can get more training/coaching and continue to practice enough to improve.

To conclude that we'll only be successful if we get approval of those around us, well, it isn't true. So, if you experience that feeling, you have to reframe it or change it in your mind, so it doesn't mean as much or represent the same thing to you. If you feel like you need others' approval, it's a different way of saying that others are more important than you, which isn't true. It's a way of saying that others' goals and aspirations/intentions are more important than yours', again, not true. That approval is more important than earning the living you want or the way you want to live. Often, there is an overuse of apology when approaching people if we're dependent on their approval, which points to not understanding how important what you're offering will be to them…meaning, if you undervalue what you're offering, you'll likely seek their approval as though they hold-the-cards…they do not.

If this describes you, ask yourself where the need to get approval from others comes from and then be patient and pay attention. The answer might pop into your head or come in a couple days later. Often knowing where it started from is enough awareness to resolve it. Other times, relying on modeling successful people who don't care about others' approval, is the place to go so you can see the lack of concern for approval in action in real time, reflecting on your own

More often than not, regardless of what endeavor a person strives in, you're 'putting yourself out there' and its unlikely everyone will approve or be happy about you living the life you want. It's just not reasonable to get approval from everyone and you would exhaust yourself and maybe make yourself sick attempting it. Take others disapproval and rejection as a sign you're on your way…build your new circle of influence (inner-circle) starting with the person you joined with and others in the same group. [The more support you have in your new inner-circle, the less other people's approval or opinions matter!].

Truthfully, you only have to live up to your own expectations (healthy) and it's not reasonable to attempt to control how others treat you. You can drive yourself crazy trying to get nasty, unhappy, frustrated, emotionally-imbalanced, mentally-ill people to treat you how you want to be treated. So, focus on what you can control (doing the [process] of your own work habits, attitudes, beliefs, values and perceptions) *and find your happiness in those processes*. As the weeks and months go by, you'll develop a great support system (*a sanctuary or an oasis*) which you can count on for morale support. But don't conclude that just because you have a few unpleasant experiences it will always be that way. Don't take yourself too seriously and let the water roll off your back, like water off a duck.

People tend to challenge and discourage people who start new things, then wonder how they did it once they are successful!

The importance of travel:

Having grown up very poor, in the trailer-court, we rarely traveled. If we did, it was an overnight camping trip. Often my parents would say that if we behaved, we would go to Disneyland, but we never did.

Once I was a teenager and started working my 'real' jobs, my time was filled up with living from pay check to paycheck. I did go camping, which is important, but it's not world class travel.

Around 1996, after years of working, working, working, working...I realized I was not in the place in life I thought I would be by that point. I realized, by looking back at my life how small decisions here and there had led me to be where I didn't want to be at all...I was on track to be on the same path as my parents, in a lot of ways.

I walked away from everything. Got rid of the majority of my belongings, just set them out by the road. Kept my dog (Dolly the beagle), my truck and a few sentimental belongings and started over. I moved to Vashon Island, in Puget Sound and began attending clinical hypnosis school.

Eventually, I even got rid of my truck. I walked, rode the bus and bummed rides to get wherever I wanted to go. Jump ahead a few years and I met my wife, Jessica. We started taking the Hawaii trips around 2005, a couple years after we met. All I can say is 'mind-blowing'. It was everything that little kid dreamed, of as an escape, from the trailer-court.

What I have found is that real vacations are not a luxury, but are essential break-state from whatever we create as the structure of our lives. In other words, regardless how good we are at designing our lives, inherent in that is structure which muffles and suppresses our own success.

By traveling, for a week, ten days, two weeks at a time, we relieve ourselves of the constraints we inadvertently build into our lives, known as structure, safety, familiarity and routine. The thing is, that you don't know which part you built into your life, which holds you back until you go traveling and you're outside your life for a week or two at a time. Once outside you own life, experiencing culture and food different than what you're used to, you begin to a sense of detachment, enlightenment, inspiration and creativity that you would never have if you didn't take a week or two to get refreshed. I believe, you actually won't be as productive or successful unless you take at least a couple weeks each year, to the exotic location of your own choosing, to see your life from the outside. Only then, will you reach your full potential in your business. To keep working your business with only the inside perspective, limits what you'll be able to accomplish. It doesn't matter how economical the travel is at first, just get away. When we started going to Hawaii, we would rent a VRBO or condo, cook all our own food for the most part and shop at Costco after picking up our rental car, but before getting to the hotel or condo to unpack. Each time you travel you get better at knowing where you can reduce costs, yet improve the quality of your adventure. VRBO and Airbnb has been amazing for that. Be sure to check that your rental includes air conditioning! Even if you simply travel to an out-of-state tourist area, it will be very rejuvenating. Then your mind starts going to work about how you can do it more often, for longer periods of time and continue earning money the whole time you're on vacation! That's where Shaklee comes in!

I remember the first time we landed on Oahu. It was about 7:30 pm by the time we got to the beach at Waikiki, in front of the hotels. We had picked up our rental car, got to our own hotel and ran down to the beach. I had waited my lifetime to feel the warm, tropical ocean...it was breathtaking bath water. I was in heaven. My soul had waited decades to feel that warm, tropical water. We returned to Hawaii every few months and got married there in 2006. In 2014, we moved to Maui and lived there eight months, until my father-in-law was diagnosed with cancer, and we moved back to Vashon Island, to help him.

Once you travel first-class, all-expense paid, your life will never be the same. It changes you in good ways that are beyond description. Things that you once thought were so important, look small and insignificant. Living in luxury gives meaning to hard work, other than doing work just for the sake of work. It puts things in a whole new perspective. For building your Shaklee business, you receive all expense paid, worldwide travel.

The Shaklee Family is hitting the high seas and traveling in high style for the Dream 2019 Incentive trip. We'll be cruising aboard the Royal Caribbean Cruise liner *"Allure of the Seas$^®$"* as we visit The Bahamas, Honduras, and Mexico! Earn this trip and spend 8 days and 7 nights enjoying exotic locales, incredible food, ancient history, and sun...LOTS of sun!

Each year a different location is available, to each business-expander.

Chapter Six

Projection

pro·jec·tion

/prəˈjekSH(ə)n/

noun: **projection**;

1. an estimate or forecast of a future situation or trend based on a study of present ones.

"plans based on projections of slow, but positive growth"

• forecast, prediction, prognosis, outlook, expectation, estimate

2. the presentation of an image on a surface, especially a movie screen.

"quality illustrations for overhead projection"

• an image projected on a surface.

• the ability to make a sound, especially the voice, heard at a distance.

3. the presentation or promotion of something in a particular way.

• a mental image viewed as reality.

• the unconscious transfer of one's own desires or emotions to another person. "we protect the self by a number of defense mechanisms, including repression and projection".

4. a thing that extends outward from something else.

In other words, you have to insist on believing in and projecting what you're building, more than believing in what others project in their own doubts, about themselves and their lives, (toward you, when you talk with them), remaining in a leadership posture/mindset...the foundational principle of leadership.

Much of entrepreneurial endeavors are "projection". In other words, you combine what the company already offers in terms of products & service and the benefits of them, and connect that with your emotional excitement and enthusiasm of what you intend to create. Then you share the vision with as many people as it takes to expand your business to the level you want. "Projection" in this context refers to "putting it out there", ...putting *yourself* out there. Risking encountering negative attitudes and beliefs in order to work through it, rise above the low-lying clouds or fog and bring your vision into reality. Because negativity is common and popular, you have your work cut out for *you*. But here's a secret: the more confident and self-assured a person, the less they are affected by others negativity. And the more you do the process, the more competent and confident you become. Each tiny success builds your confidence and carries over to the next situation, resulting in competence or skilled-ability.

When flying helicopters and airplanes, there's two terms used to describe flight: IFR and VFR. VFR means Visual Flight Rules, meaning you can see where you're going with your eyes and senses. You know what to expect for the most part. But, when the weather is less than desirable, IFR rules take over and that refers to Instrument Flight Rules...meaning, conditions are such that you can't see where you're going because of the clouds! (metaphor for others' negativity and self-limiting beliefs).

So, during IFR Rules, you have to rely on the instruments to get you where you intend to arrive (your training and instincts). Generally, pilots learn to fly visually first, because the instruments are complicated and take extra training to become competent. If you're a pilot, you know what I'm talking about. In network-marketing, its often that suggested newbies make a list and contact their people they know, first…this is the equivalent of flying by sight/visual, since you can "reasonably" expect how people you know in some way will respond…there's a warmth to it. Once you start contacting people you didn't previously know, often referred to as cold-marketing or working 'leads' (people who have requested you contact them about having a home-based business), it's more like flying by instrument, because you can't really see how every interaction will go, in advance, but you have to trust in your training, staying focused on what you see as your goals already having been accomplished and keep your emotional status calm, assertive and in control, regardless how stormy or nerve-wracking each interaction might seem in the moment. Do what you were trained to do. Let your training kick-in.

In an aircraft, if it gets cloudy or rainy or foggy, you have to rely on your instruments and the flight-plan you hopefully filed to get you through the low visibility weather conditions. In network-marketing, part of the fun is the unexpected and the requirements of 'thinking on your feet'. With each contact you make, you learn at least one new thing or nuance that you then carry forward to all future conversations. By the time you feel you confident, pretty much have a handle on knowledge, your business is built! You're never expected to fly by yourself until you have enough training and agree *you're ready!*

Different skill sets:

Although less common, there is a portion of the population who were raised in a very positive, uplifting, supportive environment, where the majority of the time they're looking forward to a bright future, regardless of what kind of negativity they encounter during their days. These types of people and personalities are often very confident, regardless of their experience level and have no reservation about anything that resembles customer service. But, here's secret #1: Anyone can today behave as if they were raised in a positive environment, they are self-assured and they don't let others negativity or cynicism affect them nor interrupt their forward momentum. They expect good things to happen, both consciously and unconsciously. They "project" their vision and dreams and when they do encounter negativity, like water running off a duck's back, they rarely notice and definitely don't remember it…like it never happened…they don't retain nor magnify nor dramatize nor sensationalize negative experiences...*because there's no tangible benefit to recycling negativity.*

The only benefit to being engaged in drama is gaining sympathy and attention from people who might feel sorry for you. BUT, one of the secrets of entrepreneurial endeavors is that you can either have drama or you can improve your income and lifestyle...*not both*. The reason being is that like heart-beats or human eggs, each person only gets so much emotional-energy each day. So! You can increase the drama in your life (and continue to lack financial and time-freedom) or you can use that very same emotional-energy ration to simply and effectively seek out the people who want and value what you offer...it's that simple...there's not room for both drama and tangible benefits. People who seamlessly expand their business without permitting space for life-sucking drama certainly don't try to convince negative people to be positive, nor do they feel at home around negativity...if they encounter it, it's more like grazing at a buffet...take what you like and leave the rest. *Hint, hint...* in case you didn't get that, positive people, naturally migrate toward positive people and environments. They don't try to stop negativity, they just notice it the same way they notice condiments they don't like at the buffet...they simply "pass".

Secret #2 is that as you stop engaging with negative people and attitudes, you inherently cultivate positivity which brings more,...*guess*...more emotional-energy! Yes, when you aren't dealing with negativity (not engaging it), you aren't wasting energy on exchanges that deplete emotional-energy and in turn you're cultivating a higher level of positivity and mental clarity, which...attracts more positive people. That is to say that some people are so habitually addicted (or at least unaware they're doing it, out of familiarity) to engaging in negativity, even if it's attempting to convince people of something, that their emotional-energy suffers and they subsequently never get their business off the ground...they keep trying to convince negative people to want or value or afford something based on positivity...it never works! You have to have more energy than your prospects and wasting energy on drama, gossip and negativity takes you in the wrong direction.

No informal moments/no non-teaching moments:

It's very common for new business-expanders to think that if they know someone, are friends with someone or are related to them that it makes sense to conversationally attempt to convince or persuade them to join them in the business. But, this proves counter-productive, takes time away from the people who would join you if they knew about you and gives those resistant people the impression that in order to build a business you have to do conversational battle with people, twist their arm to join you. That's no fun and ineffective. Whenever you approach someone about the products or business, do it professionally, the way you want them to do if they start their own business. If you take too casual approach, it gives the impression that it isn't a legitimate business. If this is the case, you can't expect people to take you seriously. In the off-chance you do gain their interest, they're going to copy the informal approach you made with your first impression.

Truthfully, what "persuades" others, is seeing you making huge monthly checks, driving new cars, looking younger, feeling better and traveling the world for free...*think about it.* And those things come from a fast, strong launch and continued expansion, throughout the first year. Truthfully, there are enough people out there to build yourself a significant business base, within 15 months, but that means making the conscious decision to not spend time convincing and rather invest your time wisely, as a clear-minded messenger planting seeds, weeding out and training motivated people who naturally see, hear, want, value and afford what you're offering. Trust me, people are praying to find this opportunity, right this very minute. Its up to us to work in ways that we locate them and show them. *More on this later.*

Especially with the first 100 people you approach, if you try to convince or persuade, you'll lose up all your emotional-energy before you get to 100...more than likely you won't get past the first three negative people...all the while, people who don't engage in negative situations will go on and on and in until they expand their business to the level they want or at least until they have 15 leaders who do the same actions as themselves...see the difference? Wasting time on people who aren't interested, versus locating the people who have been looking and value for what you offer.

Remember the story about my worm business? What if I spent my days trying to convince people who didn't enjoy fishing to buy my worms?

I wouldn't have been having as much fun (which I think is the point of life) and I wouldn't have had as much time to fish and play, myself. The point being that as simple as my worm business was, I approached it professionally and showed respect for my customers by providing the very best product I could get (and I was nine and ten years old). If I would have beat-around-the-bush and people couldn't understand what I was offering, then the burden of understanding in on the potential customer. People aren't going to buy or join what they don't understand or see how they will benefit from it. Fisherman want worms to catch fish!

When someone isn't interested, ask who they might know who wants more energy, want to lose weight, wants to feel better, etc., etc. With over 300 products, assure people they don't have to buy anything, but ask if they help you think of people who might want to use the products. If you only get one name for every product, how many more potential customers is that? Think about it.

Once you have names and contact information on them, simply contact them and tell them who referred you and that they thought of them and offer them the benefits you think they might want or need the most.

Case example:

Mary, a young, single person wanted the benefits of having a home-based business and got a strong launch, gaining a whole bunch of customers and three business partners. After about five months, the expansion of her business seemed to plateau and she talked with the person who helped her join, about it. He, who had started his business to increase his income while he was a high school teacher and football coach, had focused on finding one new business partner at a time. Joe figured, if he could locate just two business partners each year, he would have more money than he ever had before and this proved true, for him. So, Joe suggested that Mary may have very well inadvertently started to over-complicate her business and that she should come back and simply watch him demonstrating how he expands his business, *"...don't take notes, don't write things down, don't try to memorize, just watch and listen."*

Mary took Joe's suggestions and sure enough her business expansion took off again. In hind sight, Mary realized that as the months passed she had started to add more and more to her business practices, complicating the process and overwhelming herself. Once Mary went back to focusing on locating people who want, value and have the means to afford what she is offering, more people continued joining her. Mary re-focused on locating 10 customers and 3 business partners (a manageable group) and then repeating the process. Not only did she increase her customer base, referrals and number of business partners, she also qualified for the international trip, which she took her mom with her and qualified for a fancier company car. By simplifying, and re-focusing on the basic fundamentals, Mary's business is back to growing exponentially.

Chapter Seven

Attrition, Refining and Screening

1. Attrition:

/əˈtriSH(ə)n/

noun; refers to people who leave a business, job, club, organization, team, etc. In order to offset attrition (loss of people), and prevent collapse of the organization, more people (or people who are more productive than one individual), must be brought in than those who quit, leave, die, join other organizations, lack time to give, etc.

2. Refining:

/rəˈfīn/

verb; improve (something) by making small changes, in particular make (an idea, theory, or method) more subtle and accurate.

3. Screening:

/ˈskrēniNG/

verb; the evaluation or investigation of something as part of a methodical survey, to assess suitability for a particular role or purpose.

If you were to learn that only one-percent of the population would make a good customer for your products or services, regardless of the business, would that dis-courage you? The truth of the matter is, a mere 1% of the population has leadership quality and investing or trying to convince 99% of the population to join you, value what you have to offer isn't effective use of your time. But, the good part about that is that knowing that from the beginning, it shows you that your time is best spent locating and sorting. If someone doesn't follow through or value what you're offering, it isn't about you, at all. Knowing this, would you move through the 99% as quickly as possible to find your 12-15 leaders every 12-15 months to earn $100k per year?? Simple, right?

So, when you know a person isn't one of the one-percent, who are a leader in your organization, an unsophisticated, but effective person just turns the other cheek and moves toward the next person, as soon as possible. The sophisticated/seasoned networker notices someone isn't qualified, doesn't react on the outside, makes them feel good about where they are, makes a calculated decision to preserve their energy, keeps the friendship bridge built, and both conversationally and emotionally disengages themselves whilst making the prospect feel good. No harm, no foul. If a person ever does grow into a qualified prospect, they can use the friendship bridge. No one feels offended, isolated nor alienated.

In my extensive experience, as long as an organization focuses on communicating the [benefits members get for participating], they don't have any trouble "getting' people to join in. *BUT*, the qualifier is that in order to retain members, the members must feel appreciated, get the benefits they were promised and gain intangible benefits which carry over to every other part of their lives (satisfaction, purpose, confidence, competence and skills that they can use in the rest of their lives outside the organization itself; in other words, they get built up as a person as a result of being part of the organization). Additionally, asking for an agreement, from each member to pay-it-forward, by adopting newer members they naturally have rapport with, the newer members have connection, friendship and a feeling that someone is watching out for them, while they learn the ropes and gain confidence. (These qualities are inherent in Shaklee: finding people who have similar values, want similar things and desire to be shown the ropes to help assure the successful launch of their business. Paying-it-forward is inherent…its built into the system of training those who join you.)

When these principles are integrated into the organization, members get so much from their involvement that they naturally start bringing others into the group, so that more people are joining than leaving, effectively balancing out the attrition factors. That's a result of "feeling good" about their participation. [When people don't understand why they feel bad, emotionally, about their participation, they drop out].

Attrition refers to the number of people who join, but either quit or don't take action before successfully expanding their business/seeing their goals, through to the end. It can also apply to people who try the product, but don't continue to purchase. Attrition exists in every business, club, organization, etc. You can count on it and *have to*. When you have helped 100 people join, not all of them will necessarily stick around or stay involved. But here's the thing, they don't have to. Like everything else, some people will do more than average and some will do less. It's just a phenomena of nature...*predictable human nature...some people work harder and smarter than others*...it's this way at every business. From all the people who join, the ones who stick around will do more than the ones who dropped out anyway. Much of your own income will come from about 15 leaders you locate and train each year.

Even with business-expanders, some are going to flake-out, some will stop returning your calls, stop responding to emails, *basically disappear*. And that's ok, because sure enough, there's some leaders that will join way downline from you, sponsor in with someone else you might not even personally know that well...but...they'll build a business and move up closer to you and you'll be earning money from their efforts anyway.

That's one of the predictable phenomena of this business and why you fully invest your energy with each person in helping them start and get trained, but also be unattached to "who" sticks with it (insulating yourself from disappointment). Knowing that some people you train won't follow through and you won't make an income from them, but also knowing some people will move up and you'll earn huge income from your efforts getting them properly trained, even though you didn't personally sponsor them...as the cream rises to the top, you can't worry about the majority of the milk. You have to stir all the milk to get the cream to rise to the top.

See that? Hear that? Invest fully in each person, but don't be emotionally-attached to who performs or copies you and who doesn't. All you can control is your own work ethic of continuing to expand your own business and lead/teach by this example. The rest will take care of itself. 60-years of success has proven this.

Knowing attrition exists everywhere, you counteract it by bringing in more people than you think you need to and the rest takes care of itself, through the law of averages...*also known as "working the numbers"*.

Some people fear attrition because they look at it from the side of loss, or losing people. What masters know is that through attrition, the strongest team mates rise to the top and duplication occurs effectively, efficiently and more predictably…the natural screening process takes care of itself. You don't concern yourself with losing that which wasn't in alignment with your goals….quality vs quantity. It just doesn't make sense to invest in people who quit and essentially, everyone naturally picks which role they are going to play, before they even join, you don't have any say in the matter. Our job is to be the messenger, help people join and get them trained properly by demonstration, to repeat the process. It's that simple!

So, its critically important to manage what you're telling yourself, inside your head. If you think that for every 10 people you talk to, 10 people will join you and become productive leaders, there's a major misunderstanding occurring. The key concept here is to develop your work routine, (locating people who want, value and afford what you offer for 2 hours/day) and keep in the front of your mind that of the people you talk to, you're 'screening' for the best candidates based on the information you have at the time. Once those join you who are inclined to, next you're watching their ordering habits and business-expanding actions to find out which of the ones who joined are the cream-of-the-crop.

The majority of the time you'll be working with people who won't follow through, but will buy and use some products and refer other people. The majority of the population is so scared and threatened by change and anything different than what they're familiar with, as well as insecure within their daily routine that as they get closer to having greater income and enhanced lifestyle benefits, the more insecure they become.

In every field of endeavor, there's a small group of people who become exceptionally successful, at what they do. These people are comfortable/excited by change and improvement. The further they get from their comfort zone the more excited and engaged they become. These are the people we're looking for. Very, very often these people (regardless of their current profession) are keeping their options open, for a way to earn more money and have more time-freedom…they recognize the value in what you offer! With this being said, most everyone will comment that they "want" more money and free-time, but they won't be willing to do the work to work through their current limitations, work through the discomfort of change, won't let go of the past, won't let go of distractions, won't let go of the familiarity of mediocrity, to reach a new level of achievement. In short, they aren't ready to let go the past long enough to step into their potential future, nor are they willing to do something different to get a different result. So, we screen the people we locate, which is essentially like an interview, in order to make sure there's a match.

You'd be surprised to how much strategy, effort, energy and resistance people put into complaining about their lives as it is (which we can understand as wanting more ease in life), yet resisting anything that would slightly improve their situation, lest it threaten their current comfort zone. This chapter is about the concept that you can predict which people will become one of your 12-15 leaders your train every 12-15 months. Often, the people you are personally invested in joining you will flake-out, but by establishing a consistent routine of locating people who want and value what you offer for two hours per day, will come 12-15 leaders every 12-15 months.

More often than not, you'll invest in getting a person started, they'll join, use products and refer a couple people who do the same. Through this repetitive process will emerge a leader, like yourself, often many level away from that original customer. In this way, you realize the "search" isn't necessarily about the person you're currently talking with, but who will come as a result of talking to them, many levels away. That means giving every person the professionalism and attention they need and deserve to succeed, but doesn't mean you don't have sense of attachment to any one person in particular, which frees up your emotional-energy to do what was demonstrated to you, without worrying about any particular person joining you.

Knowing that in your routine includes having a certain number of people join you each day, week, month and year and that the numbers will take care of themselves. You're doing the process. That's not to say that you take such a care-free approach that you don't locate anyone who wants, values and affords what you offer and still expect to expand your group. You have to put energy in to get a return on your investment/to see your group expand and duplicate. It's just that as you're building, you don't want to be emotionally wrapped up in "which" particular people follow through….which could set you up for intense emotional ups-and-downs and disappointments, which are inevitable. You'll need the emotional-energy to invest in your business over the long-haul. It's a marathon, not a sprint.

Like an airplane flying above the clouds, you might find yourself unconcerned about all the drama on the ground. Using the same air that the ground is using, but using it to get from point "A" to point "B", without dealing with all the traffic on the ground.

Opportunity vs follow-through:

You'd think that the reason everyone isn't financially-free and living the lifestyle of their dream is because they lack opportunity. Not true. Opportunity abounds. In my book *Motivation,* I give many examples of people who made something out of nothing. People who complain about not having enough money or the free time to enjoy their money are often really good at starting things and not completing them. This goes for all areas of life and endeavor. This business is no different and you're now frontline to seeing it in full detail. People who follow through on their intent make all the money, have tons of friends, finish they education, and have the freedom to come and go as they please rather than being anchored to a job in one location. They are thankful for the American Dream. People who don't follow through complain that the system is rigged against them...that it doesn't work. And, unfortunately, most people you approach will fall into varying levels of this category. As they take some action and approach a new, unfamiliar level of success in their lives, they'll start easing back on the throttle to get life "back to normal". This is just a factual phenomena of human nature. *No one said being successful is comfortable, at first!*

You'll invest some time talking to people who won't follow through, but then from those main prospects will rise up leaders that you didn't put a lot of faith in, other than to initiate the process. The reason being that network-marketing amplifies people's natural (albeit latent) personality tendencies...the cream rises to the top. People who were successful in endeavors which require confidence and being outgoing won't necessarily be successful in network-marketing and people who didn't do well in conventional business, often do amazingly well. The reason being that network-marketing brings out people's latent skill-sets and strengths. So, if they weren't at home in politics, sales, and things like that, they'll often rise to the top in Shaklee.

What initiates this process (the stirring of the milk) is you doing your two hours, per day of locating people who want and value what you have to offer. The cream that rise to the top is the 12-15 leaders you train every 12-15 months. Many times, people you didn't personally know when you launched your business. That's not to say you don't invest your energy reaching out to people who may not follow through (it's about who they know) but rather that you get back at least double, maybe ten times more than what you put in…it's just that it isn't going to come back from the people you thought or might wish it would have been…it will return two to tenfold, just not how you expected!

Membership based on productivity:

For every industry, there are people who simply don't qualify to participate. That's not to say people can't improve themselves, thereby qualifying or improving their position for themselves at a later date. But, during the launch and expansion of your business, you're screening for people who are ready and have the means [right now]. You want a strong start. Those with such a lack of understanding and personality development that they can't be taught the fundamentals will, by default, eliminate themselves. For example, a person who unreasonably believes that if a business models works, then they should earn $20,000 their first month, in the business isn't being reasonable. And if they can't understand why, there's nothing you can do about it.

"Business" implies that you have to invest your time, energy and money to "expand" and expand the thing up, consistently, over time. Yes, some people have advantages, like internet marketing skills, for example. People who *enjoy* sales will have an advantage over people who fear talking and learning about others…not because we're looking for sales people, but because they simply have less fear about talking to people. In the right environment for a person's personality, anyone can do sales, but not if they are untrained and scared. I used to manage a GNC store and I hired a house wife and mom who was afraid of people and didn't want to sell…but, she loved nutrition. So, she simply talked nutrition with the customers and they made their own decision about what to buy. She did great. Usually, if someone says they don't like sales or want to sell anything, they're really afraid of being put on-the-spot or needing to pressure people into buying something they don't want…which I wouldn't do either. With my worm business, I just posted sign and made the products available and then the fisherman knocked on my door. They gave me money, I gave them worms. Never, did I twist anyone's arm.

People who can speak multiple languages, thereby being able to talk to a wider variety of people, will have advantages, as well. But people who only speak one language become millionaires, also! People who were raised understanding business may have an advantage. But, every person can improve their skills thereby improving their assurance of success and that goes for every industry, not just network-marketing. Every time you talk with someone you can improve a little and carry that forward, into your next experiences. It's okay, to *learn as you go.*

For many who don't reach their goals, the common factor is simple...[in the first month of launching their business, they can't accept the fact that the people they thought would join them or the people they wanted to join them the most, simply didn't value, want or afford what they were offering]. So, instead of moving on to find the people who *are* interested, they linger back there with the people who aren't interested, stuck, trying to change the reality of the past...trying to force people to want something they don't want. Duh! You could think of people who don't "get it" as wet-wood. If you're in need of a fire, are you going to wait until water-soaked-wood dries out and risk hypothermia or simply use dry wood to get a fire going immediately? People who lack inner-fire aren't likely to be successful as any business...it takes inner-drive.

If new a new business-expander emphasizes what they *aren't* willing to do, prior to learning what they *need* to do, it indicates that they're more concerned with staying on their comfort zone that going outside the box to achieve their dreams. Neurosis of attempting to do the same thing, but get different results...*also referred to as insanity.* I've always been the type of person who is more than willing to go outside my comfort zone and change as a person, but I have to see a demonstration of the skills...not be told what to do and I've found most of my group is the same way. Demonstration of what to do always works better than being told what to do...too much is lost in the "telling". The less skills a person comes in with, and you don't have to have any skills, the more important it is to show people what to do versus telling them what to do.

In the meantime, during the same time people join and drop out (attrition), others will become the next top-earners, be traveling the world for free and driving their new company car (Yes, Shaklee offers free company cars to people who locate and trainer 12-15 leader every 12-15 months; a perk)… *it may as well be you.* Did you get that? During the same amount of time that some people are procrastinating, rationalizing and making excuses, others are making a hundred-thousand in bonuses their first year, making use of *The FastTrack Program.* Your choice.

Success patterns:

Successful people tend to be adept or well-adjusted socio-economically, meaning they understand roles, responsibilities and how to utilize the system to *get along with others* and move up the ranks of society. Sometimes referred to as well-adjusted versus mal-adjusted.

People who do well, tend to understand etiquette and manners. Meaning they're on their best behaviors, especially when someone is offering them something good, useful and valuable. So, even if they aren't interested they don't pull punches or try to get something for nothing and they behave professionally, even if they aren't interested. Real Estate agents come to mind when I think of professionals. They know that a property sale can come from anyone, so it's in their best interest to be nice and professional and make connections with people, rather than be polarizing, argumentative and make people feel bad for having their own opinion…in other words, they separate their own preferences and bias from business…they aren't trying to prove anything, they focus on expanding their business without offending others' sensibilities. In addition, real estate agents are often looking for ways to increase their income and are often open to options, between property sales…*hint, hint. Can you think of any city that doesn't have real estate agents?* How many people do you think any given real estate agent knows? Do real estate agents socialize and work with other real estate agents?

The reason the concept of having a process to screen who you choose as your primary 12-15 leaders (each 12-15 month period), why it is important to take notice of, is because very often when one person among a group of friends decides to move up in socio-economic status (more freedom of time and more income) the rest of their group who isn't ready to move up will attempt to interfere, in the one who desires change progress, even if it's only through disguised discouragement. When someone decides they want "more" for themselves and their friends and family aren't interested, they literally have to choose to move forward, with their dreams or stay back, with their familiar circle of influence. This goes for fat-loss and fitness, as well as income.

Without a healthy support system, people have to choose to move forward, with the faith they will develop more friends, whom seem like family and unconditionally support their goals. If they think they'll be alone in their new endeavors, most people won't survive the potential, for loneliness. This is why you must introduce your new business-expanders to others in your group, even members lateral to them, make sure to get them involved in online meetings, webinars and conventions so, that they inherently know they aren't alone, but part of a community. Even if that person has good support, somewhere down the line someone won't have that support. If you don't have everyone involved to some degree, some business-expanders that you went to the work to have join you, will fall through the cracks (attrition). In previous decades, this meant home meetings and parties. Today, it can all be done with conference calls, three-way-calls, free online meetings, classes and webinars, which are often free to utilize.

In this way, it makes a lot more business sense to approach people outside your comfort zone, beyond your current socio-economic status than to approach people who are in the same boat as you. I remember one preacher in Texas, who didn't even have enough money to file bankruptcy and his truck was in the process of being repossessed. He started his business with a chunk of money he borrowed from a church member and started calling people in the phone book, in the wealthier part of town. He went on to earn twenty-million dollars in network-marketing and he prided himself on never wearing a suit, but rather blue-jeans.

The side benefit is that you, by default increase your circle of influence, make friends with greater resources than you might and find people who are more open to money and time-freedom than your current circle of influence. If you have a circle of influence who are very open to opportunity, money and time-freedom, then that's a blessing! Build on it! Go for it!

Another reason to stretch your courage-muscle, by going outside your current circle of influence, is that it's uncommon to build a sizable income by talking to people you already know…some do, but if it doesn't work for you, it doesn't mean you won't reach the level of success you desire...they aren't connected. Eventually, you'll have to reach people you don't know...which could be month one or two of your business expansion. If you work through your list of people you already know (warm market), and few are interested, then the emotional-brain will try to talk you out of approaching people you don't know... *"What's the use?"* the mind might say. The rational-brain will tell you to go outside your box and meet new people.

But just like the cliché, *"You can't be a prophet in your home town,"* goes, if you don't have much influence with your circle of friends and family you're still going to have to approach people you're yet to be friends with, as they gone no reason not to believe in you enough to take a look at the business. *Hint, hint*...some of your very best friends will come from your business and you haven't met them, yet! I promise.

Average of five:

There's a statistic that says every person will have an income equal to the average of the five people they associate with the most (same goes for bodyweight and self-esteem). Looking at your current income and circle of friends, do you want your income to be that average? If you want more, then it makes more sense you approach people you don't know then get shot down by people who insist they know you so well, but don't see a reason to join you. Sometimes, people who know you is the reason for them to join you, while other times it's the very reason they won't listen to you (dismissal, discredit, minimize), and it's time to increase your circle and make new friends!

Because my wife is an ER physician, I tend to get to talk to a lot of doctors from all over the U.S. Most are happy they chose their careers, but many are looking for healthy alternatives to offer patients who either don't respond to westernized-medicine or want to use natural supplements to feel better while being treated with westernized-medicine. And, most doctors want to take good supplements, but are apprehensive because they don't want to take supplements that are dangerous, toxic or ineffective. In addition, people want to be told by their doctors which supplements to take. Can you think of a city that doesn't have a doctor? *Hint, hint.*

Historically, business-expanders who [approach people with higher income levels, disposable-income and so forth, expand their businesses faster and with more ease], than people who approach people who are broke. Makes sense right? You have to be able to purchase products for yourself and for samples. The people who expand the fastest are using and having the most experiences with the products! Think in terms of cities that have a good economic growth situation. If you don't, many of the people you approach will insist they want more money, but don't want to invest in their own business to increase their income and time-freedom! They want something for nothing or think too much like employees (1/2 the population isn't hardwired for entrepreneurship). That would be like trying to install new software, on an old computer that simply doesn't have room for the newer operating system. It won't work and repeating the process will only cause frustration. Half the population will stay being an employee, even if they aren't happy with their job! The truth is that most people who earn a hundred-thousand or more, per year aren't looking for a way to earn *more money,* but have *more free time!* So, they get it! That's who you talk to!

The people who have the worst, most frustrating time expanding their business, after the launch are trying to convince people to value Shaklee, want Shaklee, invest in themselves and so on when they don't inherently do so. Then, when their friends don't join, they approach *more* people in the same category…people without desire for more money or time-freedom and people who don't have money or inclination to improve their situation…or the keep hounding the same people who have said they aren't interested, wasting time, energy and resources, while they could be locating their key 15 leaders (each year), thereby duplicating their efforts, over and over…the way it's supposed to be. Don't waste time convincing!

One of the most common objectives you'll hear from people is that they, *"…don't want to do "sales"."* I learned in my junior-high, Mr. Thompson's careers class that, *"…everyone is always selling themselves, no matter what they do."* Mr. Thompson was a Pepsi™ drinking, high school teacher, but had a roofing and rain gutter company on the side, in which he hired high school students who intended to go to college to work for him. He was the only teacher who drove a new Porche 924, *which he paid cash for.* I learned a lot from him…because I wanted to escape the trailer-court and improve my life.

What's the solution for people who don't want to do "sales"? Well, if they have enough motivation (say, $20,000-$50,000 income per month), they might drop the idea of avoiding sales. Or they might learn that most people fear what they know as rejection, not sales itself. If they had good experiences in sales (meaning, they were trained properly and received high monetary reward for doing sales, they would have a positive association to sales). In other words, they need training to be good at sales, versus being sent to the wolves without training, only to end up with PTSD.

OR, you can [simplify the process even more] by locating/screening the people who love sales and commission-based income…there's thousands and thousands and thousands of people who love sales and are looking to make more money than anyone else…get it?...think about it. You can make it hard on yourself by trying to convince people to do things they aren't inclined to do, or simply find the people who have money, love sales, don't have hang-ups about sales and are a natural fit. Get it? Every college has a business school full of students chomping-at-the-bit to take the business world by storm. You can literally build a multi-million-dollar business locating sales people, without ever doing sales yourself! Think about it this way…sales people don't mind being sold on a good idea…in fact, they appreciate it!

One of the most successful network-marketers I've ever known, mostly looked for sales people, got them their initial product orders and then told them that once they had 10 new customers, only then would their training continue, effectively gaining 11 customers for each new person! He earned tens-of-millions, in income, and he started his business being broke…*what he didn't do was approach more broke people!* So, you can see that people not having a lot of income to start with isn't an exclusive disqualifier, it's just that he had fire-in-his-belly, was skilled at public-speaking (hint, hint), only approached people who he thought had money and wanted more of it and didn't have a bone in his body that gave a hoot about rejection…it didn't phase him. Shaklee's *FastTrack™ Program* is a perfect match for this approach and appeals to all sales people…just show them the video or brochure with the payplan…the right ones will get it.

People who approach friends, family, co-workers and classmates who are broke, don't want to do anything that reminds them of their lack of experience and skill in sales, or are afraid of money and don't understand time-freedom, from leveraging their time are going to get very frustrated. It results in people quitting the business before they really get going.

Worry less about yourself or the fact you're starting out and focus on locating natural leaders, speakers and sales people.

The difference between the people who are successful and those who quit is the canyon known as perception, mindset, attitude and ability to adapt…the same person could approach people who seem "easier to approach" and dropout in the first week, in response to perceived rejection, judgement, disapproval and so forth or they could approach people who have money, are looking to increase their money and free time, looking for a way to decrease their taxes (home-based business), travel more, drive a new, free car every two years and are looking for a system that is time tested and proven without having to sacrifice their health or their family time…this person will walk away from each interaction and partnership feeling lighter, energized with increased confidence and competence. Their business expands so fast people can't believe it. 15 new leaders every 12-15 months. Think *Fast-Track!*

Same business, different approach and focus equals dramatically different results.

Refining:

A phenomena of any endeavor in life whether work-related, hobby-related, recreation, relationships and even vacation planning is that you don't know everything until the experience is over. That's part of the fun of it. If you knew everything, then you wouldn't want the experience! It's common to have a level of knowledge to get going, but it's really enthusiasm and passion for the topic or task that gets you in the game and keeps you in the game…it's what defines the high-achievers from the bench-warmers or spectators.

In hindsight, we think, *"If we only knew that when we started it would have been so much easier"*. But, if it was that easy, everyone would be wealthy, healthy, happy and free. The truth is we need enough information to get started and then refine as we go…*that's it*. The people who have to know everything to start, never start, since new information, techniques, technology and strategies are surfacing *daily*. Needing to know everything to begin is a strategy for failure called procrastination or "analysis-paralysis"...meaning, people think they need more info, but the more information they get the more they think they need and the more information they get, the more overwhelmed they get, mistaking the anxious, overwhelmed feeling for needing more information! Needing more and more information to begin is a sign of insecurity and a need for assurance...almost a phobia. In other words, the more information they get, the more insecure they become...doing and experiencing builds confidence and competence...not learning new ideas, but failing to apply them.

In traditional careers, whether after earning a college degree followed by an apprenticeship or fellowship or vocational certification, you have a level of training (for which you may or not be paid), before you enter the job market. One of the advantages of network-marketing is that you can begin getting paid from day one...even paid on your own first, personal order!

Traditional education and training has the inherent benefit of building up the student's belief and self-confidence in themselves as they progress through their training and learning-curve. Part of the reason people who drop out of network-marketing, in the first month or so (attrition), is because they set out to do the task without having built up inner-strength, resilience and confidence prior to encountering negativity or being challenged by nay-sayers. They perceive that the discomfort of what might be construed as "rejection" is about them personally, when in reality it's about the person you're talking to not being a fisherman, who doesn't want to buy worms to go fishing! Does that make sense? If they don't value or want what you offer, let it go! Don't make it a thing! Your job is to tell people who you are and what you do. Keep the topic on that! Focus!

People who "personalize" potential negativity (*take it personally*)...in other words, take it in, give it a home and then recycle it in their memory will, unfortunately perceive more negative experiences than positive ones...in their perception....they magnify negativity out of proportion. It's an unconscious habit people need to break themselves of.

On the other hand, people who place their focus on "sorting", "screening" and "locating the people who are looking" will see that people who aren't looking will often respond in what's referred to as negativity with humor and as the messenger, *"let that poop roll off their back like water off a duck's back,"* while in their mind collecting and recycling the positive experiences they have each day...*replaying and magnifying the positivity of each situation.* The most successful people in network-marketing keep their focus on their goals, visualizing the goals as already having been accomplished, collect positive experiences in their mind and feel grateful for each interaction as a learning experience, while committing to forget what might be considered negative...*take the lesson, but leave the experience behind.*

The psychology of this is that people who have (at some time in their lives) been overly criticized (or lack self-confidence/self-esteem), in life, have a habit of focusing too much on the next perceived criticism (they expect and anticipate criticism, rather than expect approval and a positive experience)...the next perceived rejection...the next time they come out of a conversation perceiving that they were "wrong" or "did something wrong"...in essence, exacerbating anxiety about a future that only exists in their imagination. They might even feel as though if they don't get a positive response from a prospect that they "are a bad person". This is also known in the psychology world as a complex-equivalent or a "complex", meaning they connect two things/experiences in their mind as related to one another, without knowing that they don't have to or that not everyone makes those same connections in their mind. How this plays out in real life is that they avoid any situation where someone might disagree with them, tell them they're wrong, discount their efforts, discourage them, dismiss them and so on, not knowing that a certain percentage of the population defaults to a negative response, rather than being positive and encouraging and that it has nothing to do with them, let alone a reflection of how successful they can become. They live in a box. They shrink and turn inward on themselves. In essence, a person who fears criticism or lack of approval will be very stunted, in the personal and professional development, since they are operating out of a model/internal strategy of "avoidance" rather than advancement.

We have found that what these kinds of personalities need is to see demonstrations of successful people without worrying how they will do it themselves...simply watch, listen and feel...observe.

No matter what area of endeavor, we will all receive unsolicited negativity, discouragement and nay-saying no matter what we're doing or not doing...hence, the importance of constructing your "inner-circle"...*a group of people who each have each others' back, united in common goals.*

A common factor of most successful people is that they have the courage to go out in the world and put themselves out there, but they also have a solid support system of people who understand and can relate to their greatest challenges and stressors...something that not all of us have the good fortune of having with our immediate family and friends, but do possess the personal power to cultivate over time. Even if you have only one person (the person who helped you join), who believes in you, supports you, backs you up, lends-an-ear and even makes suggestions, that one person can be enough to support you during the launch of your new lifestyle.

But, hear this, whether a person is a celebrity, an athlete, an actor, politician, saint or a business person, there will always be critics who criticize because it's easier than doing the work itself and the more successful a person becomes, the more vicious, mean and passive-aggressive critics can be...it never stops...you simply have a choice to let it rob you of your joy, inject drama into your life or ignore it, laugh it off and do the work to reach your dreams. Even God has critics! There's never been a president in the history of the U.S. whom everyone agreed with! Even before the U.S. was founded there were presidents, and never did anyone agree with every president! Who are we to think we should be above being criticized...it means we're alive!

I promise you that once you've accomplished your dreams, your critics will still be where they were when you launched your business and started pursuing your dreams to begin with. It's happened to me several times. You have to get to where you can operate in the eye of the storm...it doesn't matter what is going on around you, you remain calm and focused on the task at hand. I survived a helicopter crash this way.

The people in my circle of influence who behaved as if I was naïve or short-sighted or simplified the goal attainment process, are still where they were ten years ago, doing the same things, complaining about their lives, complaining they don't have enough money or free time...complaining about their boss, their benefits, their car payment...*zombies.*

BUT, the summary of this topic, is that as network-marketers, we don't have the time to do therapy and talk about improving self-esteem, self-confidence and so forth (those are not direct, money-making actions)...*we don't have to*. This is a business of doing...*not talking.* "Telling" people doesn't work..."showing" people what to do, definitely works....that's right, "demonstrating". If it seems like your group is struggling to expand at the same rate as you, it can mean a couple of different things, but comes down to the same principle. I can assure you, if you don't demonstrate, first-person, meaning they watch and hear you working your business then they won't understand how to expand their own business...they'll have endless questions (training demonstrations can be done in-person or online with a live webinar, on a weekly basis, for 30 minutes to an hour at a time).

If they haven't had a demonstration of what you "do", every time you answer a question, they'll ask the same questions over and over. If someone keeps asking the same question over and over, they're giving you a "hint" that they haven't "seen and heard" it for themselves...it hasn't been demonstrated. By demonstrating the "what" and "how" expanding a business, the questions are answered before they get asked. It leaves no doubt what needs to be done. At that point, it's their choice to continue or not, based on how passionate they are about reaching their goals and creating their dream life for themselves. If you insist on telling versus showing, you're essentially taking away their opportunity to learn and make positive connections in their own mind.

"Telling" is the equivalent of thinking for someone else...its doesn't do anything, except make the teller feel important. Showing, or demonstrating gives the student the chance to connect-the-dots and learn in their own way...rather than being told what they should experience. Telling implies that everyone learns by listening...which I do not, and eliminates learning by watching, learning through feeling and combining/integrating all three. If you only teach by talking and telling, then the only students who will thrive are the ones who learn by listening, which is 30% of the population...you've effectively stacked the odds against your own success, as well as made it unlikely that the students who learn by watching and feeling will be successful.

Here's the clincher of the story: self-esteem and self-confidence develop from "doing" and the resulting "experiences" of "doing". The more a person "does", the more success they have, and self-esteem and self-confidence are like the cream that rises to the top. Without constant "stirring" of the raw milk, the cream remains mixed in with the rest of the milk. Cheese is made by separating the cream from the milk. As people "do" more, they naturally develop self-esteem, self-confidence and competence...*belief in their ability to create something out of nothing and accomplish their wildest dreams.* Self-esteem and self-confidence are the results of [doing] and subsequently having experiences. Having skills demonstrated is like turning on a lightbulb. People are drawn to their own self-confidence by watching others demonstrate successfully what to "do", so that's why we teach that way.

By you demonstrating correct, efficient activity and use of time, they learn in a way that bypasses their own inner-critic, answers questions they didn't know how to ask, relieves their own lack of belief in themselves, relieves doubt and so on. Demonstration is the cornerstone foundation of all apprenticeships, fellowships, internships, vocational-training and so on *where senior trainers are invested in their students' success and progress.* They don't teach plumbers, electricians, doctors or pilots by telling them what to do over the phone. They show them, have them job-shadow the senior teachers and advisors and then refine through feedback. People who don't care if someone really "gets it" or not (or simply enjoys hearing themselves talk) will take up time on the phone telling their people what to do, attempting to appear like an expert and avoid demonstration that could show that they really don't know what they're doing, endangering the newbies and enabling a higher drop-out/attrition rate, chalking it up to a lack of commitment on the newbie's part. "Talking" is not doing, nor is it teaching. If you get to a point where you've attained all your own goals and want to go into retirement, then you need to either set up an automated system for all the new people who join or have a trainer you believe in and refer new people to them, rather than doing a half-*ssed job or training, leaving new people hanging and then acting like it's them who isn't putting in effort. If you truly demonstrated "how" to expand a business, you should have a lot of people who you can refer to. You'll know which ones in your downline are effective by the amount of their monthly points and bonus check.

Lack of demonstration leads to indecision. Indecision leads to break down in the morale of the group.

Case example:

The good news about launching and expanding your own home-based business is that you're not trying to get just everyone to join you. Not at all. We interview people who request information from us, to see if what they are looking for and what we are looking for are a match. With thousands of people looking to get in and start their own home-based business, each week, we're not looking for just anyone to fill spots. There's no shortage of people who want more money, more free time and to have a nice work environment. We're looking for people who are nice to work with. People who make for a nice work environment.

People leave the traditional job market, often in search of a nicer work environment and that's what you get to create with your own home-based business…you locate, select and build your team to match your ideal business partners. If someone doesn't meet your standards for how you want to be treated, you don't let them in your team. Build your team and surround yourself with people who have similar values, so that you look forward to your work days and you get as much positive energy from your team as you put in.

You can do it.

When someone doesn't join you, it points to where they are in their life, right now, not to "how" you presented the benefits to them. As long as you clearly share how they can benefit, from the business (big money and free time), if they don't join you (right now), it simply means the timing is off. Ask for referrals and keep the friendship bridge, in place. When their situations changes (and it will), they'll contact you at a later date. Everyone thinks their current family, career, and income situation is permanent (gives them a sense of security), but rarely is anyone's situation without change. Be the messenger. Share the benefits. Ask for referrals. When people do not join you, it isn't about something you could have done better or differently. That leaves you to be in an information-gathering mindset. Learn as much as you can about people, so you can offer benefits which are important *to them!* That's your best strategy for expanding your organization.

Chapter Eight

Averages & Do-ers

If you take 100 people, less than ten percent will be naturals or have prior *success* in network-marketing. Another ten-percent will learn successful strategies out of motivation to reach their life-long goals. Maybe 80% will refuse to have an open mind, learn new ways of thinking and being, fail to adapt and quit before they learn, leaving the rest of the market wide open for the 20% of us who follow through and learn on the fly. Kinda' crazy right? But, remember the rule that it takes seven (7) exposures to an idea before its readily accepted or considered normal? Well, the good news is that the people who have joined a network-marketing company, but haven't had success, the reason is that they haven't been trained properly or they didn't follow through, once trained because the timing wasn't right for them. That means that they are open to the possibilities. Unless they reached the top pinnacle of success, it comes down to either not being trained properly or not following through on their training, because the timing wasn't right, for them. Remember...we're locating people who the timing is right for them, right now...15 of them, in the next 12-15 months. That puts us square in the middle of the *FastTrack*™ Program, with room to spare...a cushion, if you will, along with all the perks like free travel and a company car.

Unlimited target market:

Even if we only took people who want to lose weight, for example. There's never been a time in history when more people are overweight, clinically obese and suffering the consequences of lack of exercise and nutrition. On top of that, the age of people becoming obese is getting younger and younger to the point of elementary school age kids suffering with what used to be adult *dis*-eases. That means the market for weight loss is expanding faster than we can fathom, with no end in sight...and we have the best weight loss products I've seen and experienced in my 30-year career as a personal trainer. Would I offer a really skinny guy to help him lose weight? Of course not! But, I certainly will ask him who he knows who wants to lose weight! (referrals). The market for weight loss is so big, no individual can serve the entire market and the market is increasing (no pun intended), every day. Even if we only had weight loss products, which we happen to have the very best weight loss system out there, all the people who don't join or follow through, are effectively leaving all those potential clients and money on the table for those of us who do. *Hint, hint*...even if you only focus on marketing the weight loss program, you're likely to reach your financial and time-freedom goals from that one product line alone, as a foot-in-the-door.

Here's the thing, motivated people maintain the course, regardless what life throws at them. Procrastinators use life as an excuse to disengage from their goals. I think that people who don't reach their goals because life-happened think that's normal...*to let problems take up all your emotional-energy, distracting from simply doing the basic fundamentals, regardless of what is going on, around them.* Using life distractions as an excuse to stop taking action is an indulgence that leads to disappointment and regret. **Focusing on all the details that aren't working inhibits the big goals from coming to pass and passage of the big goals usually eliminates all the little problems that seem so overwhelming.**

As a business-expander, one of the most important skills you can have and develop is observing, recognizing and discerning behaviors of those who aren't intentional in their actions/behaviors, regardless how convincing their words are.

The reason being, that by noticing those patterns, and investing your time in the motivated, goal-seekers you effectively, but conservatively double and stream-line your available work hours. You invest 2 hours per day in the people who want, value and afford what you are offering right now and gain referrals from the people whom you come into contact with.

As a business-expander, you receive an email each time an order is placed by anyone in your group. We all have that. So, if people join and want lots of individual training time, but they aren't ordering, then it doesn't make sense to do individual training with them. Focus on the fundamentals, but *include them in the generalized group trainings.* Some of the very best and most productive leaders start out slower and even rather unimpressive. But, at the same time, some of the most successful network-marketers started out as the worst network-marketers...me included.

Invest in your people carefully:

Romanian Tennis player Simone Halep hired successful coach Darren Cahill, to help her overcome a plateau and reach her next level of success. Even though she had extraordinary work ethic, she had such a negative attitude, her attitude that gotten so bad, her coach walked away from her in 2017, telling her, *"You can lose, but don't quit."* You see, every time things got tough and she was about to have breakthrough to the next level of her development, she would allow negative emotions to take over and she would threaten to quit. That strategy essentially utilizes the coach as an emotional punching bag, which no one with an ounce of self-worth would tolerate for any amount of money.

What kind of a message does that send to a coach who is investing their time, energy and expertise in your development, if you quit when it gets "tough"? In every endeavor, emotional-stability is what helps assure ultimate success. A moody, broody person with severe mood swings won't be able to develop consistency, let alone develop relationships needed in business. In addition, it gives new people the message that moodiness is a good strategy for success. Moodiness creates confusion, uncertainty and complications versus emotional stability. Most of the time, when a person is close to going to the next level of success, they either have to let go of some baggage, gain some skills or a little of both. Ultimate success is a lot of getting out of your own way! You don't get everything you want by staying the same. Each level of success requires inner-change. For a lot of people who insist they would rather stay the same than achieve their goals, it explains why so few become super-achievers in any arena.

In essence, if someone joins us with the skills, mind-set, values, beliefs and work ethic, there's not a whole lot we need to do with them once they understand the three steps, of the business:

1. Want more money and time-freedom.
2. Use the products.
3. Locate and show others how to do the same thing.

That's it!

Some people will want the benefits and possess less skills, which is where "demonstration" of said skill sets comes into play. It's our job to bring out the best in others. Its others' job is pay-it-forward...that's how we know we did our part.

Some people can't help but focus on the perceived problems, what the negatives might be, why it won't work. Simply plug them into your generalized group trainings, so they can be exposed to the benefits (to them), positive mindsets and habits and then leave it to them to adopt healthier habits, but don't be around them in a way where they are permitted to tax your emotional-energy, create a fog of negativity or pull other members of the group down. Negativity breeds doubt, contempt and resentment...it's toxic to progress, but some people seem to thrive on it.

As people join our business organization as an expander, we invest quite a bit of time getting them trained and up to a basic operating level. Some of the training is automated through *Shaklee University*™, some is through CD's, DVD's and online MP3 recordings, webinars, three-way-calls, conference-calls, product-talks and some is in-person. In other words, we work very closely with people and often develop life-long friendships with people we would have otherwise never known. With this in mind, this is another reason why you screen and choose your business teammates *wisely*. Part of the initial contact with prospects is to hear their voice, hear their values and to find out *about them*, to see if there is a possible match. Find out what their energy is like.

Even among the people who want to join, you have to make sure you invest your time wisely with the people who are doing the work to expand their own business. I often refer to the concept of "talking" vs "doing", especially in the world of fitness and fat-loss. [You'll know when a person is applying what you've taught them because their monthly group product volume continues to increase]. Product Volume (PV) increases through:

1. Personal use of the products,
2. Products purchased to give in-person samples,
3. Products purchased from new business-expanders joining and beginning the evaluation and experimentation phases and by
4. Establishing new customers who aren't interested in the business, yet.

From the group of people who do join, you'll notice that some people are producing better results than others. This is a natural phenomena, in all areas of life. But, as you continue to expand your business, you'll notice that you only have so many hours per day, per week, per month, etc., to invest in one-on-one, continued training. More often than not, professionals in any industry have what they refer to as their "inner-circle". The inner-circle is the group of people who have similar values, beliefs and who provide the greatest return on their time investment and moral support. The inner-circle is the people that cost you the least in emotional-output, but provide the most in return, to each other in terms of positivity and mutual moral support.

Inner-circle people are generally not people who are gossipers, engaged in pot-stirring, argumentative, polarizing, negative, back-stabbing, creating alliances, nor procrastinators, or knit-picking about the products, but rather agreeable, united-in-the-common-cause, positive, action-oriented team-players. *FUN.* Meaning, you have to look at who is producing the greatest results that are in alignment with your goals (increased PV and recruitment of leaders, for example) and provide individual attention to them, to accelerate their efforts…essentially, the next, deeper level of duplicating yourself.

That's not to say that the people who aren't producing as much or are slower-starters are to be shunned or ignored, it's just that you want to include them in your group trainings, versus individual training. Group trainings are a way to multiply your efforts, without increasing your labor output. Nowadays, Zoom meetings are a very common way to hold online classes for free and you can have up to 50 people attending, from your own computer, regardless where participants are located. You can Google 'Zoom' and sign up for a free account, schedule meeting times and then simply sent out announcements of the meeting times.

In the beginning, you don't need to run your own meetings or trainings, that's not expected. Jump in and invite your people to the meetings, trainings and webinars the person you joined with are having. Any and all meetings should have content and outline planned in advance, concise and to the point and should be systematic in that each person gets the same training at the same time in their development as a expander. If the training is inconsistent, ill-planned and different every time, your group will lack consistency and everyone will be on a different page, unable to clearly communicate with each other and confusion will reign. For example, Training Session #3 is the same every time, that way everyone knows what Training Session #3 means. If you give homework assignments, provide a date when the homework is expected to be completed and follow up on its completion. It's common for people who want to sound like an expert to give homework, but if they don't follow up to assure completion and summarize the point of the lesson, then there's no point to the homework…it's just time filler and time is of essence when expanding your business. Respect your expanders' time, by having a clear, concise plan for meetings. This is not social time, nor is it a formality to appear like you're doing your due diligence. Serious business-expanders need all the time they can set aside to locate and train new expanders, don't be taking up their time with informal, ill-planned, unprepared social time, which doesn't cover anything of value to business-expanders.

If a new expander has said they have 15 hours each week to devote to their business and you give them an assignment, but then you don't follow through or remember at the next training session that you gave them an assignment, you just wasted their critical expansion time, which to me, is disrespectful. It also sets an example of wasting time with "filler"…activities that make a person "busy" but don't create new business partners or customers. Business-expander leaders who lack focus and think they need to "manage" their expanders or attempt to come across as the "expert" attempt to get people on the phone, chat, take up time and attempt to position themselves as being "in charge"…talking *"about"* business, but not actually doing expansion behaviors.

I'll reiterate this point here and throughout the book…how you make money in Shaklee is by 1) Increasing your monthly product volume by using products and locating customers and 2) Gaining business partners/expanders, who are also using the products themselves. Your primary investment of time and energy is in those two activities. Nothing else. This means that you have to be particularly guarded with the time you set aside, for business- expansion, as well as respect the time of your new business-expanders. About 75% of your time, during the launch of your business (first three months), is invested in these two activities.

If time spent with them isn't invested in demonstrating these two skills, you're spinning-your-wheels, wasting your time and theirs. That's not to say you have to be obsessively and compulsively rigid like a drill-sergeant and be blunt and cold with people. It does mean that if you aren't investing 10-15 hours-time, each week to locate more business partners and customers, you won't get the results you insisted you wanted from the beginning. The ONLY thing that counts as teaching, is [demonstrating the expansion of *your own* business], meaning you combine your hours of expansion (10-15 hours per week) with demonstrating to your new expanders/business partners what it is you're doing to expand your business...not talking about the business, they already know the benefits and want to see how to expand their own business.

Again, that's not to say you can't be friendly and have casual conversations (that's partly how you get to know people better and build relationships) it's just that the time you set aside to expand your own business, has to be compartmentalized, "preserved" if you will, for locating, and helping new people join you. Any time outside of your designated 10-15 work hours can be used however you want. Let your group know in advance that you'll check your email or return calls within 12 hours or whatever fits your own expansion work schedule. If you want to set up social time with your members, that's fine, but don't mistake social time as expansion time on your work schedule.

Entrepreneur mindset:

You'll run across people who just have an employee mindset. Its recognizable by them saying something like, *"I'll invest if I make money first,"*...the opposite of the entrepreneur mindset. The same thing happens with people who want to lose weight saying, *"I'll change my nutrition habits, if I first, lose weight,"* (wack-bards). Permanent fat-loss comes from improving your nutritional habits. It takes money to make money, even if you are investing in your own business. People who say they'll invest if the make money first are exercising the "entitlement mentality" in that they don't understand employment is not the same as self-employment...they're missing that business owners put up the money for their employees before the work is done. In business, you do the work and invest before the money comes. They're missing the point that the benefits of having your own business are much greater than being an employee. But usually, they have to get screwed over by a couple of employers before they make the connection. Just keep the friendship bridge built, since if they won't invest in their own business, they are not part of the 1% of leaders we are sorting for, right now.

Case example:

Give yourself a raise. In traditional employment, you're pretty much at the mercy of your employer as to how much you can earn. But, with this model, you can give yourself a raise any time you want, as many times as you want! In other words, any time you want your monthly income to increase, you simply do the actions you're shown during your initial training, again…*locate three business partners and ten customers.* You can figure that for every three business partners and ten customers, your annual income will go up by at least $500, per year. It's a simple, repeatable process that you and your friends can do together. Shaklee sets aside a certain amount of money for every successful business-expander, who locates people who want the benefits of the products and business. Say you currently earn two-thousand a month at your job, but you'd like to earn ten-thousand-a-month and have a company car and free travel…you can do that…you can do that for yourself. There's no ceiling and you can have as big of a piece of the pie as you want for yourself.

You simply do the processes you learn and repeat them until you have the size of income you want. At any time, you can repeat the process and give yourself a raise.

Chapter Nine

Focus On The "Process"

"Inspired by the hustle." Bruno Mars

So, it's critically important to manage what you're telling yourself, inside your head (self-talk). From competitive athletes to Olympic Athletes to Navy Seals, what they tell themselves from moment-to-moment, especially when the facts seem bleak, success is determined by the level of self-talk moment-to-moment. That's what makes good things happen. [Successful people, from all walks-of-life repetitively rehearse their successes, in advance]. They imagine their own success.

If you think for every ten people you talk to, ten people will become leaders in your group, there's a misunderstanding occurring. The key concept here is to develop your routine, 10-15 hours per week locating business partners and customers. A lot of people simply don't qualify nor are they a match for my or your group. Remember/keep in the front of your mind, that you'll need to talk to a lot of people, who may not join you directly, but through talking to those people your group will develop in unexpected ways, two to tenfold the energy you put in, depending on how efficient your routine is.

What *"No"* means:

I was raised in a very strict household, where we weren't allowed to make mistakes. Whatever we tried we needed to do it correctly, the first time, or we would be punished for failing. If we didn't do something correctly the first time, it as considered shameful. If we asked for something and were told, *"No"*, that meant don't ask again. That strategy worked well for my dad getting his way, but didn't really prepare us kids for the real world. Nor did it coincide with my desire to be a salesman from a very early age. To me, sales were fun…a direct correlation between effort and payoff. *Do this-get this.* Offering value in exchange for $$$.

As I said earlier, statistically, the average sale across all industries requires seven contacts or exposures about a specific product or service. It's just that until we see something the 6th or 9th time, we aren't aware of the importance of the thing until it clicks in our consciousness. Sometimes we don't know we want to buy something, until we know how it solves a problem we just became aware of. *Hint, hint.* I think one of the reasons is because people have to become familiar with you or what you're offering as well as taking time to make up their mind and find ways to afford what they want to buy.

Aside from my worm business, earlier than that I had a rock business, where I would find rocks I liked, paint them and set them out by the road to sell them. I also had a marble business in the third grade, where I sold steel ball bearings to my classmates, who played marbles at school.

Just because someone doesn't take you up on an offer, doesn't mean they don't want to. It could mean they don't have the money at that moment and they don't want to say so. There's a million reasons why a person might not accept an offer, *the first time,* many reasons we may not ever know about. I had an acquaintance who was a hypnosis-therapist and charged what she thought was a reasonable hourly-fee and saw it from that one side. She had been contacted by a lady about receiving hypnosis, but then never heard back from her. Eight months later the lady called back for her appointment, as it took her that long to get the money for one appointment. Long story short, the client was in a terribly abusive relationship, walked several miles to work back and forth each day and had to give all her money to her husband. It took her that long to skim off sixty-dollars, without her husband knowing it.

Often times, people are using a product they think will work, for them and it takes some time for them to grow dissatisfied before they open up to try what you're offering. The last I heard, the average Shaklee customer has been using Shaklee products for 17 years…think about it. I've consistently been using Shaklee products since 1993 and had been looking for a Shaklee Distributor for 20 years, before that!

The point is to focus on cultivating familiarity with people, versus pushing a sale. Focus on learning about them and their lives, rather than trying to get one sale. Focus on solving problems and asking if they would be open to trying something. Most of the public has no idea there's 300+ products, but they don't need to use all three-hundred. Cultivate familiarity, so you can share information without them feeling obligated, focus on benefits (feel better, more energy, look younger, weight loss, etc.), rather than debating technical data and features. Make it easy for them to ask questions and consider your offer. If you can help them solve one health problem they have (not feeling good, lack of energy, feeling like they look old, weight gain), then you'll have built relationship, trust and opened the door to learn more about them and the concerns/problems of their family. Think about it, 80% of the population is over-weight. The only thing more people need than weight loss is breathable air.

One of the secrets of products, is to have a focus or two (more energy, weight-loss, etc.). Once a person gets results with one thing, they start asking about possible solutions for all the other problems their family has (high blood pressure, digestive problems, diabetes, etc.), resulting in even more business! Make yourself known as a source of good info and you'll be on your way.

Appointments this week were made last week:

People who lack business experience often think that you just start talking to someone and you get a new customer right there and then. But, remember the rule of an average of seven contacts. Many experts say that 6 weeks is the average time for a new business-expander to get up and running, even though they want more money, now. If you don't have any business appointments set up this week, it has to do with not making contacts and working to set them up the previous two weeks. Think in advance, work by appointment. Make sure people know you can fit them into your appointment book, but [everything is done by appointment]. All successful professionals keep an appointment book (I use Google calendar) and stay organized as well as plan their time based on this. When people know your time availability is limited, they'll respect your time a little more. If you don't use a calendar, you'll come across as casual and people won't take you as seriously. The more organized you are, the less stressful your daily routine will be because you know what to expect at what time. Staying organized is key so that you provide people the time they deserve. If you aren't organized you'll come across disheveled, miss appointments, double-book yourself by mistake and feel generally rushed, which will take the focus off the topic and you'll end up stressed out.

Perceptions vs reality:

Shaklee and network-marketing have successfully been around since before we joined and it'll be around long after we've successfully expanded the base of each of our own businesses. New, inexperienced business-expanders are often so excited that they can't imagine others "not" being interested in it. When I first joined, I contacted everyone on my contact list (warm market), family, friends, etc. Most either made fun of me, told me I was an idiot or insisted the business model simply doesn't work. I couldn't believe it. I still hear of people who have great responses from their family and friends and build the entire launch of their business around their warm market contacts. That was definitely not my experience. As I was growing up, it seemed like every week there was some kind of product party, whether it was Tupperware, Avon, Christmas-Around-The-World or MaryKay. When I started my business, many people were like, *"I know what you're up to and I'm not interested."*

Perplexed, yes, but deterred, no. I've never been a half-way person. I either do something all the way or not at all. Based on my very early experiences of how I felt after that first energy bar, at age six and my long journey of locating a Shaklee Distributor, before the internet and all the health benefits I got from the products the second time around, I just figured those people who said they weren't interested really hadn't used the products. *Hint, hint*...if people don't use the products, they will "believe" they understand the business, without really understanding the business and they won't ever have a business. They have to get Shaklee in their cells.

For me, each of my three sisters bought some nutrition products initially and my youngest, older sister has been a customer of mine since 1993. The people who try and give the products a real run end up being long time customers, who consistently re-order month after month and constantly tell me what amazing and unexpected results they get. So, it goes without saying, that the people who don't use the products say they don't understand the products and don't get any benefits from them. Duh!

I keep a list of unsolicited testimonials that people give me. Whenever someone makes a comment or thanks me for how I helped them, I write them down and add them to my testimonial pack. This builds belief in the business. It's a good idea to collect testimonials and comments, right from the beginning of your business launch.

One of the big-pictures I like people to get is that the business was here before us and it will be here after us. Whether we expand our business today or not, there's people around the word doing so and making a ton of money doing it. Not to mention free cars, free trips and free time. People are buying online more and more, all the time. Considering how many box stores are closing and how convenient online purchases are, sales will inevitably increase exponentially, over the next ten years, which is exactly what experts in the industry have been predicting for the last 20 years. This time is uniquely determined to be massive for people who want to have their own home-based, online business...in fact that's an understatement. Yet, I remember acquaintances of mine who insisted the internet was a fad that would pass. If you can see trends, then you can see how big this is going to get.

Consumers have become very sophisticated when it comes to health, prevention, quality of raw ingredients, certified-organic and GMO-free products and so on. The point being that while a lot of companies are just now getting the idea, Shaklee has a complete and successful manufacturing, distribution and logistics system in place...*in other words, perfect positioning, for the next wave of growth.* With the gap between the wealthy and the impoverished in our society, increasing and more and more people needing two or three jobs just to stay afloat, more people are opening up to the idea of earning money from home...people are praying and looking for something like this. They're waiting for people like us to approach them. That doesn't mean everyone wants it. It means we can have enough faith that by talking to people, sorting through people, locating the ones who do want it, we'll find 15 people each year, who will make up our frontline or first-level of leaders who effectively duplicate ourselves.

Think "process"...15 hours/week, 15 leaders, 15 months:

Ever hear surfers talk about the euphoria of catching waves in the tropical, blue, warm water of Hawaii? If you've ever spent any time in Hawaii or on beaches like that, you can *experience it for yourself*...they can't wait to get in the water and when they get out they are invigorated, relaxed, sometimes exhausted and they can't wait to get back in the ocean, again.

Interestingly enough, surfers never know exactly what their experience is going to be when they head out for the waves. They have faith that it might be good, but they never know exactly when the waves will come, how big they'll be, how many will come in a "set" or if they will even be in line, properly set up to catch the ultimate wave.

For eight months, in 2014, my wife and I lived in Maalaea, Maui. The harbor was at the base of the Haleakala volcano. Simply gorgeous beyond words. Beaches lined with those big, sea turtles. We were in a great condo right on the water, where surfers lined up to catch the waves. Often there would be 20-30 surfers waiting for their turn. The worse the weather the more surfers there were (the worse the economy, the more opportunities there are). We were there for a couple hurricanes and that's when there would be 50-60 people lined up for the waves. The surfers didn't know *which* wave they would catch, but they had faith, based on decades of others' experience that there would be waves to catch. We watched some that were exhausted, just from fighting the currents to get out to where everyone was waiting on the waves (lack of training). Then after a few hours of that, they had to fight the currents to get back to shore (lack of training).

The point being that surfing, one of the most exhilarating and euphoric activities known, demand people fully participate without any assurance that they catch any particular wave on any particular day (being present in the process)…they're simply operating on faith, for those few moments when they get the ride of their lives (locate the right wave and be there for it)… *"being in the moment"*…average "highs". Whether someone catches a wave or not, the *process* is *freeing and exhilarating*. Noteworthy is that the ocean was there before they started surfing and it'll likely be there long after they're gone…they simply get into the process and fully experience it. Most surfers have had the experience of falling off the face of a wave and getting washed on the reef along the floor of the ocean. Then they have stories to tell and scars to show their friends. Like the seasons that come and go, surfers anticipate the next set of waves and catch the ones they can.

When tourists head over to Hawaii, they can hire the "surf-boys" to take them out and catch their first-waves. For people that get hooked, they can get advanced lessons. The "surf-boys" don't tell people what to do, they take them out to the waves and demonstrate what to do! One of my favorite things about taking surf lessons on Waikiki Beach was that even at a half mile out, the water is a few feet deep and crystal-clear blue. If you haven't experienced it yet, add it to your list of to-dos. After you're exhausted from catching a few waves, get back to the beach, grab a snack at the snack bar and lay on the sand with a cold drink and sandwich and admire the tropical blue water. Nothing like it. Very, very peaceful.

There's a pier on the East end of Waikiki beach that the locals jump off of and body surf or boogie board into shore and repeat. When you're there, you notice that the local children are taught to *feel comfortable* in the ocean from infancy and they learn it by copying those who have gone before them. In a way, it's in their blood, generations of family members at home in the ocean…they spend hours and hours jumping in and riding to shore and it doesn't cost a dime (sweat-equity)…they're used to the currents, recognize the weather patterns, the trade winds and wildlife in the water…they're at home in their environment for the energy they're willing to put in, to the fun. Over and over and over they practice the fundamental skills. It's really amazing to see…but even more so to jump in and participate. The water feels so good, nothing like it.

"People are capable of amazing things, when they feel encouraged." Chris Leahy, street musician in New York, who sits down and plays and sings music he made, then gives all the money people passing by give, to the homeless person he was sitting with.

The point being that all those kids go to the beach with fun on their mind and if they catch the ultimate wave or do an awesome trick, cool, but if not, they were still playing in the ocean and having fun each other and creating amazing memories in the process…they *live the lifestyle* so it's enjoyable. At the end of the day, they have gotten a lot of fun in the sun, they're exhausted from all the play and exhilarated at the same time, looking forward to the next day…Hawaiians literally build their entire lifestyle around the ocean. In the ocean, there's no beginning, per se, and no end in sight…vast, yet anyone can get in and participate, enjoy it and have amazing experiences…no two days are alike.

In Shaklee, the people who seem to do the best, realize that it's a *process*...they simply get in and begin participating in the process. They find enjoyment in the known, the unknown, the successes, the challenges, the surprises, the people they meet and lifelong friends they make, the money, the travel, the freedom, the health benefits and so on. Many people realize fairly quickly that they get more benefits from their Shaklee business than any job could ever offer...and that doesn't even take into account all the testimonials they receive from people whose lives and health were improved simply by using the products...in Shaklee, people find their ultimate freedom that exceeds their wildest expectations...its like a big, warm ocean of fun choices. I've known a lot of people who are in companies which don't improve their life and health the way Shaklee does. They get their business built but they lack purpose and their health is gone. Very sad to see.

In my experience, even though I got amazing experiences from the products, I needed to grow and improve to meet my own expectations from the business. I needed to mature my understandings, before I could be wildly successful. Having grown up very shy, introverted, sheltered and financially insecure, I had my own areas of my personality that needed updating, in order to get the most from what Shaklee offers. Many people, in all industries, avoid facing their own weaknesses or insecurities...many people operate out of fear and avoidance of discomfort...they believe their fears. It's more common than you might think, but so is poverty, dissatisfaction and unhappiness. For entrepreneurs, we have the freedom to do what we want and not do what we don't want, but as our goals and aspirations increase, its common that as a business person improves their personal development, so do they recognize an improvement in the performance of their business. For me, I needed to watch and listen to the people who had mastered the fundamental skill-sets, before I would even have a basic skill-set.

For me, I'm not as comfortable talking one-on-one as I am with public speaking to groups and writing book and articles. But, I wasn't always that way. I literally dropped-out...quit high school my junior year because I felt overwhelmed with the social aspects of school. The last time I got embarrassed and my face turned bright red during a book report in Mr. Mejlaender's English class, I quit school. After a time of splitting wood, being unable to get a job or join the army without a diploma, I went back, made up the credits and graduated on time with my friends.

Many years later, in the fall of 1996, I went to clinical hypnosis school, on Vashon Island, Washington and did a lot of self-hypnosis to deal with the phobia of public speaking. As a result, I'm more comfortable speaking in front of large groups than one-on-one. In other words, I saw where a belief or habit or fear was holding me back and I dealt with it head-on. In turn, I've taught many other people self-hypnosis and they've shared their stories about how much it helped them. The first public self-hypnosis class I taught 20 people showed up.

The point being that when you focus on doing and participating in the process, without getting too hung up on the details of every single conversation, and you combine your focus of what you intend to gain from your Shaklee business, with helping other people experience the benefits of using the products your goals will likely come to pass. Even the most amateur surfers catch awesome waves. It's all about being properly positioned, when a wave rolls in and being aware and prepared, when opportunity "knocks".

People who haven't been in business for themselves before or haven't been successful in business, don't realize that [you don't need to win every single time, every single interaction in order to reach all your goals]. Bill Gates, Microsoft Founder, intended to have a desktop computer on every home in America…computers that would use his operating system…that he hadn't developed yet…that had never been made by anyone. Guess what…he failed. It's been decades and some people have numerous computers…but, some people have still never used computers or the internet. Some of my neighbors don't have a computer or the internet. And yes, they complain about not having enough money.

But, Bill Gates is a billionaire, many times over. He got in the process, aimed high, couldn't control what other people did or their level of participation or consumption of his products. Some people simply don't/won't use computers, even though it could improve their life. And yet, he has success beyond most people's wildest dreams and his efforts have made many, many people millionaires because they participated in his vision. I know people still complain about Microsoft products, and yet, millions make use of his products and it made him a billionaire. The process wasn't perfect, bugs continue to be worked out, today and yet enough of the process worked to help a lot of people. Now, the money The

Gates Foundation provides improves the lives of thousands of people around the world.

You see, to reach your goals, you don't have to be perfect, you don't have to win every time and the process itself doesn't have to be "perfect"…it simply has to be *processed*…meaning people spread the word of the benefits of the products, help people get started on the products and then, if you want to build a huge business where you have time-freedom and financial-freedom, locate the other people who want the same kinds of things and help them do the same thing! Remember?…5,000 people join network-marketing each day!

Baseball players don't hit a homerun every time up to bat. Touchdowns take a few plays to happen, but sometimes there's a turnover and the opposing team intercepts the ball and makes a surprising touch down. Sometimes, three-point shots are missed and yet sometimes a player throws the ball from the other end of the court, at the buzzer, for a swish…the commonality is that in order for the amazing plays to happen, people have to choose to participate in the process with full effort, without knowing for sure when the amazing plays will happen…but, they do happen. Some people say that success is largely based in luck, but the more you participate the luckier you get…the participation allows luck to happen to those who fully participate.

Often, business-expanders, in any industry, find that when they really invest time and energy locating people for their group, they may not get the exact people they spoke to, but somehow, they get the number and quality of people they need in order to bring about the goals/outcomes they hold in their emotional vision. Entrepreneurs often refer to this as the curvy path to success. They hold the emotionally-charged vision of what they want/intend to achieve in their minds-eye, combined with honest, smart, consistent work and the process doesn't go exactly as they thought it would, but they still achieve all they wanted and then some and the results of their success benefits others, as well. People who participate half-heartedly are, more often than not, disappointed with their dismal results, while those who do what it takes (consistently contacting a number of people each week for 10-15 hours and adjusting their efforts), end up achieving more than what they had put on their goal boards.

Hint, hint...have you heard of people coming to America to seek the American Dream? Thousands of people migrate to the U.S., on a monthly basis, and in many cases, they come from countries where Shaklee does business and they have family, friends and associates who want the same opportunity...Canada, Mexico, China and Laos are just a couple of examples...*think about it*...it doesn't matter if your family and friends are interested or not...there's thousands of people praying and looking for this and we have it in our hands...you can never run out of people to offer this too, as long as you don't sit on you're a** complaining, whining, focusing on the negative or feeling sorry for yourself.

I can't even tell you how many ways and in how many different contexts, where what other people consider impossible, I've seen the impossible come to pass. I believe, that by looking for exceptions and watching for possibilities and expecting the solution to emerge, it often does, but you have to be open to the possibility in order to recognize it when it appears...you can accomplish what others consider impossible...its like watching for a window to automatically open on its own, but at a time not previously known to the viewer...you have to be open to the possibility in order to see it when it happens, for you. I saw this a lot during my years as a massage therapist and from there it has expanded even more.

It's not uncommon for people around us to take for granted what's offered, because with so many perceived choices available, and the perception of the luxury of time, people fail to act at all, but it's common for people who have had much more challenging pasts, people who leave their homes with nothing but the clothes they wear, to appreciate an offer that meets their expectations of the American Dream...think about it. There's people who have a lot of money who appreciate and recognize quality, because they can buy whatever they want and have tried a lot of junk and there's people who have lived in abject poverty, who recognize opportunity. In between those two ends of the spectrum are a lot of people who, since they believe have a choice to make, exercise freedom of choice, over what's good for their health and their family's welfare...hard to believe, I know, but you'll see it for yourself.

When you focus on doing the process consistently, the results are free to emerge. Love the process and you'll never work another day again.

Case example:

Mark felt as though he was out of options. Broke and in debt, he thought, *"I need to beg, borrow or steal the money to start my own home-based business."* Being a man of faith, he wasn't really considering stealing the money, he simply knew that with the right training, he could become successful, so he borrowed the money from a fellow parishioner.

Many people get started the same way. There's probably fifteen different, creative ways a person can come up with the money to get started, since it's really not that much. Many people I know have a had a yard sale, or sold stuff on CraigsList or posted on an online auction, to get their launch money together. If they're really motivated, it can be done. Many people simply borrow the money to get started.

Mark was taught that it really isn't about "how" he located people who want what he offers, but more importantly [who is at a point in their life where they want and value the benefits of what he was offering]. Mark isn't the kind of person who cares what others' opinion of him is. To him, he's *"...clear with the guy upstairs,"* so that's what's most important to him…everything else is irrelevant. Mark decided to contact everyone in his city (a population of about 400,000)…*leave no stone unturned.* Mark emphasized the financial benefits and time freedom perks of building a successful home-based business.

Within six months, of working two hours per day, his income hit five-figures per month ($15k) and went up from there. Many critics insisted his success was based on 'luck'. So, he moved to another city and repeated the process. Mark emphasizes that by simply focusing on two-hours of work, five to six days each week, locating people who want what you offer, your life will be unrecognizable in a year and you won't have any income problems again. Mark does emphasize that if the business you're in doesn't improve the lives of the people you work with, you'll likely burnout and feel the affects of a life lacking purpose and contribution. He said he's seen plenty of people who made a lot of money, but were essentially broken-spirits, having reached all their material goals, but lacking mental, emotional and spiritual balance.

Mark's mentor, reflects on Mark's success, which was his success, too and explains that there is no secret formula other than [locating people who want what you offer and are at a place in their life where they realize it, *right now]*…at a place where they are ready, which you do during your 10-15 hours per week. As long as you don't try to get people to want something they aren't naturally inclined to want, your time will be well spent. (Convincing is wasting. Locating is investing).

Mark retired early and spends his time traveling the world, fly-fishing world class trout streams and para-gliding as well as teaching other how simple a home-based business can be. He said, *"… there's no shortage of people who want the kind of lifestyle I have, but most people complicate the process or simply won't work their business two-hours per day, five to six days per week."* He said the secret of the business is that, *"…it's so simple, a lot of people don't do it because they can't be their own boss. The people who want it, simply do it and reap the rewards of consistent effort."*

Chapter Ten

Confidence & Competence

I Googled the definition of competence just now. Here's the top two definitions I found, right off, from Oxford Dictionary.

Noun:

1. The ability to do something successfully or efficiently: *"the players displayed varying degrees of competence" synonyms: capability, ability, proficiency, accomplishment, ...*

2. An income large enough to live on: *"he found himself with an ample competence and no obligations"*

You'll notice, in listening to those who have mastered network-marketing in general, especially Shaklee, that they either don't build at all, build to a level and maintain that level or grow to master, relatively fast, but its still faster than a 40-year career that may or may not be there for you at the end.

The masters "do-their-do" (separate emotional-baggage, from the required actions the same as Olympic Athletes have, to do to make it to the Olympics), [without unconsciously looking for places to bring, store, attach or have their emotional-baggage acknowledged or validated.] They are aware that you can either identify as a baggage carrying, non-progressive or let all the baggage go and move onto to living their dream life. You can't have feet in both buckets (e.g. *"poor-me,"* vs *"I made it"*).

So, partly, it comes down to the network-marketers unconscious identity (how they see themselves, their role and their way of getting their emotional needs met, in the world). The person who sabotages themselves as a victim, martyr, avoider of self-work, procrastinator, etc., won't ever achieve and keep success that a victor or confessor will (martyr; the verb, means to make a martyr, or to martyrize). (Please note, although the definition is broader, in reality, there are less of successful people.). You can't undo a martyring. It results in death of one's intentions. Saving a martyr from death would not be the opposite either. There is no word to define the opposite of martyring.) (The closest words to the opposite of martyr, but these words come close: *addressor, handler, embraced, hard-worker*; powertheesaursus.org) determinist, power-house, go-getter, go-ahead, will, get and keep.

An irony of it is, the victim, martyr, avoider of self-work, [procrastinator will withhold encouragement, from an under-developed victor, determiner, confessor go-getter, meaning the person who isn't willing to do the work will avoid encouraging those who do.]

Belief in self a.k.a. *self-efficacy* is essential. If you don't have it, create it. You'll need it. People who seem to have strong self-belief come about it in one of three or four ways. Either they were raised in a highly supportive environment, by people who told them respectively that they "could achieve". Or they have taken enough risks to develop a belief they can succeed. They might have vicariously seen that everyone has the same ability to succeed. Others who didn't have a supportive environment nor have they succeeded at much, but develop an "attitude" that if not me, who? Or why not me? Either way, if you use your imagination to cultivate belief in your ability to succeed, the brain doesn't know the difference. Technically the brain houses the mind, which simply learns from each perceived/imagined experience and gathers information to prove you're correct in your assumptions. Once a person jumps from perceived to imagined to actual experiences, the brain then connects the dots and skill develops. It's as though the imagination is used to give a person a map to follow when there doesn't seem to be one, until experience (from doing a skill) develops. So, whatever you want to believe about yourself, if it's what you really want and look for hints and cues of evidence of your beliefs, certain parts of the brain Reticular Activating System (RAS) searches for and collects evidence in your environment/experiences to prove you're correct!

In other words, a person intent on not succeeding will not succeed because the RAS's role is to prove you are correct! Think about it.

So, you decide what you want to believe, go about having as many experiences, in that context, as possible (locating and training new business-expanders](in as short of time period as possible) and your brain will start collecting & retaining a data base to prove you're right, (in your new actions), establishing your own success reality track-record, whether you want to prove you believe in your own success or you want to prove you won't be successful...*your choice, you'll get the evidence you insist on having!*

Mentoring, modeling, training:

Isn't it interesting that the two definitions of competence and confidence relate to *ability* and *financial abundance*?

Out of fear and lack of belief, the un-confident person may say, *"When I'm successful, I'll behave successful, rather than behaving successful and permitting it in the moment."*

If you were to learn that only 1% of the population makes a good business-expander, would you spend as much time trying to convince the other 99%? Or would you work through them as quickly as possible to build your frontline of 15 leaders, who do the same.

I have heard and experienced the Catch-22 that confidence and competence are a Catch-22...in order to have confidence, you have to be competent, but in order to build competence you have to start with a level of confidence!

The clearest definition of confidence that I've ever heard was by Richard Bandler, one of the founders of Neuro-Linguistic Programming™ (NLP™). He referred to confidence as what comes from "doing" or "having experiences". In other words, a person who lacks experience will often lack both confidence and subsequent competence (ability). These concepts are both closely related to belief in the self, or belief in one's ability to accomplish what they want, also known as self-efficacy.

In other words, a person may require a level of confidence to start a project or business...confidence they can have some success for themselves, to start with and build on. Other people will start a project if there is someone there to help, support or train them even if they don't have any experience themselves. In this business, we'll meet people with extra confidence and competence and we'll meet people who really lack confidence, but who are looking for the opportunity to grow and improve. Often times, people who have a track record of confidence and competence, in other areas who are challenged by the network-marketing environment, while people who haven't achieve a whole lot professionally do better than average…it's not really predictable who will do well, at first glance and who will drop out, before they get going…again, reminder to not be attached to "how" things play out and for the most part, do all your trainings as a group. to allow the cream to rise to the top, on its own.

One thing is for sure, that regardless of where each person is on the confidence and competence scale, what teaches people the "what" and "how" to build the business is to demonstrate how it's done and what exactly is done. "Talking" or "telling" does not build confidence nor competence (except in the person who is talking), whereas demonstration gives people examples of what the correct, foundation behaviors of confidence and competence look and sounds like. Essentially, demonstration of skills builds a file or base of knowledge in correct actions, which all the other details will be built upon and attached to. And, for the people who think they are experts, it shows them what the reality is. There are those people who are successful in other kinds of business, who think they'll simply do the same thing in Shaklee and it doesn't often work that way. So, a novice can do better than the "expert".

If, as a leader, you aren't demonstrating correct actions, you are effectively creating unconscious questions in the mind of your new business-expanders. Un-asked/unanswered questions cause pause, procrastination and disassociation…interruption in momentum…analysis paralysis.

The definitive factor for copiable, continual success in network-marketing is based on a narrow focus, referred to as *"What the new business-expander sees for themselves/what is relevant to them"*. This is what builds the basis of their identity in the business. Without proper mentoring (demonstration of correct actions & habits) new expanders join, they expand their business with a few new people pretty quick and then everyone is in a holding pattern because no one has had proper action demonstrated "to them". Without this first-hand modeling, no one knows what to do. "Telling" them doesn't fly because it leaves too much room for variables and mis-steps, which are very difficult/near impossible for new expanders to emotionally recover from. A set-up for frustration.

So, for beginners, the time between starting and getting their first customers is the *"learning curve"*. If you don't help new business-expanders navigate their learning curve, they'll feel un-confident and in-competent...*meaning, worse than doing nothing at all.* And that's not what we want, so we don't sign people up and feed them to the wolves...in other words, we don't leave people to their own until they have built a base of success that improves their confidence and competence. We don't just blow them off and tell them to *"Just talk to people"*. This business requires more specific focus than, *"Just talk to people"*. People who are natural talkers are going to do that anyway, but that implies a level of confidence and competence! Duh! The person who sees themselves as trainer and cultivator of human potential will have much more success.

Here's the thing; as a person (does) a greater variety of "things" they naturally grow in confidence (confidence is linked to a wide base of experience). As they do more of those "things" they feel better about their ability to do more "things" and they get better at (doing) new things, taking risks and expanding and expanding their business. The ironic phenomena, is that as a person who grows and develops as a person, so does their business grow and develop. As confidence and competence improves, they expand their routine, habits and the kinds of people they feel great about talking to and hence, their business grows in size, depth, width and financially.

Ideally, what we're doing is creating an environment, where newbies can vicariously learn "how" and "what" expanding the business means, where anyone can join at their current level of competence and confidence and proceed at their current comfort level, but learn new skills and competencies as their comfort level and confidence improves, which is natural process if the learning environment is created properly.

"Telling" people to do "more" is a form of insult, since it implies they aren't okay how they are or that the effort they have made isn't good enough. But, on the other hand, a person whose confidence improves will naturally grow in the scale and nature of the skills. As a new business-expander "does" more "things" their competence level improves and so does the scale of their energy investment improve, which improves their feeling that they want to accomplish more. It's an endless cycle that feeds itself, *as long as they have a good support system to fall back on* when

142

they have an "off" day, which should imply their sponsor/upline (the person who helped them join) (emotional-oasis).

When people really know that good days and bad days are like *seasons*, in that they constantly change, and everyone has days that are better than other days, they feel comfortable with the so-called ups and downs (they get in a rhythm and ride the waves)…it's when people feel that not having success every single time is implied or somehow abnormal that they tend to drop out before they get their business really up and running, where they can see that the point is to consistently engage in the process, and know that they're going to reach their goals as long as they continue to expand their business, *by locating the people who want, value and afford what we offer.*

Note imbalances of follow-the-leader:

Now, if someone insists they want the benefits of having their own home-based business, but they won't take training, and insist they don't want help, then all you can do is morally support them and let them know that when they're ready to be trained they can do that. But be cautious, this can be a case where the role of leader and follower might be "off". It's common for people who won't accept your training, that when it doesn't work they will insist you help fix the problem they created. In these cases, you might not be able to help, and it might not be up to you. It would be like insisting a car mechanic work on repairs on your home or visa-versa. Or comparing apples to oranges. The point of training new business-expanders is to have set standard that the team agrees to play by, so when there are problems, you can actually help them adjust their course. Think if a baseball player didn't show up for practice, but insisted on practicing with the football team. Game day comes and the guy who practiced football isn't doing so well and wants the baseball coach to help fix what isn't working…*there's no base to fix or build on since the standards are different.*

Some people are naturally born with a level of confidence and unless they had their spirit morally beat out of them in some way, they'll be more willing to take chances in life, try new things, continue learning and so forth. Some people are not self-conscious and they'll likely launch and expand their business a lot faster, since they aren't inhibited. Some people simply aren't affected by what we refer to as rejection…they simply don't care! And anyone can copy that mentality, when they see it modeled for them (demonstration). If you help such a person join, who is sensitive to criticism and rejection, it's up to you as their leader to show them how to work through these sticking points, by having them "watch you", first person, expanding your business (not telling them how to get over it). Some households and families naturally support personal development and expansion, taking risks, learning over succeeding and so forth. Other families, especially like the one I grew up in, discourage change, discourage improvement, value appearing 'right' over learning and value safety & routine over learning & success. I've seen a pattern in lower level socio-economic groups (people who live in poverty, like I did as a kid), where people are less concerned about people doing better than them than they are about improving their own situation. If they grew up like me, their parents don't want them to do better than them, so instead of each generation doing better than the last, it works in the opposite direction…anything that looks like the child is growing out of the mold is discouraged and even punished.

In these cases, people may be adults and still have very little socialization, confidence or ability to express themselves. They have potential to reach all their wildest dream, but you have to be more patient with them, (create the learning environment), since many years of development as a whole, balanced and socialized person may be lacking…they're starting from ground zero. If you pursue and sponsor people at that level of development, then you effectively are their mentor, since you personally benefit from their success. If you aren't going to "show" (NOT tell) them what to do, then you have no business telling them to do more of which they don't know what to do. Get it? Telling people who lack skills and development to do "more" is neither helpful nor supportive and can make their situation worse. More is not necessarily better. The key is to emphasize in-person training, so they can see, first-hand, you talking to people expanding your business (which becomes a solid foundation of their business skills)…if there is any question in a new expander's mind as to "what' is to be done, they won't do anything and they might even quit ordering since the lack of professional training effectively creates a feeling of alienation. Do not say you agree with this or that you fully understand this, if you aren't doing first-hand demonstrations of how you expand your own business.

The general rule-of-thumb is that as long as people produce results (locate customers and/or business partners, equal to the amount of time you invest in their training) then they are worth your investment of time. When you have enough people that you're training at the same time, then it's time to combine training sessions (in-person with local expander and online for local and non-local builders), to be more efficient with your time. When you're consistent with your own people-locating and you've duplicated yourself a few times, it's time to combine as many meetings/trainings as possible...otherwise, you won't have time to continue expanding and your own business will begin to suffer...and trust me, if you re expanding, your group will stop expanding too...people don't do what you "tell" them to do...they'll do what your "doing". Repeat: if you stop locating and training new people, and change that time investment to train or "manage" your expanders, your group will also stop expanding, just like clockwork.

Expanding your own business is the greatest motivator for your group. "Telling" them to do more is "de-motivating" because it isn't congruent telling people to do something different than what you're actually doing yourself and people know it, because they can see how many people you're personally brining to the training sessions and webinars. If they're bringing people and you aren't, it gives them the impression that they are employees of you!...that they are building your business for you! That's not exactly what's happening, *unless it is*, but impressions are as real as anything.

Learned confidence:

Some people weren't born confident, but they participated in enough different activities that they are generally a little more confident, less shaken up by others' negativity/criticism and less influenced by outside influence and opinion. *Hint, hint...* the more confident a person, the less influenced they'll be by other people. Confidence comes from doing and watching others doing and being okay with the learning process, which includes making mistakes.

Confidence built in by others:

For people who were/are fortunate enough to have positive influences in our life, confidence, to a degree *can* be built in from the

145

outside. Although it borders more on inspiration than true self-confidence, when we have good people around us who intend for us to be happy, healthy and balanced, they can build us up with words of faith, until we have enough experiences under our belt, to fly on our own. **When we speak words of faith and positivity into others, we are essentially preparing/guiding their mind to notice evidence than they believe they are…preparing the Reticular Activating System (RAS) to collect/notice information/data that they are successful, important, unique, valuable and can achieve whatever they want to do, become and have.**

Once the concepts are spoken, the mind begins to discern where its true or not and collect data/evidence that matches the suggestions of positivity. Many people are just waiting for someone to speak positive words of faith over them…maybe they never had that before…the mind is wired to accept words of faith and positivity spoken over them. Once you speak positivity over a person, the part of the brain called the RAS (Reticular Activating System) goes about collecting data in its environment to prove its true, if the person is open to it and likes the idea of it. Studies of teachers who are told a particular group of students are brilliant, even though they are less than average or visa-versa has proven this phenomena…*that our expectations for others, our thoughts and words can have power to influence people's lives by bringing out the best in them,* even if they don't see it for themselves. So, we know that we can be influenced both positively and negatively, from the outside-in, for better or worse. That's why it's important to be selective who you permit into your inner-circle.

Even if we only have one person, in our life like this, it can make all the difference in the world. The goal is to build your inner-circle of people who are like-minded and speak words of faith over each other. Unfortunately, people tend to naturally migrate toward people who match their *current*/familiar level of unconscious (outside their awareness) confidence. In other words, their confidence will be the average of the five people they are around the most. So, in order to improve their confidence, they have to associate with people whose self-esteem is higher than theirs, until it's an average once again, albeit at a higher level, than previous.

Generally speaking, when a person has a good mentor who invests by bringing out the best in them, once they get where they are going, they naturally pass it one/pay-it-forward and invest in bringing out the best in others. A person who is deficient in confidence, competence or belief in their own abilities will be unlikely to invest in others. Either way, the cycle continues for better or worse. The person who had good mentoring, encouragement and moral support and develops to their full potential, regardless of the context, will naturally look for others to mentor themselves. A person who has had moral support withheld, will have trouble perceiving the benefit of morally supporting, nurturing and encouraging others. A person can't proactively give what they don't know exists!

Fake it 'til you make it assumption:

Since we now know that success or achieving a new standard of living, having time-freedom and financial-freedom is based on doing a different and particular set of behaviors on a consistent basis, (versus luck) it's easy to see that we can take years to believe we're successful and relax into success, through external proof like income and travel, or we can assume from the beginning that we are a success for each and every small effort we make. In other words, some people have an exaggerated sense of self and almost come across insincere, while others are super successful, yet come across unassuming…you'd never guess their level of success from the humble way they carry themselves…they cover their success on the inside, rather than insisting it onto or "over" others.

In between the two, is the place where we give ourselves credit for the full value of each action we take, to improve our situation, pat ourselves on the back, measure our worth by how much we contribute to others rather than others' opinion of us and these qualities in general. In other words, when we behave as if we are successful, even before we reach all our goals, the process can be easier. If we wait for others to approve of us externally, we might reach all our goals and still not feel successful. Success is a feeling that is created and validated in the mind of the person. Success can be another Catch-22 in that we might think we need to feel a certain way to take the actions of what we each consider a successful person, but at the same time we think we need to do a certain thing in order to achieve success…*a Catch-22* or paradox

Celebrate each success so the mind associates reward with doing:

What I suggest is that you view your choice to join, launch and expand your business a huge success, in itself. Something a huge percentage of the population will never have the courage or motivation to do. "Expansion" of your business goes on from the first day you make your first product order until you reach your goals and retire. Whether you're earning $100/month or $50k/month, you're in expansion mode and that's how you should talk about it to people you're approaching about partnering with you. From here out, view your progress as "expansion" of your organization, and customer base built on the base of your successful launch. As in, *"I'm expanding my business and..."*

If you don't give yourself credit for the little things, then people will attempt to put you in a place that is more comfortable for them and be less likely to take you seriously. Like I said earlier, a lot of entrepreneurship is "projection". You get to decide how the world sees you by what you project about yourself. You'll attract people to your organization by what values and goals and vision you project. If you don't give yourself credit and recognition for your accomplishments, neither will others you come into contact with.

At a certain point, you have to have or create enough confidence to do what you need to do to reach your goals. Whether it comes naturally through accomplishment, or by watching others do the process of expanding, each time you stretch and do a little more than was first comfortable, the you'll experience higher levels of confidence, competence and belief in your ability to create a higher standard for your life and your family, as well as teach others to do the same. In other words, own the small successes.

I tend to be of the school of thought that if someone doesn't feel confident to move forward and demonstrate the needed skill sets, simply have them watch and listen to someone (preferably the person who they joined with, who has also been properly trained), who is really good at that particular skill-set. That way they see and hear what should be done and they see and hear what isn't being done. Both are mutually important. Often, the person who is struggling to expand isn't doing key things and is doing things that serve to no purpose toward increasing income or free time, but they aren't aware of it. In my experience, when people understand the structure of the "how" and "what" of expanding, they naturally want to do it on their own. In other words, their confidence in their basic ability will come from watching the person they look up to do the actions successfully. Especially important is not just your new builders seeing how you help people who are interested, but in how to gracefully and eloquently deal with people who are negative, have poor manners or simply not interested. These are basic concepts that are commonly passed over, in hope that new business-expanders won't be turned off by seeing that some people simply aren't interested! But that's not reality and really leads to confusion and frustration down the road. Not everyone is a match for everything out there, otherwise there wouldn't be any challenge and everyone would be wealthy!

On the opposite side, one of the most destructive and undermining habits is to tell new business-expanders to, *"...just go talk to people"*. This is the equivalent of sending civilians into combat, who are neither tactically trained nor emotionally prepared for the horrors of war. One of the very worst things you can do that will assure people are dropping out of your group as fast as they join is to tell them to, *"...just talk to people,"* and then when it doesn't work out, ask them what they did and proceed to critique what they did or said, after the fact, as if they knew better.

In reality, this is the actions of an upline who isn't expanding their own group, so they won't show their new expanders how to do what they do…they want to sound like an expert so they "tell people" what to do without demonstration of actual skills sets, then to make matters worse criticize the new business-expander, thereby second-guessing them after the fact. In other words, if you don't train people first-hand through demonstration, then you don't have a place to criticize their efforts. In fact, its passive-aggressive. And if you're in retirement phase and refer people to a different trainer than yourself, they need to refer to that trainer for questions support and follow-up, you don't have a place to criticize what they are doing to carry out that training. Its simply too confusing for new people if they're told to, *"... just do it,"* then if it didn't go how others would have preferred it to go, criticize their efforts…this places too much irrelevant emphasis on others' opinion when new business-expanders are preparing to be independent and dependent on themselves…hence, *the concept of duplication.* You can't have it both ways…you either train people through demonstration and have the structure of training revolve around those standards, or have someone else train them, but never skip training then criticize their efforts,…that's an emotional set-up for failure and very disrespectful to new business-expanders.

If you train your own new expander, then at first you demonstrate the whole process and little by little the new person does more and more of the activities themselves, but not without discussing and debriefing what they experienced (whether intended or unintended results) each step of the way. Explain what went on and why and how you'll handle those results. There's too many nuances for a new expander to go from hearing and watching you to jumping into the whole sequence by themselves and sets them up for failure.

Seeing how elegantly, skillfully and gracefully leaders manage their emotions and situations when dealing with negative, confused, conflicted people is one skill that has to be demonstrated first-hand and passed down through each generation of the business…the lineage. Anyone can deal with positive outcomes, duh. Dealing with disappointment is a learned skill. If a concept or skill is skipped or overlooked with one person, they'll skip it with their people and so on down the line. If we assume a person has a skill, they don't. Just like apprenticeships, fellowships and other vocations, people learn by watching, listening and doing through a process of interpersonal development.

If you're going to compare the benefits and lifestyle of network-marketing and its advantages over traditional professions, they you have a duty as a leader to follow through and build your newbies up, so they can function at the level required to reach their goals. Just like the saying, *"Marriage is where the real work begins,"* so it is with network-marketing. If you sign people up and turn them loose, without taking them under your wing to demonstrate how you are expanding your business, shame on you. The exception to this is the professionals who DO know what to do and demonstrate it by finding ten new customers their first month, but this is very rare.

Case example:

Jim is an army veteran who had seen his share of combat. During his tours of duty, he fantasized about having his own business and being his own boss, once back at home. When Jim got home, he had a lot of health problems, many thought were rooted in chemicals he was exposed to during his years of service. By this time, some years later, Jim had gained a lot of weight, had high blood pressure, high cholesterol, was tired all the time, had what he describes as anxiety and depression, was on multiple medications and had a terrible time breathing and sleeping. To Jim, he was a shell of the man he used to be. He was unable to do all the things he used to love to do. He barely recognized himself any more.

He saw an ad for an offer to "feel better naturally". He contacted the person, explained what was going on and started on a weight-loss nutrition program. He noticed feeling better right away and as the week and months passed, he lost weight, his energy starting coming back, his sleep improved. Over time, his doctor reduced his medications as his cholesterol and blood pressure numbers normalized and the digestive problems he thought he had to live with went away.

As a result of the benefits Jim experienced consistently using the nutrition products, Jim launched his own home-based business offering the products he was using and found there was a huge demand among his fellow veterans who wanted to lose weight. Jim earned the first trip within a couple months and is looking forward to receiving his first company car. Jim says that even if he didn't receive all the income and perks, the return of his health made it all worth it. He considers the person who helped him join one of his best friends, now.

Chapter Eleven

Goal Setting, Goal Achievement, Visualization & The Role Of Emotions

"Don't let your lack of belief in yourself, prevent the great qualities of others from improving you." -Sov

"The smarter they worked, the less hours they had to work... to become what they wanted, the faster they realized they were already there..."

The person who doesn't commit to their dream(s) has the luxury of not working and criticizing those who do.

Have the courage to behave as if "in the now" you've already achieved what you insist you want to have, become and experience (also known as future-pacing). Behave, based on locating and training leaders, attracting those not trying to impress people, who don't "get it" or don't understand or who aren't properly wired to expand a business. About half the population isn't wired to be in business for themselves...they may want the benefits, but they won't have the self-motivation, inner-fire, inner-drive and where-with-all, to carry-through without a boss. One-percent of the population makes a great leader. Sad, but enlightening, at the same time. Knowing this from the onset, you can be at peace that when people don't value, want or afford what we offer (or even go on the offense to be critical of us), it's not about "how" we offered or presented, but simply that they aren't wired to appreciate the thing itself.

Another percentage of the population has some of the required characteristics to be successful in network-marketing, but are happy or content where they are. Another percentage are neither happy nor content, but they don't believe in themselves, so they act like they don't believe in *you* to hide or deny their own insecurity. For me, I learned to look for my own insecurity and then take action to snuff it out, like a spark, from a campfire. When people can no longer hold your own insecurity over you or against you, you become *unstoppable*. This is because the difference between having a good idea and making a good idea come into reality, is your level of security at both a conscious and unconscious level. When you are no longer concerned about others' opinion of you, then you can no longer be emotionally black-mailed with your own emotional-insecurity, which is what happens if someone allows others to talk them out of their decision to live their dreams.

Lock into your motivation, be clear about it, pursue it:

In high school, I had a side-gig (when I wasn't at the grocery store, feeding cows on the farm or mowing lawns), doing fire-watch, on logging sites. At the end of each day of logging or clearing a property, to build a house on, there would be a big pile of scrap wood, as big as a house, (scrap logs, stumps, roots, etc.), that wasn't good enough to sell as lumber or even salvage as firewood. The huge piles of scrap would be pushed together by a big bulldozer and burned. Since it was summer time, there was a chance the pile that had burned down quite a bit by evening, could spark another, unintended fire. So, I would go on the site and simply sit there and watch for smaller fires to start and put them out if they sprung up. This was before cell phones and all the tech stuff, so I'd essentially be sitting there smelling the smells of the forest, the freshly turned dirt, watching the flying squirrels floating overhead and all the wildlife that wandered through the site, for about five-bucks and hour…cash, of course. The motivation was the cash. No one was there monitoring me, checking in on me or anything. The person who hired me simply assumed I would do the job I said I would do. Where I grew up, in the Lower Snoqualmie River Valley of Western Washington, people just had a sense of who you could trust and count on. It didn't matter their age, people tended to have a work ethic and keep their word, or they didn't. It came from how they were raised, their values, work ethics and by what motivated them. It wasn't uncommon for people like this to have two, three or four different jobs, since they filled positions where there was a shortage of good workers.

When my wife and I moved to Western Montana in 2015, we found the same thing. Some people have three or four jobs, since there's a percentage of the population (in the poorest county in Montana) who spend their time acquiring and consuming methamphetamine or other substances. Meaning, just to keep basic businesses going requires a few people doing many jobs. This effectively means that for a person with good work ethics, who is motivated to do so and doesn't use a part of their time consuming drugs, they can have their pick of work and income.

Which means that a small percentage of the population (even in a small community) earns the majority of the income, based on how much value they offer or create for others. A good worker effectively establishes good word-of-mouth marketing, for themselves and people begin to see these kinds of people as the ones you want working for you if you need someone to fill in for a few hours each week. That way, the business has their employee needs met and the reliable person fills in their free time, with income-producing activities.

*******In network-marketing, you have to establish an emotionally-driven mindset that cannot be influenced or changed by external factors (use your emotions for your best interest, rather than letting your emotions drag you down), especially other people, whether from your family, friends and traditional circle of influence or prospects you're talking to. Referring back to the flying-by-instrument (IFR) metaphor, no matter how cloudy or stormy things get, *keep your mind and emotions are above the clouds…above the storm…untouchable.*

Plan ahead who you take information and input from:

Be discriminatory about what information you take in. If it even hints of negativity, limitations, what others couldn't do or accomplish, what has been done before (4-minute mile) or others opinion of you, block it out, don't take it in.

Become an **"Ace-Debater of Catastrophic Thought"**…meaning, become habitual about looking at the positive side of anything, maintain your focus on your goals already having been accomplished, maintain an attitude of gratitude and when people give their opinion or make a prediction about your success, don't take it it…redirect it away from you. In your mind, say, *"Nope…not mine, not for me,"* or *"Not my circus, not my monkeys."*

Think: Creator of Precedence:

prec·e·dence

/ˈpresədəns,prēˈsēdns/

Noun: precedence; noun: precedency

1. the condition of being considered more important than someone or something else; priority in importance, order, or rank.

   "...his desire for power soon took precedence over any other consideration."

   synonyms: priority, rank, seniority, superiority, primacy, preeminence, eminence

More important to your success, than the facts, is your unequivocal *belief in yourself.* Holding an emotionally-charged vision and feeling of your goals already having been accomplished (future-pacing). No matter what happens, which could be interpreted as an obstacle, a barrier, interruption, failure, etc., stay in the process, maintain your focus regardless of others response, reactions, opinions, how it comes about and so on.

The phenomena of [future-pacing] as described, taught and utilized in Neuro-Linguistic Programming™ (NLP™) is the concept of imagining, say a year in the future, having all the basic resources you need taken care of, seeing, hearing, feeling, smelling, tasting what you would living the reality of having reached your highest held goals and aspirations.

What the experts in human performance and development have found is that, instead of saying, *"When I have such-and-such, I'll be successful,"* effectively puts what a person wants to achieve further and further off to the future. But, when you use your mind to experience a goal having already been accomplished (in the present moment), the creative resources of the mind come to the forefront and go about making the experience come to pass. In other words, an experience that would have continued to be put off into the future, comes about in the present time. Most athletes, actors, celebrities and anyone who sets a goal an achieves them, utilizes this phenomena. People who continue to say, *"Someday I'll...,"* or *"When I have such-and-such, I'll be/have...,"* effectively procrastinate the accomplishment of their goals, without knowing it. When a person imagines and emotionally charges a desire as having already been accomplished or achieved, the creative resources of the brain become activated to bring it to pass.

If a person believes or "tells themselves" certain things have to happen (conditions) *before they will succeed* (whether related to money, time, energy or otherwise), then the creative resources of the mind are disabled, interfering in the accomplishment and realization of the very same goals, which would have otherwise come to pass. The person is effectively using their own mind to interfere, in the progress of their own goals.

True goal achievement supersedes all physical limitations. In other words, we think that 1+1=2, but in reality, goal achievement goes more like 1+1=8…the cumulative affects of focusing as though "it" has already come to pass, means the outcome of the goal itself is greater than the physical energy and resources put into making the thing come to pass. You have to believe it has happened before you see the facts that it has happened…*this opens up the super-highway to goal achievement, which transcends physical limitations* (perception that the conditions needed to reach your goal, do not yet exist). Remember, the RAS will prove whatever you believe to be true! So, if you believe you create a list of conditions that you have to perform before you can be successful or have to jump through hoops, suffer, pay your dues and so forth your RAS will show you how hard life can be (the essence of obsessive-compulsive disorder (OCD).

If, on the other hand, you believe the right circumstances will come to pass (which often defy logic) to realize your goals, your RAS will prove this to be true! Your choice! Goal achievement is more about proper use of imagination and getting out of our own way (mentally and emotionally) than doing everything perfectly, crossing every "t" and dotting every "i". If you hear yourself saying, *"Yay, but first I have to do "this"…and "…before I do that, I have to do "this"…and before I can do that, I have to do such-and-such…"* then you're likely interfering in your own goal achievement processes.

"Whatever you can do or dream you can, begin it; Boldness has genius, power, and magic in it. Until one is committed there is hesitancy, the chance to draw back. . . **What you can do, or dream you can, begin it, boldness has genius, power, and magic in it. Only engage, and then the mind grows heated, —Begin it, and the work will be completed!" (Goethe often credited with this quote.)**

Things that unsuccessful people consider/perceive as barriers to their success, which interfere with the [future-pacing process].:

• Delays,

• The season,

• The weather,

• The economy,

• Lack of money, (e.g. *"I want money, but I don't have the money to get more money"*).

• Others' opinion,

• Experts' opinion,

• Disappointments,

• People changing their mind and

• Perceived setbacks, etc., and so on.

Stay focused on your intended outcomes, feeling, hearing and seeing what you would at the moments you know you accomplished your goal (the emotions of accomplishment), use the products, expand your business by locating others who want the benefits of more money and free time want and value what you offer and teach them to do the same. Commit to working in this way for 10-15 hours, each week/2 hour each day.

One of the most significant factors to "faster" expansion of your business and all areas of your life for that matter, is remaining positive and faithful that you have succeeds...*seeing and feeling, it as done.* By remaining positive regardless of perceived external obstacles, arranges the mind to be able to recognize and capitalize on situations that people with a negative bias misjudge and miss out on. Your outside world reflects what's going on in your mind. If you keep saying and creating all these conditions have to be in place to achieve what you want, then the outside world will keep creating a list/reflecting of things/conditions that have to happen before you can succeed (OCD/drama). Anything that hints of negativity in your mind is considered head-trash, meaning it directs the attention of the creative, problem-solving part of the mind to focus on problems, obstacles and barriers that can't be helped (an often get bigger and more complex), rather than solutions and ways to take advantage of opportunities. Some of the most outrageous periods of growth in the economy took place because of industrialists who viewed *problems as opportunities*, rather than saying, *"Yay...but what the problem is..."* If you make this mindset a habit, of focusing on the thing as already completed, solution-focused, both consciously and unconsciously, your business will grow faster than others whose skill-set and technical approach "appears" correct. The person who focuses on the problem, will have an endless list of details and problems which have to be solved before they can succeed...more and more problems of greater complexity seem to appear out of nowhere!

When you focus on the positive, stay open to opportunity, remain in expectation-mode, remain in gratitude for everything you want to have, be or experience, you'll find yourself experiencing synchronicity...good things that happen that if you look at just the "facts" of the situation, are considered *impossible*. Impossibility and synchronicity are simply two sides of the same coin.

Things that successful people consider/perceive as enhancers to their success, which amplify with the [future-pacing process]:

• Speaking in faith,

• Capitalizing on the season,

• Perceived setbacks, etc., and so on,

• Reframing problems as opportunities,

• Utilizing the season to our advantage,

• Remaining positive regardless of the facts,

• Reframing down-turns in the economy as opportunity,

• Seeing what you want or need as having already arrived,

- Bias for seeing the facts as evidence of your own success,

- Interpreting people changing their mind as saving us headaches,

- Refusing to conclude that facts show interference in your achievement,

- Perceiving delays or setbacks as reality rearranging for our convenience.

People will say, *"When I'm successful, I'll behave successful,"* but what they don't get is that by doing so they miss locating many leaders by posturing themselves as an amateur, rather than a professional…they effectively keep putting-their-success-off in the future. It comes down to how a person positions themselves, how they see themselves, what they project about themselves. Which came first the chicken or the egg?

"Your imagination is your preview of life's coming attractions."
Albert Einstein

You are your own genius:

To be honest, I've been studying goals since I was a little kid. Being primarily visually-oriented by nature (meaning I learn by watching and then listening), I always had pictures in my mind about how I wanted my life, to be. Mind you, much of my childhood and part of my adult life I spent in poverty. Poverty means different things to different people. To me, it meant that during the 1970's and part of the 80's, as a family of four, we were living in a trailer-court, on about one-thousand-dollars per month. My dad was on disability/social security and my mom wasn't working. From about 1975 until about 1984 we had a route of 25-30 garbage dumpsters which we collected everything we could possibly recycle including bottles, aluminum cans, cardboard, newspaper, copper-wire and so on. We went to all the grocery stores in a 20-mile radius and collected outdated breads, cheese, yogurt, fruits and vegetables from all the dumpsters we could and even use the local food banks. Our 2nd freezer was full of foods we salvaged from dumpsters. The reduced price for school lunches was twenty-cents. There was also a free-lunch program, but we were considered to earn too much money for my sister and I to qualify for free lunch.

With all the recycling my parents brought in about another $500 per month, in cash. We had a 70's model Ford pickup with homemade sideboards and a two-wheeled, homemade, utility trailer we towed on the recycling-route. With a pickup and trailer stacked high with cardboard, and tied down with ropes, we would get about $40 per load of cardboard, at the recycling center which was about 15 miles away. This was before stores were bailing and recycling the cardboard themselves and there really wasn't anyone else doing it as organized as we were and gas was about .80 cents per gallon. We would take several loads of cardboard each month and a load of aluminum cans and beer bottles whenever we got a load full. All we did was use box knives to flatten the boxes down and pack them flat into the truck and trailer. We knew which days were freight-days and so we would plan our route, based on which stores were unpacking freight on which days. The store employees loved us because back then all the cardboard was going into the garbage, so we created more room in their dumpsters. Some of the dumpsters were 40 feet long and as an elementary school-age kid, I'd jump up in the dumpster and start throwing the cardboard out, to my parents on the ground.

Many days, I skipped school and went with my parents, on the cardboard route. I kind of liked it because you never knew what you were going to find in the dumpsters. Many years after the fact, I went around on the same route and took photos of the dumpsters we used to frequent. I was very shy and introverted until my late twenties, so for me, skipping school was a huge relief from social anxiety. Sometimes, at the end of the year, stores would clear out toy inventory, for packages that were damaged or opened. Once we got a car trunk full of toys, including a lot of unopened Matchbox Cars™, which I was fanatical about. My head about blew off.

Unique to me, I thought we were doing the dumpster-diving until we found something better…to my dismay, I learned as an adult that my parents didn't aspire to ever do anything different. It was like it didn't occur to them. For me, the whole time I was growing up, I was watching and comparing what others were doing for a living and what they were doing to live beyond survive and more in thrive. For my family, you could say we lived month-to-month, but even so, there were days at the end of each month where we literally didn't have any money. But, there certainly were people who were worse off then us. I noticed the kids with single parents had even less money, but often, substance abuse was involved, meaning their priority was cigarettes and alcohol first, food was lower down the priorities.

As I said earlier, I also mowed some lawns for money and had my worm business from about age nine for a couple years or so.

For me, I could see that others around us, whether neighbors or relatives had a lot more money, better food, vacations, nicer clothes, ability to go to movies without taking away from the food budget, way more presents at holidays and less stressed, in general. In other words, I could see a difference, wanted to have a life more like them and actually thought that that's what we were trying to do.

To me, I could see that others were doing different things to get a different quality of life. My dad frequently referred to people who had money as having stolen it or robbed someone or acquired it in some illegal way. So, in a sense, he was convinced that his lifestyle was a moral highground. My mom's viewpoint was that if people had money it was because they had *luck*. Or that, *"...everything they touch turns to gold,"* which she affirmed over and over. My dad liked to antagonize people and I watched him ruin opportunities that could have really helped our family, but combining his belief that anyone who had money got it illegally combined with his false pride of being unable to accept help, he interfered with anyone who tried to help us out at all. My mom was perfectly capable of working, but my dad wouldn't give his blessing to this, so my mom really didn't have a job until I was about 15 years old, when I got my first real job, as well. My mom and dad managed the trailer-court and apartments on top of all this, in exchange for a discount on the rent for the space that our mobile home sat on. If you can imagine, the rent was about $250/month and we got a discount on that. In exchange, my parents mowed all the lawns, enforced all the rules, did all the managing of the applicants and rentals, collected rents, evicted tenants when needed, ran classified-ads in the local newspapers, called the ambulance and police when needed, *which was quite frequent* and so on. It wasn't uncommon, at all, for me as an elementary school age kid, to answer the phone and give rental applicants directions from Seattle, which is about 25 miles away and the other surrounding towns, so they could come and look at the rentals and fill out rental applications, while sitting in our living room.

This part was very interesting, since we didn't do background checks, it was very interesting to see how people behave when they apply for a rental and how they behave once they move in and are your next-door neighbors. That's a study and whole book of its own. Some people lived in the trailer-court because it was so cheap it was all they could afford and others lived there even though they had great jobs, but kept their expenses very low. The state penitentiary was about ten miles away (we could see it from our front yard), in Monroe, and we definitely had neighbors who had just been released from "The Pen".

So, for me, I began studying (informally at first), the differences between the "haves" and "have-nots," from a very early age. I guess you could say I was very "success-curious". Whenever adults were around I listened to everything they said, for hints about the differences in their lives versus ours. Especially today, I've become more and more opinionated about this as time has gone on, meaning the differences between the financial status of people, their happiness level and the differences between the people who are chronically impoverished and the people who may start out poor, but improve their situation as time goes on…often to the degree that you wouldn't recognize the person from one decade to the next.

As an adult, I even had a time where I was on food stamps, homeless, living in a 1970 Ford Pickup. I jokingly tell my wife that if I ever was homeless again, I'd be the wealthiest homeless person out there, because I know how to scrap, dumpster-dive and work my way out of bad situations, one-step, one-day-at-a-time. I've done it more than once. As a kid, it never occurred to us to stand beside the road begging for money…maybe we should have. But, even today, when I see homeless people and how they are navigating their situation, there's a part of my mind that is calculating what I would do differently, to improve my situation, if I were in that situation, again.

"Good day, Sir! Good day, Ma'am!"

In Seattle, they have a small, local newspaper that covers topics about homeless people and all the challenges they face, entitled, *Real Change*. There's a non-profit publishing organization that sells the papers to homeless people, who sell them on the street for double what they buy them for. When my wife was doing her undergraduate and part of graduate school, at The University of Washington, there was an older man that sat on a bucket in front of a Safeway store on Brooklyn Avenue, by the UW, selling those papers.

"Good day, Sir!..Good day, Ma'am," Edward McClian greeted every person that passed him on the sidewalk. He didn't sell a $1 paper to everyone who passed, but he made a point to be noticed and create value through a nice greeting (making sure every single person knew who he was and what he did). There had been many stories written about him in Seattle, he had been there for years. It started, when he wanted to have some money to spend with his grandkids and his daily goal was to make a hundred-dollars, each day. He started early and was generally out way after dark, right in front of the store entrance. We bought papers from him frequently, mainly to support his motivation. He was very consistent. As new students came to the U-District each year and others graduated and moved on, he just kept selling papers. But, he was a senior citizen and was making a hundred-bucks a day, in cash. He bought 600 paper each week to sell and gave 100 of them away to other homeless people, to get their own start.

Now, again, I've lived both sides, from a blue-collar family with benefits to living in a trailer-court and dumpster-diving for a decade, to working up to four jobs at a time in high school, to working full time and attending school full time, being self-employed, walking away from my life in 1996 and starting all over again from scratch, ending up homeless and rebuilding my life once again to eventually being a published author, being married to a wonderful woman who is an E.R. physician and, to where I am now finishing up my bachelor's degree in aviation and being enrolled as a student in helicopter school. In the last years, since 1992 I've earned ten different vocational certifications on health, fitness, massage, hypnosis, Reiki, personal training and so on. I've experienced things that people simply find difficult to believe.

With my extensive and varied experiences, and I continue to stay open, to learn more. I've found that as long as mental illness or substance abuse aren't immediate focal problems, *anyone can dramatically improve their financial situation in a relatively short period of time.* In many cases, even those facts don't interfere in people's success...the other day, I watched a pet pig online, that is earning ten-of thousands of dollars, for charity, painting pictures!

With my parents, mental and emotional problems definitely interfered and prevented us from doing better. This is important to note, because we'll all encounter people who have every reason to want to improve their life, but if mental, emotional or there's substance abuse going on, there's really nothing anyone on the outside can do for them until those key issues are improved. Meaning, you can give a person a fish, but they aren't going to learn to fish for themselves. This is where charity and philanthropy come in to play.

When people have their wits-about-them and they can think clearly and track thoughts without internal emotional-conflicts, people are very likely to improve their situations, given the opportunity, the tools, training and support. This is important to note because you will come across people who insist they want your time and energy, but they either haven't done enough personal development to be capable of accepting your help, or they have mental, emotional and substance issues that prevent them from being capable of accepting your help. How you know the difference is whether they produce results (PV) on a monthly basis or not…does their PV improve? Are they willing and capable of using the products themselves?

Assuming that a person has the ability to focus, set goals, aspire and visualize their own success and has the drive to take consistent action, even if based on baby-steps, education, training, modeling and/or mentoring, anyone can dramatically improve their own life and help others do the same. It's a systematic-process. My formal goal-achievement training and experience has occurred since 1996, but I had already been utilizing these techniques, since I was a little kid, without knowing exactly what I was doing. Everything since then has been refining the process of goal-achievement. Many people who have achieved the life of their dreams, having started from a place of deficit, have shared the key tips that got them where they wanted to be. Based on the environment I was raised in, statistically I should have been an addict, abuser, dys-functional, self-destructive or a combination of all of them.

For me, the difference was that instead of shutting down and being stuck inside my head, I always observed what was going on around me…what others were doing to add to the quality of lives they had. For me personally, this gave me hope and gave me a lot to look forward to. [I believe that if people don't have something to look forward to (hope for a brighter future) they are in deep trouble, because their actions, choices and behaviors will be rooted in immediate gratification, rather than what they are looking forward to, in the future.]

People who don't have anything to look forward to, in the long run, make choices on feeling satisfied or better *in the immediate moment* (escaping the pain of their current conditions, even if it means checking-out from life itself). Someone with a lot to look forward to will make decisions based on protecting the vision of what they look forward to. *This is also known as hope.* People who have hope and faith that their must be a way to improve their conditions, even if they don't know what that way is, will take actions based on long-term success and happiness versus immediate gratification in the moment…even if it means making choices that don't interfere or limit future choices…even if they don't yet know how they will improve their conditions, they unconsciously are looking forward to things improving, thereby opening themselves up to opportunity. *THIS* is a primary difference I identified, between the "haves" and "have-nots".

Beyond that, is the concept that because attempts to improve in the past have failed, that future attempts will also fail (learned-helplessness). Using my parents as examples, they believed "others" had better opportunity to improve their lives…that others were more blessed than them…that they weren't "permitted" to get ahead…yet, at the same time, they had inner-conflicting beliefs that if someone did have good income, it was because *"…everything they touched turned to gold,"* (superstition that earning money is almost a magical power) or that *"…they must have stolen the money…wealthy people are thieves,"* or *"…they're nothing more than a used car salesman…a shyster,"* and that they were morally "higher", by working hard, but earning less…the point of working hard was not to earn money and improve the well-being of the family, but for the sake of doing the work itself…that working, not earning makes you a better person, than people who have wealth and freedom.

With these kinds of inner-conflicts and unresolved beliefs about money conflicting with each other, it would be near-impossible for a person to improve the living conditions of their family, and regardless of the quality of opportunities that presented themselves, one would be either unable to make use of an opportunity or self-sabotage whatever advances they did experience. The same kinds of phenomena occur with people who want to lose weight, as described in my book, *Weighting To Wait* (2018).

The fundamentals of goal-achievement:

First and foremost, is that you can pretty much have whatever you want. It doesn't matter how "big" the thing seems, *size doesn't matter with goals*. A big goal is as "easy" as a small goal, except in perception and self-talk. Exceptions that I've seen to this is that if it means taking something away from another person or hurting someone else to get the thing, one might get what they want in the short-run, but they won't be able to keep it or sustain the gain. This implies letting it happen naturally, rather than forcing it to happen unnaturally…*getting out of your own way*.

The good news is that most of the things people want, there's not a shortage problem…*meaning there's no shortage of money or resources*, just a certain mind-set and emotional-set that can help or hinder. If its free travel, it's there for you. If its to help or provide aid or charity to others, its there for you. Maybe you want a huge house, free cars, or something else material…its all there for you. Maybe you have an ideal relationship scenario…the principles are the same and I'm going to share this with you. Maybe, you want more time-freedom…you can have that. The list is endless and the principles are the same.

First and foremost, is to know exactly what you want, in full detail…*specifics*. Specifics about how you feel having gained that thing or experience. Without attaching the feeling of already having it, it gets projected into the future as procrastination, rather than it being here and now. This requires you to get specific with yourself…*commit with clarity, to what you want*. Some of the processes of goal achievement are hard to put into specific words, because we're essentially creating something out of nothing…an emotional feeling we want to fully experience. Meaning, everything we know of started out as an idea…they weren't in physical form in our reality to begin with.

Goal boards/dream boards:

Goal boards, also known as "vision-boards" or "dream-boards", work really well for the goal process. A goal board is essentially a piece of foam board, say 24"x36" which you tape pictures of what you want on the board. The board itself isn't magical per se, but makes use of the creative part of the mind, also known as the "goal-seeking mechanism". Whatever it is you want to have, become or experience, collect pictures from magazines, or newspapers or simply Google images and put them on there like a collage. They don't have to be organized in any certain way, but put them on there so you feel good when you look at it. You can put them all on there at once or add to it as you come across them. The idea is to create the "feeling" with the pictures of what you want your completed goal/situation to be, which creates a point of focus, for your creative unconscious….which controls unconscious habits/behaviors.

The world, the universe, God or whatever power you rely on will provide the thing, situation, scenario, people, relationships that match what the feeling of you want to have, be or experience in your life. So, say for example, you want a specific rare coin that only one exists of. When you follow through, that coin represents a "feeling" you want in your life…you'll either get that coin, or you'll get something you enjoy more or represents a higher level of appreciation than you originally knew existed. If there's only one coin and you know who owns it, you might eventually get *that* coin or you'll discover something you want more and that becomes your focus, during the process (refinement of your goals). Sometimes what we insist we want represents something that is missing in our life and as our awareness of what's available grows, we might change our goals. See how that works? It comes down to what is most important to you at the deepest level of yourself…what feeling you consistently desire to have the most, on average. Sometimes we think a thing will bring the feeling, but then serendipitously we get something else which fulfills that feeling and the first thing falls away from our awareness.

Some people can easily visualize (if you're like me), so there's always a movie running in your mind picturing what it is you want…the movie is attached to the feelings of satisfaction and resolution of having gotten, attained or experienced the thing (people who don't achieve their goals are rehearsing/recycling the feeling of "wanting" versus "having", which pushes the thing further into the future.). Some people do visualize, but they insist they can't…they just don't recognize it when it happens spontaneously, or they call it something else. Labeling "visualization" as something else, inhibits the benefits of visualization itself. Some people go by their feelings. Some people go by what they hear in their head or heart and some combine all them.

One of the keys to successful goal accomplishment is having an image of what you want, but then you attach the other sensory experiences to the vision, meaning feeling, sound and even the sense of smell. The whole point is to create a sensory experience of your goal [having already been accomplished]...*its already done.* People who have trouble reaching their goals tend to keep putting the experience off in the future, out in front of them, so no matter how hard they work, it keeps moving further away. I saw this with my parents many times. My dad always wanted a 35mm camera with a telephoto lens, but he still wanted it the day he died. He could have had one, but he kept putting it off in the future. Even in the event he worked toward it slowly, he could have had the highest quality camera within a year...*but, he was working against himself.* There were a few other things like this too. He always wanted a Henry, *GoldenBoy* Lever-Action .22 Rifle. I remember on some road trips and camping trips, he would stop into sporting-goods stores and ask to look at these rifles. He wanted one so bad. He never did get one, but he could have easily afforded one. With my mom, she had a belief that if she was to get anything, it had to come by way of gift from someone else...she couldn't imagine putting energy toward a goal and then working to earn it, *for herself.*

In the big picture, how you use this thing you create in your mind, these things and situations you want is, first, make your goal board. Secondly, as you're drifting off to sleep, fully experience the key things you want in your life, as already accomplished...once you finish, create the feeling of being grateful for having received it (habit of gratitude-attitude)...drift off to sleep with a feeling of gratitude, for having received things one could say you actually do not have, in reality, yet. Do the same thing just as you're waking up in the morning. This is enough to get yourself going in the right direction, but if the thought of what you want crosses your mind during the day, briefly do the same thing...create the feelings of gratitude, as though you already fully have it.

If you or someone you know is in an unimaginable situation, where it would make no sense of how you could get to where you started from or currently are to where you most want to be, don't worry about it...*the facts don't matter.* What matters is holding the image and feeling of what you want in your mind and heart (as having come to pass/completed) regardless, what your current reality appears like.

One of the major differences/mistakes/misunderstanding between the people who "have" and the people who "don't have" what they most want is how they manage/operate their emotions and connect them to their vision, for their future. People who have trouble getting what they want, always behind the eight-ball, life filled with one drama after another and the people who seem to have "the magical touch" is how they operate their emotions…operate their emotions versus riding emotions that come up.

In all my decades of personal and professional experience with all the modalities I do, I've noticed that the people who think/behave as though emotions "happen to them" randomly and without order have a lot more issues, stress and drama in their lives that they can't seem to get ahead of….like they are constantly trying to keep their head above water. Its common for this to be passed down through family generations, since we learn about the skillful use of emotions (or lack thereof) from those around us, before we even know we're learning (unconscious modeling).

On the other hand, people who direct, guide and utilize their emotions like fuel that runs the engine, seem to be more emotionally clear, able to focus, able to make a plan and work the plan and follow through on their intentions. Life seems easier for them. Things happen easier for them. Happiness and fulfillment is easier to attain and sustain. Problems that ruin one person's day just seems to roll off their back like water off a duck's back. I am saying that one of the differences between the "haves" and the "have-nots" is being aware of their current emotional state, how they got there and what to do from there. The people who have the most trouble let their emotions run them (or they hold onto emotions like possessions), like a roller-coaster and they learned it without knowing what they were learning or the consequences of the lesson.

Emotions are meant to be experienced to enhance life's events, but then released so they don't continue to run the show. It's like the difference between having an anchor in a boat so you can "drop-anchor" while in stream, or having the anchor available in the boat. Retained emotions are like a boat anchor holding the boat in one place, even though the stream is flowing under and around the boat itself…time has moved on, but the emotions are locked to a specific time/event. Emotions are meant as tools to help get where you want to go, cherish the great moments and grieve the sad times, but sometimes people get so used to the intensity of their emotions, without a specific goal and ways to monitor progress that they use the wrong tool for the situation…like wanting to drive your boat with the anchor dragging along, effectively holding you in one spot. Sometimes people unconsciously and inadvertently create intense negative drama, so they can have emotional intensity/importance, not realizing they could have just created the life of their dreams, without all the negative drama.

People often are not aware of how they are using their own emotions, but they notice they aren't happy where they are and don't know why. The person who is unwittingly using their emotions in ways that are opposite of their outcomes will turn people off, versus brining people close, since they are too focused on how they "feel" than helping the other person and responding to the other person's feelings.

In relation to expanding your Shaklee business, there's tons of potential situations, which might be considered ups, down and disappointments, but the people who manage their emotions don't hold a focus on the disappointments…they keep their focus on their goals, work the processes (the particular strategies to expand their business) and learn from each interaction, but don't let intermediate steps pull them down…they don't conclude anything about intermediate events, but rather by their PV level (this month)…no matter what happens, they [interpret] it as evidence that they are [in the process] of succeeding. Goal achievement requires a consistent, stable, mental-emotional mindset. The person who is up one minute and down the next, will be wasting a lot of energy (like being in a foot-race, but then stopping and starting throughout the race), that is required to attain said goals. In a sense, it's like letting the emotions run you is an indulgence …it's like you can either have ups and down through the day or you can have emotional-stability and goal achievement. *Your choice.* Goal achievement requires a consistent energy output. The bigger the goal, the more consistent you have to be in maintaining an emotional mindset. That doesn't mean you don't celebrate the highs, that's actually helpful and good for the mind. It does mean training yourself so that when you experience what might commonly be considered a "disappointment", you maintain your focus of feeling your accomplishments having already been attained…the facts don't matter. The roller-coaster type person will be wasting the energy of those around them, as well, since the ups-an-downs pull other people through their own imbalance.

The reason is (and I didn't make this rule up) that what we picture tells the goal-seeking part of the brain/mind what it is we want/desire/intend, but the emotions "charge/activate" the part of the creative brain that charges the imagination to carry out the actions, behaviors, habits, synchronicities, coincidences, etc., to bring it to fruition...often, outside your conscious awareness (synchronicity). One of the funny things, is that the more faith and belief you have in this process, the easier the things come to pass (affect of having your head above the storm). One might think that to get the hundred-dollar shoes requires having a hundred-dollars to spend on the shoes...*but it doesn't*. When you are clear on your intent, experience it as already completed and then let it go, repetitively between each morning and evening session, a different process occurs to deliver what you most want to feel/experience. The things you want don't have to come about in a linear fashion (1+1=2)...meaning, spend a hundred-bucks to get hundred-dollar shoes or (1+1=8).

At first, I wasn't convinced this worked, but I put it to work with my honest intention and stayed open and found that it works, beyond my conscious expectations. And one of the cool things is that whether you believe it or not, your mind will prove you're right either way. There's a part of the brain called the RAS (Reticular Activating System). As far as the experts can tell, this part of the brain monitors for "difference", meaning things that are "novel" or "different", in our environment, but also does this to collect data to prove you're right. This is part of the reason it's challenging to change a person's mind about something...the RAS pulls and collects data in each of our environment to prove we're right...no matter what we think or believe (that's why it's critical to be careful about what you believe, since your brain is going to collect the information to prove your perspective is right!). This is also a reason why trying to convince a person that their beliefs aren't valid doesn't work...their brain is collecting the information to prove they are "right"...and they have the evidence to prove it!

If you want to be right that you can reach all your goals, you're right. If you want to prove life is hard, you'll never get what you want and you can never get ahead, you're right! Two people could live in the same house and have completely different experiences and end up in completely different conditions, based on how they utilize the information at their disposal and in their environment...ever hear of making lemonade from lemons?...uh-huh. The same thing happens when two people have different short-term goals/outcomes.

If all things are equal, two people are raised in the same environment, but one of them insists on portraying themselves as a victim/martyr, in order to gain sympathy and attention, in the moment and the other one sees themselves as overcoming all the obstacles and gaining recognition for long-term successes, both of them will get what they want, in the same environment. One will stay in a horrible situation, since the worse it is they more attention they work to get and the other will change their situation, shaking up the variables to allow improvement to occur, albeit over a period of time.

When my wife was completing her family medicine residency (three years of training) in, we were strapped for cash. I had a 1999 Toyota Runner and I wanted a spare tire that was the same as the other four tires, but it was going to cost about $200. I initiated this process of being thankful that I had received a tire that was just right for my truck. Instead of saying, *"I wish,"* or *I'm going to have,"* I kept creating the feeling of being grateful, for having received the tire.

One night, I left the house and a couple blocks from the house, at an intersection near Greenlake, in Seattle, I stop at a stop sign, look to my right, and right there on the corner of the intersection is a tire! I looked forward, sat there for a minute and drove away. I literally couldn't believe what I saw. After slowly driving for a few blocks, I turned around and went back. It was the exact size tire I needed. It was kind of dirty, but it was brand new, still had the little nubby things that wear off as a tire is used. I still have that tire.

In 2014, my wife got hired as a physician on the island of Maui. Jessica had since graduated from medical school, graduated from her family medicine residency program. Our housing, car and gym membership were all covered and we lived right on Maalaea Bay, right on the water. We had moved over there with what we could carry in our big suitcases. I thought, *"Man, I wish I had brought a small set of tools with me."* You know a screw driver, pliers, etc., just to use for small projects. I heard myself saying, *"I wish I had,"* versus, *"I'm grateful I have..."*

I looked at them at the local hardware store, but I figured it would be like $30-$40 for what I wanted. I kept feeling grateful for the tool set I had (which I didn't actually have). Sounds ridiculous, I didn't have a tool set! I kept saying, *"Thank you, for the tools"*. Our condo was about a half mile from the main highway and we frequently walked along the sidewalk, which was lined by a hedge bush. One day, I was walking along, look over at the bush and there's a multi-tool hanging in the bush! It was one of those all-in-one multi-tools that cost about $30-$40.

The property manager there wasn't very nice or cooperative and eventually the faucet handle got loose in the kitchen sink. I thought, *"If I only had an Allen Wrench set."* They were about $10 at the Ace Hardware Store on Maui, across the street from the clinic my wife worked at in Kehei. So, once gain I started giving thanks and creating the feeling-out-of-nothing, that I now I have an Allen Wrench set. Anytime I noticed the loose faucet handle or it crossed my mind, I imagined I *had received* an Allen Wrench set and said, *"Thank you"*. I generally took my wife to work and picked her up from work. One morning, after dropping her off at work, I pull up to the intersection, a couple miles from our water-front condo, and in the middle of the road is an Allen Wrench set! Right in front of me! The one I had seen at Ace Hardware. I pulled over, ran out into the intersection and grabbed the wrench set. A perfect fit to tighten the faucet!

We lived in Maui for eight months and I joined the CERT Team (Community Emergency Response Team) to become certified to help out in natural disasters for light search and rescue, first-aid, etc. On the list of things, they said would be good to have is a big screw driver to use for a pry bar as needed. The large Craftsman™ screw drivers are like $15. So, I started the process again, since I wanted one for my CERT kit. One day we were having sandwiches as a natural food store in Kahului, Maui. As we were pulling out of the parking lot, on the right side of the road is a huge Craftsman™ flat head screwdriver, lying on the side of the road. I pulled back into the parking lot, ran over and grabbed my screwdriver. It was so big that when we moved back to the Seattle it was too much to take with in the luggage and donated it to the CERT organization, along with some other items.

I still have the tools, other than the big screwdriver, as well as the tire which are great reminders about how to use the emotions to get what you would prefer. Nowadays, I find tools wherever I go. I think what happens is that once you open up, for something you thought was so difficult, the channel stays open (tools for example) *and we call this abundance*. Whether money, time-freedom, vacations, material-possessions, relationships, the process all works the same.

The creative part of the mind wants to be directed toward specific goals…the front of the brain (pre-frontal cortex) is a goal-seeking mechanism. Emotions are to be used to fuel what you're grateful for, even if you don't have the thing you want (the amygdala, [behind the pre-frontal cortex] is the part small, almond-shaped part of the brain, which adds emotional-fuel to what you consciously pick as your main, most important goals)…what you're grateful for increases, even if you started out with none. (The emotional "charge" is the difference that brings the thing into existence, versus continuing to be procrastinated, off into the future, wishing and wanting.) Being grateful for a thing, attracts or pulls what you want to you, bypassing all the reasons a person could come up with the facts) as to why they can't have the thing or experience, right now. Behaving as if you already have the things you want speeds up the process of getting them. The RAS proves you are right…so choose/believe carefully. Just because you have an idea doesn't mean the idea is the best one, for you. Repeating an idea out loud, simply brings with it the evidence of the statement, as a potential truth within all the other potential truths.

If new business-expanders say that they aren't willing to do such-and-such, prior to seeing the "doing" of the business demonstrated, it indicates they are more concerned about staying in their comfort zone and avoiding self-development to achieve the life of their dreams…a neurosis of attempting to do the same things, but get different results.

Case example:

Janie lives in the Hawaiian Island of Maui. She had always been conscious of the environment and ways that she could reduce the amount of pollution she contributed. Being a single mom with two small children, one of the other moms from her children's play group asked her if she was interested in a way for moms to earn extra income, working from home.

When Janie realized she could offer Earth-safe, child-safe, pet-friendly products, get a discount and have a clear conscience about the quality of the products, she was all in. She joined, got her own products, learned how economical the products were compared to other stuff and started talking to other moms about earning money working from home, the way she was.

Within a couple-months, Janie was earning an extra couple-thousand dollars a month on a very part-time basis. She loves it!

Chapter Twelve

Get 10 More

If in doubt, go back to your foundation habits routine, for business expansion; *locating the people who want, appreciate, value and afford the benefits you offer.*

If your bonus checks aren't big enough, *find 10 more people who want, appreciate, value and afford the benefits you offer.*

If your customer base isn't big enough for you, *find 10 people who want, appreciate, value and afford the benefits you offer.*

If you feel like people are taking up your time, but it isn't paying off (not resulting in greater PV), *find 10 more people who want, appreciate, value and afford the benefits you offer.*

If you want a higher level of rank, *find 10 more people who want, appreciate, value and afford the benefits you offer.*

If you're not sure what to do next, *find 10 more people who want, appreciate, value and afford the benefits you offer.*

If your group isn't copying or duplicating your results (indicates you have people who joined, but they aren't doing actions that match what they insisted their goals were), *find 10 more people who want, appreciate, value and afford the benefits you offer.*

The implied part here is that YOUR PRIMARY "job"...your focus...your priority...is to continue expanding your group. That way, no matter who joins you, there's no question as to whether you're doing your "job" and behaving as a responsible trainer, mentor, leader...your responsibility is to simply do the actions to expand your group...NOT "tell" your group what to DO...but, to show them by expanding and continuing to expand your own group. If you start thinking that "telling" your expanders what to do is adequate, you're wrong. Teach by demonstration through mastering the fundamentals and refining your processes through repetitively expanding your own business. Through this process you'll train others by demonstrating what to do...not telling them, but by *demonstrating!* Without demonstration, new expanders always think that they have more skill or are better prepared than they are.

The idea is to keep stirring the milk, so the cream rises to the top. But, the amount of cream is based on the amount of raw milk. If you don't have enough cream (product points), it means you haven't added enough raw milk (people who said they are interested), into the bucket. The cliché, *"You can't squeeze water from a rock,"* applies here. The majority of people rarely do or follow through on their intentions, *in any industry.* Most everyone wants the benefits of money and time-freedom, but the percentage who make it a priority are few...small percentage. This goes for any area of endeavor or industry and that's why there's so few masters in any field. If we use weight loss as an example, everyone "wants" to be lean and healthy, but very few make it a lifestyle and give up sloppy living, junk food and commit a few hours a week to exercise to make it happen, hence New Year's Resolutions. The cliché, *"You can lead a horse to water, but can't make him drink,"* applies here as well. People have gotten such a short attention span that most everyone wants the benefits of money and free time, but when it comes down to establishing success habits which lead to the attainment of goals, a lot of people don't pay attention long enough in the first month, get a great bonus check and realize what they could get from the *FastTrack™ Program*, to make the connection between doing and getting. The solution is to keep expanding the number of people you locate for your group (the raw milk), in order to get the amount of cream (product points) you want. Even with dairy cattle, each cow produces a slightly different amount of milk fat (the most valuable part of milk). A thousand-gallon tank of milk has cream made up from all the cows in the herd that were milked during any given shift. The better the nutrition level the cows are getting and the less stress they experience, the higher the milk fat content the dairy farmer gets from them.

People can get themselves all discombobulated, by starting out by locating and training new group members, but then once they get two or three expanders they start acting as "managers" of their two or three people and all progress halts! ...*remember*, if you start managing your current group rather than continuing to expand, by finding more new people, you've inadvertently demonstrated that to expand a business you're managing people as though you're a boss at a conventional job versus "expanding" and demonstrating this process. If you're "managing" two or three expanders, rather than expanding to at least 15 leaders each year, who also expand to 15 expanders each year...what are you demonstrating?! You're demonstrating a stalled-out behavior...a stunted group. Those two or three people will perceive and interpret you spending so much time managing them, as a sign that to be successful they should manage people too...the emphasis switches from locating and training to talking "about" business-expansion. The heart and soul of success in network-marketing is an ever-expanding group, (market-share), which makes up for the people who want the money and lifestyle benefits, but don't follow through with the behaviors required to get those benefits.

Believe me, there's more people who won't follow through than people who do follow through (spectators)...otherwise, everyone would be rich! As long as you know this ahead of time, it's not a problem and additionally, you learn who to invest time and energy in and who will use your time and energy but produce little to nothing, in additional product points. BUT, the greatest gift you can give your prospects is the gift of demonstrating properly how to continue expanding, rather than getting a couple and then misunderstanding that your time and energy should be spent "managing" them. If people wanted to be managed they wouldn't seek the freedom and independence of network-marketing, duh!

The way that people get into managing a couple people is that they have a misunderstanding, in the back of their mind that, at a certain point, they don't have to work anymore. Instead of continuing to prospect, they conclude they can sit back on their two-points-of-contact, and get to pushing others to "work for them". Again, the opposite of network-marketing. In truth, the freedom and independence comes in you locating more people, who already want what you offer and afford it for themselves!

YOU!

LOCATING MORE PEOPLE, who want, value and afford what you offer for your business. Telling people who you are and what you do...the heart of all business.

The default or safety mechanism in this is that when you do have expanders who are motivated, but they lack leadership and/or marketing/sales skills, all you do is have them spend a couple or few days watching you expand your group....NOT tell them what to do or what you do...nor tell them to do more, simply have them spend your work day with you watching and hearing how you EXPAND YOUR OWN GROUP!!

Now, naysayers or negative-nannies who have gotten under the radar will likely say that this isn't reasonable...that training people in person isn't reasonable...too time-consuming. Yet, every professional school utilizing this very concept of mentoring, whether it's the field of medicine, law, aviation, or any of the professional trades, they all require the student to be present with the teacher/professor/mentor. Personally, I believe that the people who would negate teaching in person (even when its online, through webinars, etc.,) are the incongruent professionals who aren't congruently expanding their own business...they lack a system, other than throwing ideas around or brain-storming, without having ever applied them themselves and so they fear their group seeing that they don't know what to "do" themselves...by "telling" people what to do they can appear like an expert, but in real time they can't teach, train or mentor.

Anyone who has actually expanded their business and are actually expanding are going to be exited, proud and motivated to pass on what they have proven works (reflected in the size of their group, the size of their monthly bonus checks and by the amount of free time they have based on the efficiency of their system). When people don't know what to do, they rely on "telling" others what to do, rather than showing others what to do. And you don't have to train every single person *in-person*. The threshold for growth is to personally train about 20% of your business-expanders. The reason being that some people will join you having network-marketing skills, some have sales and marketing skills, some have enough business sense to know not to chase people, but keep locating new people and so forth. The in-person training relates to people who have potential to be natural sales, marketing and leader types but they've simply never been exposed to the particular skill set required to expand a Shaklee business. Those with potential will take a couple days-worth of training and *RUN with it*. They take off and expand their group. They connect the dots and repetitively repeat what you showed them without you needing to "manage" them.

This is a business of creating value for others by showing them what to do to get what they want. People who need to come across sounding like an intellectual expert, in order to gain a false persona of expertise and recognition among peers aren't generally expanding their own business. But truthfully, those who would have been successful as managers would likely have been employees as executives at a company. But, people join network-marketing because employment doesn't offer the benefits of network-marketing...so don't try to run your network-marketing business as a successful employee manger! It doesn't work and sabotages your groups progress by showing them habits that don't work...if you aren't finding, building, expanding you're inadvertently teaching your people bad habits that will spread frustration through the entire group. The system works, but it's dependent on you continuing to expand. If you decide to retire, write to your entire downline, tell them you're retiring from expanding activities and tell them who in the group they can count on for continuing training and support...by no means should you mistake distancing yourself from the daily expansion habits as or busy work as a cue to start "managing" people and "telling" them what to do. You're either teaching through demonstration of expansion of your business or you're not in business...the two are exclusive. And they can't be collapsed in your mind without confounding the members of your group. Simply put, people will be attracted to you to see if you're really living the dream you claim to be. After that, it's about the "how" they can get there, too. Once you know their goals, it's all about "demonstration" of the "how"...then getting out of their way and letting them run with it...*nothing else.*

Expanding a network-marketing business is so different than anything else, no one can visualize something they don't have a reference for. Meaning, they can't imagine what they can't imagine.... *talking is just jibber-jabber.* Talking just gives people a chance to mistakenly combine what they don't know with what they have experience with. In other words, telling people what to do leaves it to their imagination to make mistakes, misunderstand, make mistakes and get deeply frustrated...telling them to do more, is suggesting to do more of what didn't work or caused a lot of frustration...think about it! More is not better, unless the "more" is correct to begin with! It doesn't work. It leaves a group fractured, compartmentalized and inconsistent results, to say the least. Remember, people who want to sound like an expert tell people what to do without any way to measure or equalize every participants progress.

Truly successful network-marketers have huge bonus checks because they don't care if the sound like an expert...the demonstrate what to do and their bonus checks continue to grow...bigger checks means more time-freedom!

There is no single professional vocation where students are mentored by being "told" what to do without first, seeing in person the foundation of the success habits in-person. It's foolish, short-sighted and misleading (even selfish to tease people about the benefits of the business without firsthand experience of how to do the business). If you've been responsible, you approached your expanders the way you expect them to approach others. Complete without cutting corners. In reality, they see the "how" before they even know they're learning or being taught. The "teaching demonstration" is simply review of what you did with them (from the first conversation with them), but with a perspective of them learning to teach vs learning to personally experience. In other words, people don't usually know they're being taught something, unless you tell them they're being taught ahead of time, then summarizing by telling them what you taught them/what they learned.

If you think about it, this work can be lonely. When you're teaching by demonstration you have company while you're duplicating yourself. The only reason a person wouldn't teach through demonstration, is if they lack the skill themselves and they don't want anyone to see that they don't know what to do, other than helping a person join and point them to the products, which in itself builds product volume.

There's not a single professional or vocational skill that is passed on through classes, homework, study, apprenticeship, and application and finally refinement with people having to read, watch videos, study in-person, travel to class whether in the same city or in a different state! When my wife was in medical school we moved 25 times between Seattle area and Montana from 2006 to 2013. With the technology today, that level of travel isn't required of people in network-marketing, on a regular basis. Technology permits us to do live, in-person training no matter where two or more people are located. But, once or twice a year is reasonable. If the trainings are done online, weekly is better. In the 1990's it was considered unreasonable to use a computer to do presentations or overviews, because it was considered unreasonable to expect people to have a home computer. Nowadays, most everyone in the U.S. has "access" to a computer and the web, even if they don't have their own. And, a good, smart-phone can be enough in itself

As I'm in helicopter flight school, I commute over 300 miles to take flight lessons in Seattle. I have to pay for gas, housing, meals and the expense of flight training is on top of that..*for the opportunity.* In other words, to become a helicopter pilot I have to inconvenience myself to get a different result. No guarantees, just the opportunity!

From 1991-1992 I attended massage school, in Seattle. I was living in Duvall, Washington, some 25 miles from school. And, I was working 80-100 hours a week as a horse veterinary assistant in an equine ambulatory hospital. Massage school was 700+ hours of training/30 hours/week with a requirement to do 1½ hours of massage exchanged, outside of class time each week, plus study time. The total cost over 12 months was about $7k. I never thought to question how much I had to do, I just did it. Today, that same level of tuition runs about $40k.

So, if people say business-expanders won't want to do what it takes to grow a multimillion-dollar business, something is off. Either the leader is undervaluing the business, projecting that others won't value it enough to do what it takes, or the person doesn't want the benefits deeply enough to do what it takes to earn the benefits. Simple.

Case example

Carl was working at a national chain nutrition store, when a customer asked him if he would like to double his income, working in the nutrition industry. Carl had been managing the nutrition store for some time, but was only earning minimum wage, which was barely enough to get by on.

Carl looked at a video, looked at what the earning potential was for the same hours he was working at the nutrition store and immediately saw the potential. He got on a basic nutrition program, noticed an increase in energy right away and went on to expand his own customer base. Now he earns twice as much working half as many hours and gets to set his own schedule. He expanded his business by simply showing the same video to all the other people who were working at the same nutrition store chain.

Chapter Thirteen

Being Clear About Your Goals And Intentions

There's the phenomena of inner-conflict.

Inner-conflict is when a person either feels two different ways about one thing or has at least two different goals/outcomes, that are in direct conflict, with each other. For example, say a person says they want to expand a business, have financial and time-freedom, but they believe they need to follow in their parents' footsteps, in order to be viewed as a "good" child and gain their approval. Obviously healthy, balanced, secure parents and family would unconditionally support their child's vision, dreams and goals, but not everyone is that fortunate or balanced. The same kind of thing can happen with insecure, jealous spouses…co-dependency.

Entrepreneurs tend to be and need to be fairly independent thinkers and be very focused, especially in the launch and expansion-phases, of their business. If a person feels deep down that they are defying what their parents see for them, or defying their parents' expectations…well, most people want their parents' approval or want to avoid dis-approval. But, creating something new and unique to *you*, requires independent thinking, without the slightest inner-conflict. Otherwise, any progress that is gained will likely be difficult to sustain, due to inner-conflict, within the subconscious mind. It's not at all common for entrepreneurs to hear those words, *"…get a real job,"* somewhere along the way by someone in their circle of influence. Those kinds of comments are known as "discounts" or "dismissals"…as if you aren't able to think for yourself, make good decisions for yourself or that you need others' approval and validation to live the life you want. Most entrepreneurs, including some of the most well-known billionaires have gone through this very same phenomena, experiencing it first-hand.

When a person isn't really clear about their choice, the value of what they are offering, what they are contributing and how they are helping others improve their lives, the inner-pressure can be picked up on by their customers and potential business partners and make processes more difficult than they have to be.

Here's another simple example. Say a person intends to go grocery shopping and get in on the current sale (time-sensitive event), but they don't want to get off the sofa. If they don't find their motivation, the sale will come and go but they won't get off the sofa. Or, a person who insists they want to lose weight, but they haven't made a commitment to exercise and improve their nutritional habits, which support healthy fat-loss. As a trainer with close to 40 years nutrition experience, I can tell you that I am contacted almost daily, sometimes more than once a day, who insist they want to lose weight while they simultaneously want to maintain their current daily habits and lifestyle that got them fat to begin with…in other words, in their mind (since they haven't congruently decided to change themselves, in order to get a different outcome) they insist on attempting to continue living a fat lifestyle, but also insist they want to lose weight. See the dichotomy there? Inner-conflict.

In every category of goals there are people who, even at the top of their game, experience some level of inner-conflict, which can interfere in progress or sustainability of past progress. The underlying factor is "values"…in other words, which thing do you value more…*want more*? Which do you want more? If a clear, concise, definitive decision isn't made to strive for one outcome over the other, inner-conflict will likely cause the success to move further and further into the future (a form of procrastination, since the mind can't make two, conflicting things come to pass at the same time)…hence, two different people who take varying times to achieve the same goal with all relative factors, resources and skill-set being the same.

In this business, the example would be, *"Do you value gaining others approval or gaining income and free time, more?"*…you can't have both, all the time, just like you can't please everyone all the time, anyway. You can't please everyone or appeal to everyone and gain customers and business partners, at the same time…you have to focus on one or the other. If you're on or have been focused on maintaining your public appearance, you'll burn out…it isn't sustainable. No one is meant to be a match or gain approval from every single person. It just isn't natural.

"Do you want to be liked by people who have no relation to your success as a Shaklee business-expander, or do you want to sort/locate the people who are a good match for your business?"

"Do you want to sell worms to fisherman and use your money to buy fishing lures and go fishing yourself, or try to convince people who don't like to fish that they should buy your worms or go fishing?"

Let's think about this for a minute. If 80% of the population is overweight (and they are), does it make sense to simply ask people if they would like to see a healthy weight loss program...or try to convince the 20% who are healthy and fit people, they should lose weight? Hear the pattern, there?

How about skin care. Most women and many men use various kinds of skin care products to help keep their youthful-self youthful, as long as possible. Millions-of-people want to look younger and spend hundreds-to-thousands-of-dollars each year on products that often don't do anything...would it make sense to ask people if they want to try a healthy, youth-enhancing skin care product or try to convince people who don't prioritize skin care to start doing so?

Lucky for us, Shaklee has the best weight-loss program and skin care products money can buy, but their prices are in the middle of what either of them cost on the open market. In other words, there are other products that cost way more, but provide way less results and products that cost less but don't work and often contain unsafe ingredients which speed up aging!

Here's an example in sports: Swiss tennis player Timea Bacsinszky started tennis at age five and went on to become a professional tennis star. But, in Romania, her father pushed her really hard to succeed, which could be a good thing. She did become a successful tennis star on the international circuit, but as time went on she started getting the feeling that her father was invested in her success, more for himself than for her. Timea resented that her father pushed her so hard she quit the game and went on to a job in management in hotel services. She has said, *"... she resented him for this and remains estranged from him after her parents divorced"*. Timea turned pro in 2004 and has earned prize winnings close to $5 million.

While working her hotel management job in 2015, Timea received news that she qualified to get into French Open Qualifier Rounds, but at the same time had the (inner-conflict) that if she did well, it would reflect her father's intentions, rather than how hard she had worked (two different outcomes/prevent her dad, from getting credit for her work, versus really enjoying her winning process), regardless how it actually was.

Timea hired Dimitri Zavialoff, to help her resolve the inner-conflict through the use of sports psychology, because she felt that every time she shined it looked good for her father, whom she is estranged from and resented. Leading up to the 2017 season, Timea made some great placements and needed to take some time off to recover from injuries.

Whether in business, relationships, income level or Olympic Athletics, clarity of purpose means the difference between struggling to get ahead versus reaching your goals and maintaining progress for the long run, without serendipitous interruptions. Being able to get along with yourself, be at peace with your own decisions and taking suggestions from yourself is of utmost importance. Nothing interferes in progress much more than worrying about pleasing everyone else, all the time…*it's impossible to do so.*

Decide on your highest held criteria (what you want most) and put your energy toward that. If you notice moving forward followed by moving backward, it could point to inner-conflict (competing outcomes).

Case example:

Anthony had a very successful massage therapy practice when one of his clients asked he would like to increase his income. Anthony replied, *"Of course!"* His practice was full, but if he took off any time, his income stopped coming in. He watched the video, joined and took suggestions from the person he joined with. Each month he watched his income increase, until it was higher than the income from his massage practice. He still practices massage, but cut back by about 75%, while his income went up by 75%. When he returned from the company trip, there was a notice in his email saying his company car was about to be delivered and he noticed that during the time he was away on vacation, his income actually went up!

Chapter Fourteen

Unabashed And Unapologetic Bias For Action And Speed

When anyone is passionate and excited about a particular topic, product or service, its unmistakable. How a person becomes this way in Shaklee comes from four primary results:

1) Keeping track of your personal experiences with the products.

2) Hearing the experiences (and keeping track of them) from your customers.

3) Noticing your income and time-freedom increasing.

4) Helping others and hearing their satisfaction, with what they have gained from you helping them use the products and/or from the income and time-freedom they gain from their own participation in the business.

All four of these results come from focusing on, locating and servicing the people who are looking to improve their situation, in some way and who *want, appreciate and value the benefits you offer.*

For me personally, I needed help with my digestion, allergies, energy level, immune-system and so on. I joined Shaklee to "feel better"...*real simple, right?* Hint, hint. I had been looking for Shaklee for 20 years. There's a lot of people out there who have used Shaklee, but due to poor customer service or some other reason they lost touch with their Shaklee person and love the quality of Shaklee.

Think for a moment, about the concept of you helping some people, then they help some people and the process goes on and on. Shaklee has a 60+ year history of improving the lives of everyone who use the products and helps others use the products...its infinite. There's more business out there than any individual can handle. For me, my health has improved so much over the years, from consistent use of Shaklee, that I couldn't imagine not using Shaklee, even though some people simply aren't interested. People have different values and priorities. One time I saw a man purchasing a thousand dollars-worth of Marlboro™ cigarettes, *so he could get a ten percent discount*…a whole cart of cigarettes. The store clerk said he does this, three or four times a year.

It's not very likely he would be interested or "value" or afford himself the benefits nutritional supplements or skin-care products. I heard of one guy who was a chain-smoker and his dog got lung cancer and died. His wife asked if he would quit smoking now, and he said, *"No…I'll get another dog."* This would be an example of trying to sell fishing worms to someone who doesn't fish…its possible…just probably not a very good use of your time.

Another gentleman, "Brian", who is now a spokesperson for the CDC, started smoking at the age of eight. By the time he was eleven, he was smoking a pack a day. By thirty-five he had his first heart attack, for which he had bypass surgery. He went on to have chronic obstructive pulmonary disease, lung cancer, part of his lung removed, stents placed in his heart and so on. Eventually, he needed a heart transplant, but he was taken off the list because they found nicotine in his blood stream, as he was waiting for another heart. His doctor took him off th donor list. Eventually, he actually did quit smoking and got a heart transplant. Even as he was waiting for a heart, which was destroyed from smoking, he was smoking!

Some people will never buy supplements from you! Move on!

The point is that when you encounter people who behave as if you're "too" enthusiastic or that you *couldn't possibly* love Shaklee *that much,* it simply means they aren't a customer, yet (they haven't developed or they aren't aware of their own need, for what Shaklee offers). Shaklee has always been a word-of-mouth business, so that money that would otherwise be spent on advertising goes to us business-expanders. The enthusiasm for the products, driven by the unabashed and unapologetic bias for Shaklee products is exactly what made Shaklee a multi-million-dollar business. I keep my Shaklee supplements on a shelf next to the refrigerator in our kitchen. Right now, I take quite a few different supplements, so there's a decent row of supplements there. One of my relatives asked something to the effect of, *"You can't possibly be taking all those supplements…you just have those there because you sell them…".*

My reply? Silence. I've found over the years that, you can insulate yourself from negativity and being emotionally dumped on (rejection) by pre-screening people, before approaching them. In other words, if someone outright tells me they don't believe in nutrition or supplements, you think I'm going to line myself up for their poop? Remember, I'm selling worms to fisherman. If someone is pro-active in their discounting, dismissal and minimization of my efforts and/or my habits to prevent *disease* in my own body, I simply go silent. If I engage them at all, I'm essentially giving them permission to give me their opinion…which I have not granted them. By going silent, it's a one-way conversation they are having with themselves…they're essentially talking to themselves for their own satisfaction, not to have a conversation to learn new stuff or improve their situation. And if they think that their opinion of me matters that much, then they probably have more problems than I could ever help them with, anyway…its above my pay-grade.

I've found that by approaching the public in generic terms, e.g. "feel better", "weight-loss", "fitness nutrition", "more energy", etc., I sort through the people who are actually looking versus approaching people whose values are in smoking themselves to death or intent on starving their body of nutrition. With nutrition, you're either willfully putting enough nutrition in your body, or actively withholding nutrition. There's no gray-area. Much of the public doesn't even do what their physician suggests, why would they do what I suggest? Think about it…if someone has a self-stated health problem or health goal, its much more likely they're open to options. Having five or six questions you use to screen people before you ever mention Shaklee creates a sort of insulation from what's commonly referred to as "rejection". Remember, people don't do what they need to do or should do…they do what they *want* to do. With that in mind, some people are motivated by moving away from things (suffering, pain, loss, emotional pain, etc.) and some people are motivated by moving toward things (more money, more free time, love, affection, good health, goals, etc.). By asking screen questions, you locate the people who want and appreciate the benefits you offer.

Think about it yourself. Do you move toward having more money or are you more moved by avoiding poverty? Are you motivated by having more free-time or more so about avoiding other people having control over your time? Are you motivated by avoiding health problems (prevention) or by moving toward relief (treatments). The point here being that people who are 'avoiders' might spend thee or four times the amount of energy to avoid their problems than a person who works to create solutions or a brighter future. Addiction, obesity, junk food, medications, etc., are examples of avoidance-type personalities…in other words, they use substances to block out the experiences they wish to avoid. Some people will transition from avoidance to moving toward a solution (as the market for natural alternatives is expanding annually) and how you find out where a person is by asking them questions in a conversational manner and listening intently (listening more than you talk).

For me, since I tended to be introverted, especially one-on-one, I started teaching nutrition classes in the 90's and from the people who attend these classes comes people who like what I offer and ask for help. See how that scenario is different than approaching people who may or may not be interested? People are already screened by who signs up and attends the classes. If it's a weight loss class, people who are interested in weight loss generally come or attend to gather information for someone they know.

When you teach a fitness nutrition class, people of all levels of fitness from beginner to advanced attend. Competitive athletes show up, since even professional athletes need help with their nutrition and they're more likely to be open to suggestions, since so much is on the line/they have more invested, clearer goals, greater intentions. Remember how I talked about people's values and how they help or hinder them? Well, if someone has tiny goals that they think they'll reach with or without nutrition, they aren't as open to supplements. For competitive athletes, most already know they need something, it's just that there's 85,000 different brands today, so they need more information as to why Shaklee is so different and better for them, in order for them to give them a shot.

A serious athlete isn't going to do anything that might let the whole team down…there's more at stake. They want every bit of edge they can get and Shaklee supplements go far beyond increasing the edge. But, that also points out who is watching out for maintaining their fat, un-fit lifestyle and a difference between an athlete who will do anything to improve, versus someone who will do anything, make any excuse to avoid interruption of their fat-lifestyle. Once they try them, they'll be certain of the differences. For people who are active and don't use supplements, their body will begin breaking down within about three-months of consistent exercise/training (including pros). So, if they aren't open to supplements now, they will be later.

Once the body starts breaking down, then they open up to things that might give them the edge. I've written six books on the topic and those books are available on Amazon Kindle and in paperback form as well, so you can read my approach to the topic. Even if someone is using some kind of supplement(s), it's unlikely they are getting very good results. You can feel good letting them know that they will definitely feel the difference by using Shaklee every day, in very short order, even if it's a basic program (protein and VitaLea™). All Shaklee products are unconditionally guaranteed, so there's no risk other than the price of the items, but if they use them up and don't like them they get their money back, anyway!

Anyone who really loves a product is the same way about the products they like. I'm that way about Toyota 4x4's, certain brands of firearms (I was a firearms salesman for years, in Seattle and have been shooting for more than 45 years), dogs, certain foods, certain movies, certain books, exercise equipment and so on. When you combine things you love with work or a business, you have a winning combination, since it's fun and exciting to see and hear others getting results and thanking you! The average Shaklee customer has been using Shaklee for 17 years! People make fun of me for my interests (especially my wife), but that doesn't discourage me, I am who I am and there's room for everyone! What do you think that means if someone tries to discourage another from liking what they like?

The point is that your encouragement will be appreciated by those who become customers and especially your own organizational business-expanders. Your enthusiasm is *FOR* those people…not the people who attempt to discount, discredit, dissuade or diminish your efforts and motivations. If people are not emotionally and morally supportive, more often than not, it is reflective of them feeling inadequate in themselves…it's not about your worth, your clarity, your intentions, your dream, your vision nor your motivations nor whether you're a good person or if your intentions are pure…people on the sidelines love to yell at the athletes on the field…back-seat drivers. Many times, people are so self-absorbed in their own drama and poverty-consciousness and trying to fight their way out of their own problems (which they have created), that they don't know how to morally support someone who is on their way to success. (Asking the opinion of someone not qualified to give you their opinion!). Once in a while, people will try to discourage you out of fear of being left behind, combined with fear of attempting something new (inner-conflict), although it's unlikely they'll look inside themselves to tell this truth or put words to it. Your greatest super-power is in demonstration of your own happiness on your own journey…the people you can help will jump on board…if they don't, you couldn't have helped them anyway.

One human phenomena is that in order for person "A" to help person "B", person "B" has to have "identified" person "A" as someone they will allow to help them. I know doctors who have over 20 years of education (high school, 4-5 years of college, 4-5 years of medical school, 3-5 years of residency and even an additional 2-year fellowship of medical training or more), patients insist they must get in to see such an expert and then refuse to do what the doctor suggests. With that I mind, why would that kind of person do what a non-doctor suggests!? Well, honestly there a few good reasons, but the point is that decades of education doesn't mean people will do what you say. It does mean that our job is to relate to people, systematically locate and sort the people who are looking, will try something we know works and then develop an opinion about how the products made them feel.

Allow yourself to love the products, share your enthusiasm and get as many people using the products as possible. A good rule of thumb is to find ten customers and three business-expanders and then repeat this cycle (5 times each year), until you have built your organization to meet your goals and financial expectations. When you do, you'll have the opportunity to save files worth of testimonials, from satisfied customers, who can't imagine life before Shaklee. But, it takes getting in contact with people and helping them get started. Notice, I said find ten customers, *first!* The combination of your own personal experiences with the products and having ten customers of your own is a winning combination for a solid foundation (belief in the products, the business model and your ability to combine the two). Do you know anyone who *doesn't* want to lose weight? Many times, people you're interviewing will want to know if the products are good before they begin. Having 10 customers shows that there is a demand for the products and even a new person can do it.

The point is that I can assure you that you can feel really good and have a clear conscience about promoting Shaklee products and the business model. As you get more and more testimonials this will be a realization for you. In the beginning, you'll rely on help and support from the people who helped you join and as you expand your own customer base and organization of business-expanders, you'll do the same for the people who joined with you and so on. Allow your unabashed and unapologetic bias for Shaklee products to come through. Sell worms to fisherman. I have 40 years personal experience and 30 years professional experience with nutrition, using Shaklee for 24 of those years (my anniversary for Shaklee products is September of each ear)…there's nothing that comes close to Shaklee, but you have to put them in your body and let nature take over.

Case example:

Jerome has been a successful personal trainer for some time. He loves his clients and the industry, but has found that each time he breaks his own sales quota for the month, his employer raises the minimum quota for him and implies that if he doesn't increase his sales, they'll replace him. He has seen many trainers come and go this way, as its standard in the fitness industry. Hint, hint. To him, the added pressure takes away some of the fun from personal training and he has started to dread coming into work at the gym.

Jerome watched a video one of the gym members, (who is an elementary school teacher) sent him and he could see the potential right away. Being his own boss really appealed to him and the opportunity to offer nutrition was very exciting to him. He ordered a sports nutrition pack, from the website and right away could feel the difference. Jerome mainly focused on offering the same income opportunity to other trainers he knew, which was a list of 53 trainers, some in the same gym and some were in different cities and states, to begin with and within seven months, seventeen had joined him, and they began repeating the process.

Seven-months after watching that first video, Jerome is seeing that he can be his own boss, set his own goals and do it working, from home from his cell phone and laptop. Now his focus is on helping trainers everywhere be their own boss and he is looking forward to the Bahamas trip.

Chapter Fifteen

Would You Eat One *M&M's*™ Or One *Lay's*™ Potato Chip?

When I re-found Shaklee, in 1993, I started with the Energizing Soy Protein™ and VitaLea™. I had been taking other supplements for decades. I was spending hundreds-of-dollars-a-month, on supplements because I believed they helped me feel better and that I would get better by using them. I was still having digestive problems, allergies, fatigue and getting sick often. When I started in 1993, I was told to take those two products for 30 days and if I didn't notice a difference...if I didn't feel better in some way, I would get my money back. To me, the labels looked plain, compared to the other products I had used. I didn't see any health claims or anything like that. I did remember trying that one food bar when I was six years-old though and how much better it made me feel, even at that age. But, even though I had been using supplements for a long time, I felt a difference in about three days. That was more than 24 years ago, yet I remember exactly where I was living, where I was standing in the kitchen and the moment when I turned toward the fridge and felt "plugged-in" for the first time in my life. That's what you want you're your customers...*that moment when they notice the difference.*

Do you ever see anyone eat only one *M&M's* or one *Lay's* Potato Chip? Doesn't happen does it!? Shaklee is the most nutritious, most digestible, most absorbable nutrients I've found, in close to 50 years. When someone puts them in their body, nature takes over.

The body delivers them to the cells via the bloodstream...*it's clinically measurable.* But, just like putting gas in your car, charging your electric car, flicking a light switch, etc., it takes consistency. Very few things in life only take a one-time effort for it to work forever...I mean really!

Your customers who get the best results are the ones who put Shaklee supplements in their body consistently and *let nature take over.* You don't have to think about it beyond putting them in. From the people who do this consistently will come a line of customers and business-expanders...and you can have as many customers and expanders, as you're willing to earn...there's no limit!

I've had customers who buy the supplements and never even take them, including a lot of family members. Don't worry about those people, you can't make people take them. You can inspire and encourage them, but ultimately you can't make them unless they're your children or close family members you're caring for.

The main technique I've found that works the very best for starting new customers is...*drum-roll, please*...demonstration...sound familiar? People's ego will often get in the way of their own good. People don't do what they're told, but the often do what they *see*...regardless of their age or maturity, because "seeing" bypasses the ego. Unless you have buckets of money to throw away, sending out samples doesn't work so well. You don't have "control" per se over the situation. People don't have the consciousness (usually) to link your passion about the products with your desire for them to experience them and then for them to link that to a sample you send with them. Would you send someone a single M&M or a single Lay's chip? I think not. But if you open up a bag of M&M's or chips, everyone's mouth starts to water...seeing is different than hearing or being told, is it not?

The majority of people will never use a sample you send them or send with them, even if they promise to. If you follow up and continue to badger them to use the supplement they may even become resistant. A 'single use' of any products isn't any more effective than putting a drop of gas in your car...think about it..."trying" isn't doing. Real benefits come from putting the supplements in the body consistently...*daily*. So, you're locating people who will give them an honest go. As a personal trainer, I screen and expect potential clients who will stick with a program, for one-year.

Think about weight loss products. Do you want to attract people who want to 'try' all kinds of different products all the time and don't lose weight or someone who is serious and gets the program, uses it like its supposed to be used and loses weight and has more energy, resulting in more referrals? Which person will result in more referrals? The one who loses weight or doesn't lose weight? The one who 'tries' or follows through?

Unless it's one of the drinks and you want someone to 'taste it' in person, but again, customers come from those who use them consistently. With the skin care products, if you're set up with a whole system and you present them in an organized manner, a single use will likely lead to a sale, knowing all the products are unconditionally guaranteed. And of course, a business-expander is going to use all the products and change brands anyway. Business-expanders give the products a serious go, since there's a few reasons behind their *motivation*. People considering expanding their own business, want the products to work!

An interesting phenomena that has emerged, is that people tend to suggest the products they personally like. Did you hear that? This goes for health care providers, too. My wife did a study while she was working at Children's Hospital, in Seattle, around 2012. She found that whatever supplements or integrative modalities a doctor or nurse gets results with are the ones they feel good about recommending to their own patients. If they have used supplements and gotten little or no benefit, they don't recommend them. Lucky for us, Shaklee is proven to work. Shaklee has a 60-year track record of producing better results than any other products. In fact, the wider range and the longer someone takes them, the better the results you get (see *The Landmark Study 1 & 2*).

http://www.Landmarkstudy.com

Your customers will likely use some of the same products you love. See why it's so important to have a wide range of experiences with the products? Your customers will rely on your experiences to help them *fine-tune* their purchases and help them with their family and friends' concerns. Serious business-expanders will use the widest range of products anyway, since their business is the products. But, as a word-of-mouth marketing business, about 30% of your customer base will be based on your recommendations, which are based on your personal experiences with the products. You still have each customer fill out the *HealthPrint*™ questionnaire, right away, since it's unlikely you're a nutrition expert and being an expert is time consuming and not duplicable. The point of the *HealthPrint*™ is a simple, duplicable way to get a start, even for someone who knows nothing about nutrition, but wants the benefits of the supplements and/or the business. See that?

AND, even if someone new to the business thinks of themselves as a nutrition "expert", I can assure you, they've never experienced anything that comes close to Shaklee. If one person presents themselves as a nutrition expert, its likely their new business-expanders will feel the need to be nutrition experts, which is the opposite of the truth. Being an expert in the products is different than being an expert in nutrition.

At one class I taught at North Seattle Community College, around 2008, I was presenting what I consider a very simple, do-able approach to getting amazing results with nutrition. One attendee asked, *"You mean I didn't have to get my Master's Degree in Nutrition?"* I said, with complete confidence, *"That's right"*. Knowing the intricate details of chemistry explains the 'reasons' why we get amazing results with Shaklee, but you still have to simply put the nutrition in your body and let nature take over...**knowing why neither helps nor hinds...knowing isn't power...doing is power**.

Being a nutrition expert and expanding an amazing Shaklee business are at different ends of the spectrum. Expertise implies "knowing" stuff is the outcome...the more one knows the "better" off they are. But, I've known tons of overweight, low-energy, registered dieticians who have their text book, nutrient content tables and calorie counts memorized. They know a lot, but everything they "know" doesn't necessarily improve their health. On the other hand, I've seen just as many uneducated people who share Shaklee (share products designed by 60-years-worth of the top scientists this planet have ever known)...they're some of the healthiest people on the planet...they don't have to be experts, they have an ongoing team of experts like no one has ever seen backing them up...and as Shaklee business-expanders, we're the messengers on the frontline, for the products designed by the experts, who do know what's real and valid and what the body truly needs. Knowing nutrition does nothing if you don't put adequate nutrition inside your body, which most 'knowers' do not. These expanders don't necessarily know everything, but they have huge businesses, financial freedom, time-freedom, free worldwide travel, free cars every couple-years and on and on, and they're healthier than a lot of nutritionists, nurses or doctors combined and we're in control of our time. The reason they don't have to know everything is because they didn't design nutrition...nature did that! But the more people you help, you more you learn what works! Often what people believe and what works are two very different things.

That's how you sort it out in your mind, so that you congruently feel good about promoting Shaklee products. And the way I look at it, my job is messenger and to help people get started. Whether a person follows through or not is partially my responsibility, through customer service and follow up, but I can't control others. Secondly, worse case scenario, if they don't like the products from their first order, they can get their money back or exchange them for a different selection of products. If at first you don't succeed...

So, it doesn't matter if potential customers/potential expanders say they believe in you or not. Using products and helping others get benefits are the main keys to building and expanding your business to the size you visualize. But, MOST of the time, if potential business partners or customers attempt to position themselves as "above" you, superior to you or as if "they will be your judge" of your sincerity or the truth of what you offer, it's USUALLY a mask for their insecurity about their ability to make a good decision, in their own life. Many people find it difficult to make life decisions and in order to cope, they try to kill the messenger/teacher, most people are in some kind of pain or discomfort, whether it be emotional or physical. In the absence of being able to make a bold decision like you did and launch your business and then go about expanding it, they'll attempt to challenge your own congruity...your own commitment. And that isn't about you. They can't take away the 60-years of success Shaklee has already had! That's their "fluff," like a fart...*hot air...makes noise but doesn't produce anything.* Simply keep the friendly bridge built, take the high road, make it easy for them if they approach you later when they change their mind and say a prayer for them...feel grateful we have the opportunity to help those who identify us as someone they will *let* help them. Eventually, they'll recognize they want and value and need what you offer and as long as you were professional and friendly (keeping the focus on benefits to them), they'll feel fine about asking you for help.

Thinking of yourself as the messenger simplifies the process. "Knowing" stuff doesn't assure success. "Knowing the key benefits" for each product (more energy, weight loss, sports performance, etc.) attracts people who want those benefits. Customers want to know, *"What do I get for using this product?"* Proof of this is the billions-of-dollars spent each year, by consumers, on stuff that people use to feel and look different, but which are not necessarily healthy for them. Once a person uses the products and gets basic benefits, they often start asking about other "things". Like I did...digestion, energy, allergies, itchy-eyes, bloody-noses, sports performance and so on. But first, you help them get a primary benefit that you suspect is relevant/important to them. Make sense?

"Everyone is provided the seeds of greatness, within themselves. It's up to each person to recognize this, take those seeds, invest in them, nurture them, build the environment, circle of influence and circumstances where they'll flourish into great forests. Some people are born with what appears to be advantages, but those who take those advantages for granted are no further along than those born with just the seeds of potential greatness. The ones who truly have an advantage are the ones who have mentors who demonstrate "what & how to do" vs being told what to do, for them. Advice being ideas, demonstration being the gold standard of success. Those who recognize their own latent greatness and invest in their own progress are the ones with the true advantage, since they neither take it for granted nor put it off until later."

Case example:

Jessie is a fire-fighter and paramedic. Although she is passionate about her job and absolutely loves what she does, her shifts permit her to work seven days on and then have seven-days off. So, she was looking for a side-gig to do to earn extra income on her weeks off. Having known that most other EMS and fire personnel have side-gigs, this was a natural fit for her.

A person who approached her at the annual, community parade offered to send her a couple videos. She watched them and loved the idea. It seemed like a natural fit and she could see how her fellow EMS work buddies would also be interested. Jessie got a nutrition pack for herself and some Earth-safe cleaning products for her home and laundry and some to offer samples at the firehouse, now a few other of her co-workers have joined and are making their own weekly schedules on their weeks off from EMS. Jessie sees how she can earn the same amount from her side business that she earns from her EMS job and she has a lot of fun doing it!

Chapter Sixteen

Momentum And Urgency Are Keys

Artist Kerry James Marshall is changing the face of American art.

"My introduction to art history was like everybody else's," said Marshall. *"You see an art history book that has works by Rembrandt and Leonardo da Vinci and Michelangelo. Yes, these things are great. But I don't see a reflection of myself in any of these things I'm looking at,"* says Kerry James Marshall, at The Museum of Contemporary Art, Los Angeles, reported on CBS News, June 4, 2017.

So, for decades now, Marshall has been working on that reflection. His figures aren't just black; *they are jet black* -- bold, proud, undeniably black. And he wants to fill museums with them. *"That body of work has to reach a critical mass so that it's no longer an exception to see things like that in a museum,"* he said. *"You can't have one picture of a black person or two pictures of a black person. You've got to have a lot of them."* His trademark style has catapulted him into the stratosphere of the art world: 72 of his paintings were displayed earlier this year a New York's Metropolitan Museum. That exhibit, a retrospective, originated in Chicago, and is now at the Museum of Contemporary Art in Los Angeles.

Expanding your Shaklee business is the same way. Regardless how much experience you have to begin with, each success expands your base, which is the next step to success. The people who seem to have remarkable success are the ones who launch, then expand [with a sense of momentum and urgency; bias for action]. Like any skill, the more you do it and the more often, the faster your skills develop. A reason being that each success carries over as confidence, competence and positive expectation to the next interaction…the more you have in the shorter period of time, the faster and easier your business launches and expands. You carry the positive experiences with you and forget the rest. [A higher quantity of correct practice is better than very infrequent correct practice.] The reason being that we learn from doing…there's no failure, just feedback…*refinement through action.* If you wait until you're perfect, you'll never have a business, it just won't happen. But even in practice, you learn one thing from each interaction. The people who have remarkable success are the ones who have enough faith that they'll [think on their feet and pick it up as they go]. There is some training, but even the most seasoned network-marketers get surprised, once in a while, since no human is exactly the same and that's partially what makes it so fun and interesting and prevents it from getting boring. [Training is to simply connect the dots between your personal experiences...confirmation]. Some training tips help, to build a base, but nothing works every time like a recipe. Nothing is guaranteed, even for seasoned masters.

The point is to do so much activity locating people in your first three-months, that even though some people aren't interested, aren't a match, don't follow through, can't see the potential, respond with poor manners or are downright negative, you have enough positive, productive responses on the top that your belief in your ability is solid. The quantifier is getting 3-9 business-expanders and 20-30 customers in the first 90 days of expanding your business, which leaves no doubt in your mind that the business is real for you. If the same level of success is spread out over 12 months, it simply doesn't build enough [depth of belief] in the new business-expander to, (isn't concentrated enough) for you or them to get the big picture...*urgency is key*. That means moving fast, which means not wasting time trying to convince those who don't "get it". Move fast locating and sorting the people who get the idea and apply what you teach them.

The people who have the most remarkable success are the ones who launch strong, in the first three-months of expansion.

When I learned to ride a bicycle, I was told to turn toward the way I was falling and that balances you out and prevents you from falling over....as long as you keep moving...if you stop moving, you tip over even if you turn the handlebars in the correct direction...if you're not moving, steering simply cuases you to go in circles...there's nothing to control or adjust. Then, one sunny day, I was riding on a baseball diamond that had red-rock gravel on the ground, like you see on running-tracks. I did turn to the left, but the front wheel slid out to the right, as I turned and down I went. I still have a scar on my left elbow and that was over 40-years ago. I didn't quit riding my bike and I had a war story and blood to show my friends. You couldn't give a person instructions, for riding a bike, for every possible situation. A few years later, I was riding across a muddy field at a different school that was very slippery. The front wheel went up along a little, muddy, slippery tire mark. I started to fall to the right, but couldn't turn the handlebars because they were in a rut. I got dumped and the metal corner of the handlebar jammed into my chest below my collar bone, with unbearable pain. It hurt so bad I couldn't cry. My breath was taken away. That left a scar too and I was covered in thick, stinky mud. I thought I was going to zoom through the mud without putting my feet down. Not even close and the mud smelled really bad, from stagnant water.

 Part of the excitement of expanding our businesses, is that we have our goals and vision and we combine that with matching people to the products and business…it's that simple. We develop a routine of how we prefer to approach people, but people being people, no two people are the same. People will surprise you. I can't tell you how many times I've talked to people and they sound like they're going to be really negative, but once they have a little information they open up and jump right in. The opposite can happen too. It doesn't have much to do with you or me. It has to do with where a person is at in life, what they want, what resources they have and that's not anything we can control. It's always fun to do new things. You'd think the more experienced a network-marketer gets the easier it gets and a lot of times that's true because we develop a routine and we're used to doing what we do. Truthfully, the process gets easier because we learn to think on our feet more efficiently. But, I've also seen highly successful network-marketers get shut down too! It happens all the time (but it has no affect on their overall success).

 Often, the general public lets their emotions control their day, so much that if they had a bad afternoon, they walk away from an opportunity that could have improved their life forever, because they mainly had the outcome of venting-off negative emotions, rather than improving their situation…people get caught up in their own drama without ability to cope or gain any perspective…it doesn't have anything to do with you or me. When people are at the right place in life, once they know what you're offering, they come to you, as long as the know what benefits you're offering and you assure them that you'll help them and be there to support them.

Case example:

LeAnne and Susie are both school teachers who love their job, teaching second graders, but both want to really travel the world during the summer months. Problem is, they don't earn enough to travel on their months off. They heard about a lady who helps teachers increase their income on their off time. They got her number from a friend at work and watched a video she sent them. They could see the benefits right away and thought it was exactly what they were looking for. Once they got all their questions answered, they joined, got their own products and started taking the trainings.

They not only earned enough to take whatever vacations they wanted, but earned the all-expense paid travel, on top of all the extra money they earned and took full advantage of the seven different ways you get paid in Shaklee. They love the combination of their teaching job, their side business and being able to write off some of their household expenses that they normally incur, since they have a home-based business.

The best of both worlds!

Chapter Seventeen

Let The Paint Dry!

People come into Shaklee for the benefits and quit for lack of training and experience (how they feel emotionally, after approaching people they 'thought' would be excited, to join them).

The top reason people say they didn't succeed in network-marketing before they joined Shaklee, was lack of training. Someone "signed" them up and left them to their own, telling them to, *"....do more."*

We think of locating, helping them join and training them as the hard part. In reality, where networks fail or fall short is in the training. Of course, part of this is that people have to be coachable and willing to learn.

But teaching means demonstrating, not telling people what direction to head in. People get new results in life by doing new behaviors...after the decide to change. People learn new behaviors by watching and listening, until they have the urge to do it themselves. If you aren't demonstrating to at least 20% of your group, how people learn has been lost on you, as the leader.

People come in for the benefits and quit for lack of training.

There's a cliché I coined over the years after having worked with many different employers: *"You can pay people sh***y or treat them sh***y, but you can't do both."* This goes for relationships, too. Meaning, you can ignore a person or outright treat them badly, but if you do both, they disappear from your life without warning. Meaning, people's tolerance for low pay is high if you treat them well and their tolerance for being treated bad is high, if you pay them well. But, if you do both you're behaving arrogant and expect too much from your employees...you're taking them for granted and behaving selfishly. Ultimately, you'll box yourself in, be figured out and be unable to find new employees (word of mouth). It happens to a lot of employers. The employers who pay well and create a nice work environment have people lining up and knocking down their door to get in. I can't tell you how many times I've seen small companies go out of business, practically over night from this. What happens is companies like this find really hard-working individuals who will tolerate a lot because, in part, they have high work ethic and low self-worth and esteem. The company finds a super hard-working, dedicated person who literally makes them being in business and profitable possible. But, the employee with low self-esteem, gets their self-esteem, from working hard and doing a good job...see the paradox there?

The more the employee works the higher their self-esteem grows, until the employee outgrows the combination of poor pay and treatment. In a relationship, a person will often grow from the relationship itself, (whether the relationship is nurturing or unhealthy), but if the appreciation level is low and the emotional pay-off is low, they outgrow the relationship and leave with little warning. Initially, often the employee will attempt to reason with their unreasonable employer (like the story of the frog trying to safely carry a scorpion on its back, across the water without getting stung), and realizes the reason they have that job is because no one else would take the job. The requirements of the position are so unique the employer can't find anyone else to fill the position. When trying to get a pay-raise fails, the employee begins putting feelers out for a better job and other employers start attempting to recruit this lowly-rewarded employee. Or, the employee starts getting additional training, education and experience, on the side, which matches their new level of self-worth, opening the door for greater pay and benefits somewhere else.

At one point in my life, I had a retail job at a hardware store, which paid about $8/hr. Way too little to live on. The building that the retail store was housed in was owned by the grocery store next door. Even though the pay was low, I just kept showing up for work. After a year, I asked for a raise and got twenty-five cents. The employer really treated me like I was the scum of the earth…as though I needed them or couldn't find a job anywhere else, or that no one else would hire me. The fact that I worked there was in relation to my self-esteem at that time…not that no one else would hire me, but they thought they held the cards. At the same time, the grocery store manager, next door, routinely came into my workplace and asked me to come work for him. A few of my friends worked there and kept telling him about me. I didn't think I was good enough to work at that huge store, so I procrastinated. After getting a twenty-five cent raise, my employer wanted me to begin doing additional work, as a cashier. To me, a slap in the face. About then, the grocery manager visited me again and said he would start me at $10.21/hr and I would be up to $18/hr in 18 months. *Hello!*

I gave notice at the hardware store and they seemed resentful I would leave them, but they treated me poorly, wouldn't pay me more and acted as if I was a burden to them. I joined the grocery team, was up to $18/hr in 18 months and met my wife working there, who went on to become an emergency room physician (1+1=8). Yay. Even today, some 17 years later, when I go in that first retail store to shop, they treat me like I'm *"less than"*. Oh well. They saw me as someone who needed them, but in actuality, I had a vision for myself far greater than what they could offer, while they were treating me as though I was "less than".

This same phenomena can happen in network-marketing. The "pay" (beyond the obvious financial and time-freedom benefits) is [competent training, appreciation and acknowledgement of their unique qualities and strengths] through demonstration and modeling of how to do the business by the sponsor/upline. The "treatment" is the upline sponsor showing each new recruit how to use their innate and often latent talent, to rise up to their full potential and be independent, as soon as humanly possible…*bringing out the best in them.* Not recycling "about" the business, but "how" to expand the business.

I firmly believe that everyone has strengths and everyone has something they want to improve about themselves. Often, strengths show up when you least expect them, are very specialized and surprise you. If you're open to finding strengths in people, they'll often surprise you. Insecure manager-types look for where people need to improve, while true leaders take a person's strengths and show them how to capitalize on them. The hardware store seemed to enjoy focusing on what they perceived were my inadequacies, while the grocery store manager knew good help was hard to find and saw a place for me among his 120 or so employees…he saw strengths in me, that he could use to reach his goals, as well as improve my living. At $18/hr, time-and-a half on Sundays and holidays, plus benefits he tripled my income in 18 months (1+1=8), doing the same stuff at the grocery store I was doing at the hardware store! The doors to the hardware store and the grocery store were about 20 feet apart. Two very different realities existing very close to one another.

A couple weeks after I started working at the grocery store, I found a handwritten note on the windshield of my car. It said that the people at the hardware store wanted to see me. I thought maybe they wanted me to fill in on my days off from the grocery store, which I would have happily obliged. But, I was very wrong. They called me in to say that someone in the community had over heard me telling someone that I really enjoyed working at the grocery store and that they were deeply offended by this, especially considering *all they had done for me*. They felt that my comments had hurt their ability to find and keep good employees. I explained how sorry I was, if that's what I had done and moved on realizing the reality, of the situation.

Arrogance and lack of appreciation for new business-expanders shows up as neither demonstrating the "how" to expand a business (telling them to do something rather than showing them how they are successfully building), but rather signing people up, sitting back until someone starts building and then attempting to "swoop in and take the people their downline signed up" "under-their-wing" instead of working to expand their downline themselves, taking credit for what their downline created.

You see, if you aren't actively expanding a front line/first level, you most certainly are not acting responsibly and with conscience to demonstrate the "how" of the business. *Your business* is your business. Duplication comes from you teaching your business partners/business-expanders (downline) (through first-hand demonstrating how to do the business), then releasing them and them doing the same and so on. Anywhere that the upline starts attempting to cherry-pick from their downline, not only is it going to back-fire because the downline will get a gut sense that something is off, (that they're being used) the upline has effectively created dependence vs independence and the whole duplication process has collapsed, before it has a chance to take off. The upline will likely wonder why people come in so excited, but just stop communicating or participating with them...in part, it's because the upline is expecting their new expanders, to do work *for them* that they aren't doing themselves... *"Bring me more people,"* is the underlying meta-message and feeling vs *"Go build your group and teach them to do the same thing."* This same phenomena can occur if the upline is simply attempting to feed off the recognition they would get from their group doing the work to grow and expand. That's why it's critical to acknowledge everyone's successes.

Anytime an upline is dependent on the downline to bring new people to reach their goals for growth the point of leveraging has been lost on them. It's a subtle aspect of laziness, arrogance, show-boating, incompetence and *"...what's mine is mine and what's yours is ours."*

So, show yourself and your downline respect by investing 75% of your time in locating the new business-expanders, who have been congruently looking for what you offer. Demonstrate how to do the business to create independence and work with your downline by being inclusive, (serving them), but, not by insisting to have contact downline. As a leader, you should be making yourself and training meetings/events available to help new business-expanders get on their feet and including them in training as much as they want to be, but this is a very small percent of your relative time.

But, if you're insisting on inserting yourself/being included yourself in the downline, you've lost the point of duplication, maybe attempting to get people to work for you (they're supposed to be working for themselves) and attempting to show-boat and show up as the know-it-all expert scooping up spoils. Not cool, nor productive. Very few people will have tolerance for that level of interference, unless they suffer from very low self-esteem and lack of belief in themselves, which means they probably won't stick with it anyway.

Like any employer, that's not an employee position very many people want nor will they stick with it once they see the pattern. There's no shortcuts to fast, major action to expand your own group. If the leader kicks back and gets hesitant or lazy, they're demonstrating how to be lazy, which in turn will train new expanders, to be lazy in expectation, of the star showing up to do the work the upline isn't doing.

Telling vs showing:

Never underestimate the power of someone watching you handle different types/kinds of situations. Doing so allows otherwise incompetent people to connect-the-dots and release their inner-talents. Watching you gives them permission to think on their feet, improvise, create, make mistakes, be successful and surpass you. Telling someone how to do the thing does none of the three. Telling is about you being the expert. Letting them watch you work is about releasing their inner-potential, latent potentials and creating a space for them to rise to their fullest expression.

If you aren't demonstrating, then you're creating questions in the mind of your new business-expanders. Unanswered demonstration causes pause, procrastination, analysis-paralysis, disassociation…interruption in momentum…bad feelings and conclusions about interactions with people who aren't interested in what is being offered.

Don't question or expect more than a person's nature:

If you're doing weekly/bi-weekly presentations, webinars, classes, trainings, etc., you darn well better be bringing new people to the meeting *yourself*. If your downline shows up or brings people to your meetings, but you aren't bringing people yourself, it points to either an unconscious pressure on your downline to build "for you" or you have an unconscious expectation that others should bring new people in, but you don't have to. This sends a message to your entire downline that their role is to find people to work "for you", the antithesis of network-marketing. No matter what size your network, if you're attempting to use your personal group as an example for success, you better be showing that you're still bringing new people in, versus pressuring your current downline network to "do more". This is a business for self-motivated, entrepreneurial, independent visionaries. If you're pressuring your downline to do more, you're acting as a "manager" and the point of network-marketing has been effectively lost on you and you'll find you're working hard, attempting to get others to work hard, losing effectiveness and increasing frustrations. Encouragement and pressure are two very different things with very different effects on morale.

For many who don't reach their goals, the common factor is simple*…they have funny feelings about/or they can't accept that the people they thought would join them or the people they wanted weren't interested*, so instead of moving on to find the people who are interested they linger back there with the people who aren't interested, stuck trying to change the reality of the past.

Busy vs productive:

Speaking, training and managing are amateur activities, which pay nothing to independent network-marketers. The challenge today, if you can define a single challenge, is locating the people who want the benefits and who will focus on locating, helping join, training and helping customers get started with the products (which has been the challenge in network-marketing since day-one)…it's the point of every business!

Doubt leads to indecision:

"When you don't have experience to back up decisions it can lead to getting emotional about things."
Parker Schnabel, *Gold Rush*, Discovery Channel.

Doubt creeps in where action is lacking.

Because the creative part of the mind is a problem-solving or solution-seeking mechanism, when a person doesn't follow through on their ideas, the mind starts coming up with reasons to not take that action. There's a saying that, *"Ideas are a dime a dozen"*. Meaning, anyone and everyone comes up with "good" ideas, inventions and money-making ideas, but very, very few actually follow through before they begin listing all the ideas why, *"…it won't work"*. The truth is that many people who aren't happy with where they are in life come up with ideas to simply distract themselves, from their current life, situations…then, when they have expressed their idea versus following through with it/them, they have momentary emotional relief from the boredom of their daily routine and they go back to their daily routine.

Success is simply working toward a goal, a little bit each day (consistently). Again, using the model of professions such as doctors, lawyers and aviators, if they knew everything they would have to do along the way, they might not have the courage to jump in. But, by breaking the big thing into smaller, daily tasks which are cumulative, the process seems doable. When you consistently take action toward your clearly defined goals, there's little room in the mind for doubt.

Indecision leads to breakdown in group morale:

In the leadership role, there's an expectation by those dependent on your experience and leadership to be decisive, meaning make decisions quickly and adjust your course as you go. Indecision creates a perception that you don't know what you're doing, which is the opposite of confidence. It can be said that leaders make decisions quickly and if they find they made a decision that doesn't result in taking them to their goals, they simply make another decision and adjust course. An example of indecisiveness and it's effect on a group is when you pull up to a four-way intersection and everyone is taking their turn based on the order they arrived at the intersection, but then one person misses the point and either sits at the stop sign waiting for cues (other than the traffic laws themselves) or they imagine they're doing others a 'favor' by skipping their turn (passive-aggressive behaviors) or in order to have a greater sense of 'control' they forego the decision to go themselves and motion for someone else who arrived at the intersection after them to go, interfering with the cycle of the intersection, yet insisting they're being self-sacrificing by 'letting' someone go before them (they don't have the right to make a decision to forego the right-of-way, for the entire group)... a short-term favor to a long-term *dis*-service.

Whenever a person who wants the "title" of leader behaves indecisively, those who are dependent on the leader for guidance, role-modeling and mentoring, will likely be affected in their morale and motivation, since it leads to the members of the group questioning their own practices. One of the most destructive things a leader can do to the overall morale and momentum to the group is to announce or insist on specific set of actions, for a specific time frame, but then changing the actions they're doing before the time is up, without updating the group.

For instance, a leader says to the group, *"For the next three months, we're only going to utilize Technique "A", so we can measure the results."* But then, the next week when someone downline calls their leader to update them on their progress, the leader says something like, *"Oh, we aren't doing Technique "A" anymore."* This type of willy-nilly, ADD approach causes confusion, and worst of all, doubt in the leadership role and gives the impression that nothing really matters. In marketing, consistency is of utmost importance, so that averages can be tracked to see what works better than something else. It's not just about throwing out ideas to sound like you know something, nor for the sake of brain-storming, but rather to refine your system to be the most efficient with your time (time being what you can't get back). Not only is flip-flopping from one idea to the next an indulgence you can't afford, it's really disrespectful of the time, for those who have signed up in good faith to follow you. Make decisions as best you can, based on your goals and the best information you have and then monitor the results you're getting from the decision you made to the actions you are taking.

There's a hierarchy of problem handling:

In network-marketing, your main purpose is to expand your business organization, not manage the people who joined you. Within "managing" is problem-solving, for others. Shaklee is set-up so each business-expander has access to the majority of the information that everyone has, as long as its relevant to their business. Meaning, for example, you get a printout of your group, your product points, your expansion stats, etc., each month…you don't need stats for people who aren't in your group, since it's not your business.

A lot of the people who have trouble growing their business think that as soon as they have two or three business-expanders, in their group that their time spent finding people changes to managing their business-expanders, while ignoring their own expansion habits. There is a certain amount of training involved with each new business-expander, to get them up and running, but most important is to teach your business-expanders "where" to get the information, not spoon-feed every minutia of detail…you want to get independent and train other to be independent, ASAP!

The phone number for Shaklee is toll-free and every question that can come up can be answered with phone call or email to Shaklee. Most questions new expanders have are the same questions everyone else has had. If, as a leader, your time for expanding your own business is spent answering the same questions over and over, that doesn't make any sense at all and sets a precedence that everyone who joined you should follow your example and the overall growth process comes to a halt.

Shaklee pays countless employees as our support team to answer questions when those of us in the field are doing what we're paid to do…*meet new people through word-of-mouth-marketing, to locate business partners and expand the customer base!* If you want to be the "answer" person, then go work at Shaklee headquarters and answer phones for those of us working in the field. But, the support people at Shaklee headquarters are not expanding businesses, for good reason. The disclaimer here is that during your group, weekly/bi-weekly online training sessions, you can open up part of the designated time for question and answers…but, you see the difference (limiting the time frame and designating general questions in ways that it doesn't take away from your personal, expansion routine). If you don't designate specific times like this, you'll end up playing phone tag, answering questions, responding to emails, your business-expanders can get the answers to themselves and eliminating a big part of your own business expansion time. Learn to discern whether you absolutely need to be the one to answer a question or not, but by all means, refer business-expanders to Shaklee headquarters and field support whenever possible (giving a fish vs teaching to fish).

Complaining, gossiping, whining:

If you happen to help a person join you whose bias is to complain, gossip and/or whine and blame others, don't be afraid to set some boundaries with them to clarify the point of this business is to create something we enjoy, versus what is unpleasant and what we would rather avoid. If someone's identity is really wrapped up in negativity, they'll likely behave offended by your frankness, but that's a part of the refining process…locating and training 15 new, productive leaders every 12-15 months. There simply isn't enough time to spend on what we aren't happy about or what we wish was different, but rather doing the actions to find business leaders and customers. That doesn't mean you can't deliver the message gently, but if you try to stop that behavior three times without change, it's not likely the person is what you're looking for as a leader anyway…they're looking for people to co-miserate with. The reason being that this business requires behavioral flexibility. If a person isn't flexible enough to notice the harm they are doing by being negative, recycling the past disappointments and/or they aren't able to accept coaching from you, it's not likely they'll reach their goals anyway, nor sustain any success they gain. If nothing else, limit your exposure to their negativity by limiting their training to group sessions. In addition, this business requires immense emotional-energy, which is cultivated from positivity. If you're working to convince a person to be positive, you're dumping energy that your business requires elsewhere and it isn't sustainable.

Case example:

Jerry is a small business administrator, for the city where he lives. Although he gets to use a lot of the business skills he learned in college, he felt a little cut-off from the business world. Meaning, he was involved in business, but he wasn't making the kind of money he wanted and he didn't get to take his wife on trips like they thought they would.

Jerry was so excited someone would think of him and watched the video that was sent to him, within minutes. A local person came into his office and asked if he would be interested in looking at a way to earn extra money on-the-side. He couldn't believe he hadn't heard of this before. He knew a lot of other business people he thought would be interested and after getting his own product pack and starting to use the products, began contacting other business professionals in similar situations as him. Several joined right away and he as a great group developing. He agreed to invest 10-15 hours per week, simply locating people like himself, who were smart business people, but weren't earning as much as they wanted to.

Having qualified for the upcoming Bahamas trip and having received three monthly checks which exceeded his expectations, Jerry finally feels like he's "home".

Chapter Eighteen

Be Respectful
Of Your Group's Professional Boundaries

There's a fine line between supporting, training and cherry-picking downline from yourself. It's not our right (as leaders), nor is it efficient to work downline (meaning, working with people we haven't personally trained or had some agreement with, that we would include the whole group in our weekly and bi-weekly training sessions), unless they express wanting help and they can't get it from the person who directly helped them join. For instance, maybe someone joined four levels below you, but the person who helped them join is no longer active or decided to focus on being a customer versus a leader. If you have an agreement with both people, have the person who helped them join introduce you and invite all involved to your weekly/bi-weekly training webinars. What is offensive, destructive and lacking in integrity is failing to expand your own business, but then inserting yourself into your downline to make contact with those who your own downline brought into the group. Including your entire group is a positive, healthy attribute, but you darn well better be bringing your own new people to the trainings/meetings. An unhealthy tendency in the industry is for leaders who insist they are providing "service" yet aren't providing what people really need to have demonstrated…that's right, you locating your own new business partners and customers.

There a fine line between providing contact information and attempting to mooch off your downline, to gain business partners and help others join. If you're a serious leader, you're investing your time expanding up your frontline (1st levels), not trying to interject yourself into your downline's business. Provide contact info, in case someone below you drops-out or become inactive and they need help and demonstration of the fundamentals, but don't be making up reasons to contact them, to establish a relationship that isn't there to begin with. Include them in training, but don't be contacting them to mooch off your own group. Its up to your expanders to work/develop their own business-expanders!

"Growth is actually contagious, so if you want to reach your goals, you've got to get around people who are going in the same direction you want to be going, and you will catch the success." —Dr. Henry Cloud

One of the keys to successfully and efficiently expanding your business is consistency in locating and training new business-expanders. The only place you don't need to be consistent is in improvising or thinking on-the-fly, when interacting with potential business partners and customers. Meaning, if something isn't working, whether in the moment or over the course of months, do something different!

Consistency:

When it comes to training, demonstrating and being there for your expanders, be consistent! For example, if you give a Business-Expander a homework assignment or something to do before you talk the next time, you better darn well pick up the conversation where you left off. If you give an assignment, say make a list and have it done in seven days, you darn well better put it on your appointment book to follow up at an agreed upon time and at that time, cover what you said you were going to cover.

In your own world you can be as distracted and attention deficit as you choose to be, but in businesss, it's a business-killer. Partly, because people are counting on you to help them get a base of knowledge, built up and partly because you're supposed to be demonstrating how to do that. People develop their instincts (in any area of endeavor) by doing correct actions and seeing the results *of correct action.* If their actions aren't consistent and don't show them how to produce results, they effectively become *de*-pendent rather than *inde*-pendent…which is the opposite of the primary outcome of duplicating yourself in network-marketing. Inconsistency creates confusion!

If you can't keep your word long enough to have continuity between trainings or appointments, it not only says you don't respect their time, it says you lack respect for the structure of your own business and that sets a precedence for your group losing respect for you. If you don't take what *you say* seriously, no one else will and you'll find your serious builders flaking-out and making excuses to not talk with you. Managerial-minded expanders think that time spent with new expanders is an investment, but if you don't follow through on your word or you take time to chit-chat when you're suppose to be locating new people for your group, well, pretty soon all your expanders will be chit-chatting with people who already joined and wondering why people aren't finding new expanders…the group's growth comes to a halt. Often, its at this point that managerial-minded leaders panic, begin "pushing" people to "do more" and give the impression that they are employees…WRONG!

Let the paint dry…meaning don't give instructions, forget what instructions you gave and then change the instructions, without regard for the first instructions or without finding out what the results of the first instructions were! If you lack focus, then don't behave like you're a credible leader. I heard one upline tell his downline that they should start a conversation, with potential business people or customers, by paying a sincere compliment. One of his new business-expanders did this and the prospective business partner didn't follow through with the appointment and the "leader" asked him the sequence of talking with the prospect. The new expander started to say he, *"…paid the prospect a sincere compliment,"* and the "leader" said, *"No, no, you don't do that…"* and went on to say what he would have done, instead, which was different than what he told his new expander to do, before.

Obviously, this leads to confusion and lack of confidence in the "leader" as well as anxiety, about interacting with the leader, business people and customers…it breaks communication down. Ultimately, the leader failed by "telling" his expander what to do instead of demonstrating with his own (the leader's) prospects. But again, since the "leader" wasn't actually expanding his business, but rather attempting to position himself to "manage" a group that didn't need managing, gain recognition through "expertise" and he didn't have any prospects to demonstrate to, so he was resorting to "telling" about fictional situations that didn't exist, attempting to insert himself as the expert and interfering in the new expander's learning processes. Make sense?

I've heard so-called experts and leaders discourage their own expanders, by telling them their goals are too big to be reasonable. Anyone who knows anything about human progress knows that every goal was once an idea that hadn't been accomplished, by anyone else in history. If it weren't for people setting unattainable goals, nothing would change. Even the four-minute-mile was considered too dangerous to attempt…"experts" insisted people would die if they ran a four-minute mile...a 4:01 minute-mile was safe, but a 4.00 minute-mile would kill you. Bicycles used to be considered too dangerous, for women to ride. **Every day people say something is impossible, while others are accomplishing the impossible.** In the months after Roger Banister first ran the four-minute mile, others also ran sub, four-minute miles. It was first achieved in 1954 by Roger Bannister in 3:59.4. The "four-minute barrier" has since been broken by many male athletes, and is now the standard of all male professional middle-distance runners. In the last 50 years the mile record has been lowered by almost 17 seconds, and currently stands at 3:43.13, yet someone who hasn't heard this might still say it's impossible.

The truth is that when someone says a goal isn't realistic, it means they doubt *their own ability* to do it. That's it. They might even be unconsciously fearful that someone will build faster than they did or go beyond their personal sticking point and make them look bad...this is the anthesis of the mindset and outlook they should have. You should want your expanders to do better than you...*THAT'S THE POINT!* You get paid by expanding your customer base and by duplicating yourself/expanding your business leaders by 15 every 12-15 months. If you attempt to talk people out of their goals, you're interfering. If someone believes they can get *20* new business-expanders, per month, let them do it. If they don't succeed the first time, they'll adjust and run again until they do make it. That's the point of refining processes...figuring out the limits of the current ways which didn't work...*not to limit what will work!*

I've seen leaders who got 30 new customers in one day! I've seen "leaders" who were so adamant about interfering in their own business that they insist new business-expanders can achieve all their dreams in Shaklee, but once a person joins them, they insist the rate at which they intend to expand is unreasonable...*which is sabotage.*

I've seen "leaders" who ask their expanders what their goal for the month is, tell them it's too high, set a smaller goal for them, then as the weeks go by, continue to raise the bar even though the new expander hasn't seen a "demonstration" of how to effectively expand a business. That's how you create a confused and schizophrenic business partner! Meaning, as the month goes on and the so-called "leader" wastes their time telling their expanders to "do more" instead of expanding their own business, they get anxious about their group product points and start pressuring their new expanders to do more of what isn't working! Eventually, the expanders stop talking to their sponsor and disappear, contributing to the attrition rate. I've seen "leaders" ask new expanders what they plan of action was (having not shown them a demonstration), only to say, *"That didn't work for me and it won't work for you…assuming the new expander's skill set is the same as theirs or as limited as theirs, effectively shutting them down.* The sophisticated network-marketer locates and trains people who have more skills and talent than they have themselves…*not find people who have less skill and talent and then tell them they won't accomplish more than them! Duh!*

If you don't demonstrate effective strategies, you have absolutely no business critiquing a new business-expander's creativity, ingenuity and attempts. The ideas people get are *for them* and come from their own creative unconscious.

If a "leader" is so effective at expanders, they wouldn't have time to waste telling new expanders what doesn't work…they would be showing them what definitely works. We have no idea what won't work if it hasn't been accomplished (four-minute miles).

Some people say calling lists of people deosn't work. I'm here to tell you they can, [if you use the skills that are needed for reaching out to people on the phone]. On the phone, people can hear your intentions as well or better than in-person, because they don't have visual stimulus to be confused by. On the phone, you have to be able to build rapport quickly and honestly, within the first couple seconds. When I was a personal trainer at Gold's Gym, Capital Hill, Seattle, we had to get our own personal-training clients.

My first day, they showed me my monthly quota and handed me a list of 30,000 members and their phone numbers. I was so good at calling that the managers and other trainers were attempting to steal clients away from me to pad their own quotas. How did I learn to do it? I watched and listened to my manager call about five people. That's it. Call them, tell them who I was and what I was offering and offer to meet them at the gym. Some of those clients I'm still friends with and that was in 2006. And yes, I got my personal-training clients going on Shaklee products.

When I got to the end of the list, which I worked on between clients, I started at the beginning of the *same* list and worked my way through it again! By this time, some people were no longer members and many new members had joined. Eventually, I was training other trainers how to call, *from the same list*. We were all calling the same people, but it didn't matter…the members responded to which trainer they wanted to and a lot of that was based on what they saw of the trainers, in the gym…they wanted to work with a professional, not a muscle-head who was on his cell phone or ignoring the client. The manager who taught me, left shortly after he taught me. These clients would purchase $600-$6,000 worth of training at a time.

So, the point is that when someone says something doesn't work, *take it with a grain of salt,* but know that [you need the particular skills for whatever approach you're using]. Just because you get an idea doesn't mean you have the skills to make it happen the way you envision…but the only way to get the skills is to start! AND if it doesn't work, that doesn't mean you quit…it means you adjust course and go again. Make it happen! When a person says something doesn't work, it doesn't take the current market trends, technological advances or individual strengths, intuition or ingenuity into account…it says they didn't develop the skills to *make it work!* Often, when a person just goes a little bit further, they learn a detail that the person who quit early didn't learn. A person who sponsors a new expander might be good at that skill, but that doesn't mean they know what you are capable of. Not at all.

For decades business "experts" said network-marketing would never work, while billions-and-billions, of dollars' worth of products were being consumed, through network-marketing and being redirected away from the brick-and-mortar stores. They said it wouldn't work, *AS IT WAS WORKING!* Malls used to be the thing, the place to go and hang out and shop, but now they are closing all over the country in record numbers, because consumer's buying habits have changed to online shopping, so much. Now, network-marketing is even more relevant. For me, much of my shopping is online, having stuff delivered to my door!

We don't know what doesn't work. What works for one, works for another with a nuance of difference…a minor change, who cares? Remember my worm business? I was selling all the worms I could get. When my dad took it over, it all went away. When my next-door neighbor tried it, all his worms died. We were in a trailer-court, so we lived about 20 feet from one another and were collecting worms from the same yard at the same times, a lot of times. My business worked, theirs didn't. I was nine-years old. His parents were spending about $1,500.00 per month on fishing tackle!

Your role (as a leader) is to teach, through demonstration, what you do. If you aren't expanding, building and bringing new people to your group, refer your people to someone you can count on to demonstrate. But definitely, do not tell people what to do, then critique the way they do it or the results they get…its none of your business and interferes in their own creativity! People don't join network-marketing to be told they can't act on their own creativity! They should be encouraged to stretch and use their imagination. If you demonstrate and they have further questions, that's fine to clarify or "show them" again, until they can do it themselves. If you position yourself as an expert, you'll be talking a lot and likely producing very little while patting yourself on the back.

Now, the qualifier here, is that if someone refuses to receive/participate in your demonstrations of how you're expanding your own business, but then they call to complain that their business isn't expanding, that is a double-bind. They can't have it both ways. If they won't accept training, there is nothing for you to help them improve upon…nothing to adjust course. If they did accept training, then they just need clarification and refinement (mentoring), which comes from watching and listening you MORE.

I heard of one lady in Shaklee that lived way out in the woods during the 1970's, long before cell phones. She built a very successful business by calling people in the phone book. But yet, people who don't have the same vision and skill set will argue it's not possible…that you can't build from calling people on a list or from a phone book. Think about it. The people who aren't putting in full effort and follow-through, will insist it can't be done…because they're insistent on not doing it correctly!

The intellectual "expert" will insist on not showing you a thing, and criticize the approach you are working to master. It's a process. (Everyone is an expert about things that are uncomfortable to them). Everything we have now was an invention that started with an idea that [someone insisted they had the market on expert opinions of] and that it couldn't be done. *Get real.*

If you aren't demonstrating, then you're always correcting people *after the fact*...which at its essence is criticism and not-constructive criticism. If you intend to be constructive be preemptive and preventive, by demonstrating what to do and how to do it...not by withholding teaching and then asking your downline how they handled a situation, *after the fact,* and then telling them what they *should have done*...which is the opposite of building on success and comes across as demeaning, but makes you feel like the all-knowing expert.

Show people what to do, from the start, which brings out the best in people. Telling them what they should have done after the fact is weak and focuses on inadequacy.

The difference between telling and doing is having a few people who "nail it" vs a lot of people who struggle along and don't develop. Which one do you want?

There are self-starters, natural-networkers, people who are naturally-outgoing. But, just like how people have different learning styles, some people learn from watching and listening to the thing being done. If you aren't willing to train these people by taking them under-your-wing to demonstrate what and how to do it, then don't have them join them! The market is flooded with people who were sponsored or signed up and then all that happens after that is disappointing and negative word-of-mouth from upline, who don't follow through but tell their new business-expanders to follow through! How ridiculous is that! When you run into people who have a negative opinion about MLM, networking or even Shaklee, that's what happened!...whether they know it or not!

If you aren't going to demonstrate how to do the business in real time, don't have people join you, people who need demonstration to learn and then make the excuse that the business isn't for everyone, essentially "cherry-picking" the self-starters!

When you sponsor someone you're responsible for training them properly, regardless of what their beginning skill-set is!

The right vibe:

When you're making enough contacts that your return on investment yields you a good ratio of new customers and expanders, the energy you put off is, *"Hey, I want you to join me, but if you don't it's ok since a lot of other people already are and have since the last time we talked."* Prospects get a sense that you don't need them, but you could be good partners (mutually-beneficial/win-win).

On the other hand, if you only talk to a couple people here and there and no one has joined, since you last talked to a prospect the energy is more like *"I neeeeed you."* (needy).

The energy you put out is the unspoken vibe people get from you which reflects how well your business is expanding. The vibe you put out can't be faked since it is a mirror of your actual progress, at an unconscious level, which is projected to those you're speaking with.

You always want to stay ahead of the vibe-curve, by doing enough people-contact hours (locating, helping join and training), that people get the success-vibe instead of the needy-vibe.

For instance, if you're trying to prospect your downline's customers and expanders, the vibe is that you aren't busy enough to prospect recruit and train your own group.

If you run a group training that you offer to your entire downline, in order to help them launch this is different (the vibe being generosity vs desperation).

But, if you aren't busy enough continuing to expand your own business, people will pick up on it and take their foot off-the-throttle of their own business.

Prospects and new expanders expect to hear about the people who have joined you since you last spoke to them. If you haven't helped people join you in the meantime, they interpret that as struggle and lack of success/progress (neediness).

If you aren't willing to demonstrate how to do the business, it speaks to your belief in your ability to expand your business. It's disrespectful to new expanders. The message is that they aren't worth your time. In this business your success is dependent on your new expanders' success, why would you hold out on them?

New expanders are successful or fail within the first few approaches. Not that they will or they won't approach people, but how they "feel" about the interaction, after the fact. If you don't demonstrate how to handle, "No's" and smart-ass remarks, you're literally setting them up to be an attrition statistic. Do yourself a favor.

If you don't demonstrate (show) how to do the business, you don't have any place criticizing your new expander's choices or actions. When your new business-expanders watch and listen to you demonstrating how to do the business, then they have a way to channel their own innate creativity toward similar outcomes. Demonstration is leadership. Criticism is "know it all, back seat driver, attention seeking behaviors".

Don't question or expect more than a person's nature:

In the same sense that attempting to control other's ideas of you is like a rabbit-hole that circles around and goes nowhere, so is expecting something different than a persons' inherent nature. If a person doesn't follow through in other areas of their life, don't expect them to in business. If they don't keep their word, they won't in Shaklee either. If they lack loyalty, they won't in Shaklee either. It's been said that network-marketing is the greatest self-improvement course you'll ever experience. For better or worse, in those same ways, network-marketing amplifies whatever a person's [latent] personality traits are. As long as you don't expect people to do anything more than what they already have demonstrated, you'll be ahead of the game. With this in mind, it means being very specific about the kinds of people you approach as business partners, since whatever their natural personality, the process of network-marketing will amplify it. Choose wisely.

Case example:

Jose is a hard worker who came to America seeking the American dream. Working as a day laborer, in the back of his mind he thinks there has to be a better way.

He heard of one of his cousins who has a home-based business, earns a great living, gets free cars and free trips. It sounds like it might be too good to be true, but he reached out and his cousin sent him a video. He noticed that all the brochures and videos were available in English and Spanish. He went over to his cousin's house, found that it was real. He looked through the photo album of 23 different trips and 12 different company cars his cousin had earned.

He immediately joined, got his own product order going and contacted everyone he knows. Not everyone was interested, but within the first month he had 23 customers and six business partners. He says his only regret is, *"...not knowing about it sooner."*

Chapter Nineteen

You Cannot Possibly Run Out Of Prospective Customers Or Business-Expanders

When I started using Shaklee, back in 1993, my understanding was that all I had to do was make a list of everyone I knew, was friends with, or was related to and that would be the successful launch of my business because all I had to do was contact them and they would join me. Boy, was I mistaken!

Here's what I mean by that. Growing up, anytime anyone needed help, was moving, was in trouble or just needed an extra hand, I was there. From standing up to bullies, to using my truck to help people move, to working for family members in their businesses, to giving people a ride whenever needed, I was there.

Remember, I had been looking for Shaklee for close to twenty-years, all that time. When I finally joined, I couldn't fathom that anyone *wouldn't* be interested or at least hear me out. My youngest sister joined as a distributor and my two older sisters bought a couple products to show their support. My mom bought supplements, but never took them. Ten-years later, I found them sitting on her shelf, unopened. Today she is taking more than twenty different prescriptions for medical problems that creeped up over the years.

Everyone else either made fun of me, told me, *"...those things don't work,"* that they *"...knew what I was up to and weren't interested,"* or simply discouraged me. Now, excuse me, but people in my circle of influence had been having product parties for all the top companies since I could remember. Somehow, what I was doing seemed different. My experience was completely different than what my mentors insisted it would be. *"Just talk to people,"* is what I heard over and over. I couldn't believe the cold responses I got.

I have heard of people who literally launch their success just in their warm market (people they know), and often I've heard them say they never even finished getting through their initial list because they got so busy.

I know this can happen, but for the new expanders, who it doesn't play out well for, it can be very discouraging. In fact, most people, regardless how dedicated and committed they insist they are, their first week of enrolling, drop out before the first month is over when the three people they knew would join them decline and make fun of them...[they quit based on how they felt after their offer being declined and not knowing what to do with those weird or embarrassing feelings].

For me, being a hard-worker at heart, having had that initial product experience at age six, looking for Shaklee for 20 years and having great products results, in the first week, I don't think anyone could have talked me out of it. And most tried.

Hint, hint...if you really give the products an honest go, no one can talk you out of your business goals. Many of the people who made fun of me were people who I had looked up to, much of my life...but, that was when I was admiring *them*. When it came to me doing something I was passionate about, the perspective wasn't returned and that's ok. They say network-marketing is the greatest self-improvement course you'll ever participate in and I believe that because whatever your greatest fear, or phobia is, you'll have to face it down and work through it on your path to success. I found that much of my circle of influence wanted me around when they wanted something from me. How to know you've actually worked through a personal issue is that your business suddenly takes off and grows to a new level you haven't experienced before.

For me, I was caught up in trying to get others' approval and got very little. I really didn't know how important approval was to me until I started my Shaklee Business. Mind you, I was 24 years old at the time, had a long road of self-improvement ahead of me, but I faced-down the challenge and improved myself and my personality, piece-by-piece. What would have helped me the most was belief in myself which I lacked. In other words, I've heard from a lot of people (mentors I had later on), that I didn't know how good I was. In other words, I seemed to require a lot of [external] evidence [from others] that I was a good person and on track for great things. The side effect of this is that when I had an idea, I would start to work on it, but when I encountered negativity or naysayers or people who tried to discourage me, I would be surprised and retreat emotionally. I'd have to just escape the environment. Eventually, I'd work my courage back up and get back to work (persistence). Without the persistence, I wouldn't be where I am now.

Personally, I think new expanders should refrain from saying a single word to their warm market, until they have been trained how to do it and how to gracefully handle negativity from people you believe would support you. **[Without these two skill-sets, most people drop out, their first-month].** Unfortunately, most new expanders tell themselves that since they were excited about Shaklee, that "knowing" about Shaklee means they know how to talk to people about Shaklee...not true at all. If a person isn't trained, they are unwittingly relying on their particular skillset, which could be zilch [in relation to Shaklee] and results in little more than throwing mud at the wall and hoping some of it sticks.

[100% of the people who join think that because they joined, they inherently have the skill-set to talk about Shaklee successfully and be successful in the business...they do not]. Talking "about" the business is not the same as "doing" the business expansion strategies.

For many who don't reach their goals and become attrition statistics, the common factor is simple... they can't come to terms with the fact that the people they thought initially would join them, during the launch of their business (or the people they wanted to join them) and they weren't interested in moving on to locate the people who definitely are interested (they are out there). So, they end up lingering back with the people who clearly aren't interested (indicated by their behaviors), stuck attempting to change the reality of the situation...they don't bounce back from disappointment, but rather retreat to emotional safety. New expanders think people declining their off is related to how they asked.

[After reading the above paragraph, you can probably hear how unreasonable it sounds to think you could join a company for a small fee, have the potential to build a multi-million-dollar business and then assume that you could talk to three people and become a millionaire...and that if those three people don't want or value what you're offering, there's no possible way you'd ever succeed at your initial goals!]

But that's what attrition is!

From the company's standpoint, even an untrained-person talking about Shaklee is better than someone not talking about Shaklee. But, for the newbie who is serious about launching and expanding a serious business, many don't survive the learning curve of approaching their peers and within the first ten people they drop out, being unskilled in handling so-called/perceived "rejection" gracefully…they think that a lack of initial success means it isn't going to work…that they won't be success!...that they can't survive people's sarcasm or criticism…that if they were going to be crazy successful, it would happen with the first people they talk to. AND, its unnecessary. People dropping out in their first month (attrition) is like people walking into a pack of wolves…again, this comes from people thinking that because they know "about" something, they are qualified to talk about it, professionally.

Opinion and professionalism are two very different things. One pays the big bucks and the other doesn't pay a dime.

Based on my personal experiences, I would encourage new business-expanders to avoid the people in their warm market (family, friends, co-workers, etc.). A main reason being that as you're launching and expanding your business, you still have to have a family and friends who are "neutral" and who aren't going to put undue pressure on you, make fun of you, antagonize you and so on, at family gatherings and holidays…think about it!

I personally wouldn't even tell people, until I have already established 10 (ten) customers and 3 (three) people who have joined you as business-expanders, outside the people you personally already know. A main reason being that a lot of family and friends will ask you how your business is going…you need to have a base of business that is completely and utterly separate and independent of your warm market (family, friends, co-workers, class mates, etc.). That way, you'll have your own experience with the products, as well as testimonials from your customers and business-expanders, regardless of how your family and friends respond to you.

This is completely opposite of what most network-marketing companies teach to their new expander, but again, the perspective is that of the company wanting the public to speak about their products, versus the fact that most new business-expanders sign up and quit within their first month…within the first ten people they approach (attrition)…because how the experience leaves them feeling, emotionally-paralyzed. Every company, organization, employer, school, etc., experiences attrition, but the reality is particularly harsh in network-marketing. Personally, I would rather insulate and prepare new expanders properly, so you know what to expect than to throw you to the wolves, throw mud at the wall and "hope" something good happens.

With this in mind, you don't need to contact your warm-market, in the beginning. Once you have some success going and have a track record of success, believe me it's a lot easier to approach family and friends knowing in the back of your mind that you don't need them for your business to be successful. I believe that people who don't know better erroneously believe that approaching family and friends is "easier". But, I assure you, this isn't necessarily true. And [if it doesn't hold water], it's very, very difficult for most people to get their head and heart back in the game.

The truth is, it's a lot easier to approach people you don't know (can't be a prophet in your own town). When someone who doesn't know you says, *"No thank you,"* **it simply doesn't matter…**you can go home to your family at the end of the day and no one has to know any better. But, people who don't know anything about you are often more open to new ideas. This is wackbards to what many people think, but after decades as an entrepreneur, I assure you it can be true. There are people out there who have a natural talent for marketing and/or a naturally supportive support system, but this is less common than you would think.

I had a friend who joined a network-marketing company who insisted it was awesome, but his mom told him that she wouldn't join him until he had some customers on his own. He never sponsored a single person.

A lot of times, people take for granted what you're offering them. In America, opportunity abounds and people take it for granted. There's so many opportunities to use up time, energy and money that people can't make up their mind and don't take any action at all. But, people who just arrived in America, do not seem take opportunity for granted, as much. They have a better ability to discern value, because they have experienced so much scarcity.

The last statistic I could find stated that a new person comes to America every 57 seconds...*think about it.* Think about people who have been doing everything humanly possible to get to America for the *American Dream*. They are praying and hoping to run into someone like us offering something like this. And much of what they encounter will neither be as credible nor as legitimate as Shaklee.

And, if they happen to be from one of the countries that Shaklee does business in, they already have a massive network of people who are also looking for opportunity. Meaning, we can sponsor them in America and they can sponsor their entire circle of influence from their home town/country. Canada, Mexico, China, Malaysia, Japan and Laos are some included in this program. Think about it...you can't run out of people because more people are constantly arriving. Often, people who said, *"No,"* their first-time hearing about network-marketing say, *"Yes"* with subsequent offers, whether by the same person of a different person and a different opportunity entirely. Think about it.

It doesn't matter if they aren't completely fluent in English or if you're fluent in their language as there are brochures in each of the languages for the countries we can sponsor in and online translators that work fast and well. It's not uncommon for people who speak different languages to be in the same group.

Many of the people who are refugees of war, are so good at making something out of nothing, that I saw on a 2015 Netflix movie entitled *Salam Neighbor*....within the refugee camps, people who had nothing with the clothes on their backs now have a multi-million dollar economy, within the refugee camps! One lady, who had lost two of her sons to war on the same day, but a year apart, starting noticing all the used plastic bags blowing around outside and began making art out of plastic bags, selling them for the equivalent of $70/U.S. each.

In Mafraq, Jordan, a single mom named Ghoussoon, with three children she is the head of her household, her husband killed and thrown into a mass grave didn't want to live in the refugee camp, (one in four households are lead by women because so many men haven't escaped Syria), so living outside the refugee camp, because she arrived there before the refugee camps were set up and she believes she can build a more traditional home for her kids, outside the camp where they can go to public

Jordanian school. Without any other family for support, she starting making hand-made hairbows (which she had learned to do school) and selling them for $2 and is making a living, to put her kids through school...*resilient, hungry and determined.* She said, as she was sitting on the floor cutting fabric and attaching it together, referring to her home, *"...it's still there, but with nothing in it. I wish I could be a bird, to go see what is happening there and then come back."*

Ghoussoon said, *"My biggest challenge is that my children are still so young. I want to raise and teach them everything. In Syria, I was working as a nurse. But after I moved here, to Mafraq, I applied to and receive aid from the nonprofit organizations, but the support wasn't a lot. The aid was enough for my basic needs. In my head I was thinking, what is something I can do for work, so I can stay at home to protect and take care of my children. I thought of this idea I learned in school. It takes me about 30-40 minutes to make one of these. And every month I sell about 200 pieces. It is true we are considered refuges not only in Jordan, but anywhere in the world, but Syrians, even if they are refugees are productive and hard workers and will be creative with everything and anywhere."*

When asked, *"Even now when you have to provide for your whole family, would you ever think about going to the refugee camp where they give you free food or different services?"* Ghoussoon's reply, *"No"*.

Remember, people can make up for lack of skill or knowledge by getting in action, and refining their process as they go, as long as they have the mentorship and support, when they ask for it. Is this making sense? A person who knows very little details about the business, but is unresponsive to negativity will likely build incredibly faster than a person who knows all the facts, but can't handle hearing, *"No, I'm not interested, right now"*. I've seen it over and over and over again.

Case example:

I had digestive problems from day one of my life. Everything anyone could experience from the top to the bottom. On top of that I was a very picky eater and didn't get enough vegetables. I was constantly taking OTC meds to relieve heartburn and indigestion. Constant cramps and gut pain in my stomach and intestines. Before Shaklee, my life was very interrupted by my digestion problems. When I joined Shaklee, no one knew about all my gut problems, it was kind of embarrassing.

Little by little, using Shaklee, all my digestive problems went away. I use OptiFlora™, Alfalafa, Herblax™. I'd never go without them now.

Chapter Twenty

You Don't Need To Know It All.
Low-hanging Fruit, *First*

You're a quarterback. You do the play. Regardless how it works out, let it go and move forward with the next play fast and without thought for how the past worked out or whether someone caught the ball and made a touchdown or got tackled, fumbled, or penalized, which resulted in temporary lost yardage. To do your best on the next play, your mind has to be focused on what you want the result of this play to be. As soon as this play is done, regardless of outcome, your mind goes to the next play. Make it a habit. Do not focus on what didn't work or didn't work out.

The mind is made to lead *and* follow. Followers follow leaders, regardless of credibility. If you lack complete belief in yourself, you'll follow others' beliefs and vision…it's a natural law. The ignorant person who believes in themselves, will lead those who don't believe in themselves. The educated person who lacks self-belief will follow a person who is full of crap because the person full of crap believes in themselves, even though it's irrational. It comes down to which person believe in themselves.

I worked at the gun store, in Seattle, where I was a salesman and worked with another salesman, named Rich. Rich would do anything to make a sale including misleading, lying, bait-and-switch and so on. When a customer approached the counter, Rich would place both hands on the counter, lower his voice firm lean over the counter and talk down to the customer, telling the customer what he wanted them to do. There seemed to be two types of customers…one who had self-doubt or who lacked information, did exactly what Rich said, whether it was in their best interest or not. The other kind of customer, who believed in themselves or knew more than Rich about the products, neither liked him nor wanted to work with him and downright avoided him and going so far as to tell the other sales people about it. Rich never seemed to figure it out. He made a lot of sales, but he missed out on a lot of sales because he didn't pay attention to why the people who avoided him were avoiding him. He was the kind of guy who would park so close to others' car that he couldn't get out of his own driver's side door and the other person couldn't get in their car from the driver's side. At this particular sporting goods store, we had customers who spent fifty-thousand dollars, per year, on firearms and that's not uncommon among collectors and enthusiasts. Rich simply rubbed people the wrong way because he came across like he was talking down to the customers and they should follow his command. Eventually, he was let go and on his way home, someone pulled up next to his car at a stop light and fired several rounds from a handgun into his car.

It's not so much about knowing everything.

But, it is about knowing where to direct others to get the information they want and need to move forward and get the benefits we offer.

Business-expanders who insist they need to know it all, in order to begin or move forward, never develop a business. The reason being that the key concepts of 1) Using products, 2) Locating people who want more money and free time and 3) Teaching them the same things, are unchanging. The "means" change and evolve (technology evolves), meaning the internet and related technologies are relatively new, but these same three steps have been the same since Shaklee started, in 1965.

For me, after my initial attempts to share with my relatives didn't work like I thought it would, I decided to start doing public classes at libraries, school, college campuses, health stores and so on, to meet people I hadn't met yet…people I hadn't exposed the benefits to. Continuing Education programs at colleges has worked really good for this and often thousands of people see the class listed in the CEU catalog. Think about it. For me, this process works great. I aim for about 15 attendees for each class and you can either charge a small fee or offer them for free, depending on the rules each school or location has and whether they charge me to use the space. I've had as many as 60 people in attendance at my small classes, this way.

Additionally, creating a web presence for yourself works really good too. Kenny Keller of *Build Your Business Online* has a great program that teaches entrepreneurs like us to build a web presence and become really well known on the internet, regardless of your niche or topic. Here's a link to his website:

www.byob.website

The point is to pick three or four processes to share the products, three or four for the business-expansion and three to four target markets that you're already familiar with, to present to. For example, I've been a personal trainer, massage therapist, hypnosis therapist and so on...I have rapport with these groups of people. We have a lot in common, I understand the psychology of their personality and goals and we have stuff to talk about besides business. In other words, whatever your background and experiences, these build the basis of your target markets, if you choose to make use of them. I also grew up in a trailer-court, but people in trailer-courts are generally scraping by and don't have money to buy groceries, so not necessarily a good target market. Not all cases are the same. I grew up in a very small town, but that doesn't mean everyone in a small town will join me...it means be very careful about your target-markets...they have to [be able to afford what you offer, want what you offer and appreciate what you offer!] If you're going to talk to 100 impoverished people, or 100 wealthy people, which group has the [ability to buy products] more than the other?! If you're going to approach people about the business, would 100 business-minded people be better or 100 who are happy working at the grocery store? (Me and a lot of people in my family have worked in grocery).

For me, I enjoy speaking to a group more than an individual, *in the first conversation*. From the people who attend the classes, through questionnaires, surveys and knowing what people want help from me, as far as health and wellness, I gain connections with people who want my help in some form or another...*or they refer me to someone else* (very important hint).

For example, I did a talk at a health food store. One of the customers was in the local, college, Army ROTC program and so she told her commanding officer about me. The military branches are having trouble finding enlistee and officer candidates nowadays, who aren't overweight in the military (hint, hint) (80% of the population is overweight now) and there's a lot on the line. Meaning, if someone can't meet the army weight and fitness standards, they can't get into the program and have to pay for their tuition themselves. (The army recently announced that throwing hand-grenades isn't going to be part of the core training in basic training anymore because they can't find enough people who can throw a baseball size object.)

https://www.cnsnews.com/blog/craig-bannister/army-basic-training-drop-hand-grenade-competency-graduation-requirement

So, the commanding officer of the Army ROTC at MSU Billings came to my class, loved it and asked me to speak at the university to the ROTC group. From them came customers for products. So, you can see from this example, often luck comes into play. The more work you do, the luckier you get! You don't need to know everything to begin and you couldn't possibly know everything. If there was a way to know everything there wouldn't be a challenge, and everyone would be doing it…this is reserved for people who have some ingenuity. The truth is, that even once you have reached all your goals, you still won't know everything…you'll simply have a base of knowledge you rely on that supports your work ethics and business expansion habits…*your routine.*

As I've said, just because the first contact isn't interested doesn't mean more leads won't come from them. The classes I did at that store started out with about ten or fifteen in attendance, but within two years, I was having more than 60 people, in attendance. They were the most attended classes the store ever had. Part of what made them so successful was that the town had about a hundred-thousand population and there weren't many trainers and none of them had any good nutrition expertise (*hint, hint* on many levels). The truth is, that by the time you master the topic your business will be built, and you'll likely have a million-dollar business and no longer need the information, you thought you did! What's most important (more important than knowing everything), is simply crossing paths with the people who want what you offer, right now and the ability to get it/work for it. That's it! That means crossing paths with enough people to locate those ones who are ready, right now! No being an expert. Not knowing everything about nutrition. Not answering every single question without pause or research. Simply crossing paths with the people who want what you offer and has or gets the means to get what you offer! That means being protective with your time and not spending time on people who either don't want or can't get what you offer!

Earlier, I spoke about no need to be a nutrition expert and you don't. If you are an "expert" you end up attracting people who want to debate and argue minutia of their "beliefs" about nutrition, regardless of how rational or irrational they are. Especially the people who are never going to hire you or consult with you or utilize your expertise, being an expert attracts "information-addicts" and gives the impression that if they do hire you or ask for help, you're likely to spend the appointment debating minutia of detail...not helping them get started...remember, talking is not doing and you want people who are looking to "do" nutrition, not talk nutrition...customers! A big mistake for newbies is thinking that people who want to argue about nutrition are customers

How you get customers is to talk about the "benefits" of what you offer, e.g. "more energy", "fat-loss", "improved endurance", "lower blood pressure", etc., etc.

You see, info-addicts want to use their time and yours to debate and argue which information is relevant, but there's hundreds of nutrition models. Shaklee is a "do-this, get-this" business and in the first year of expanding your customer base, you don't have the luxury of spending an appointment debating with someone who has no intention of changing their habits or simply strives to be told their ideas are "right"...even worse, those people aren't going to get results because they think "knowing" produces results...so, they definitely won't be referring people who want what they got from you, since they turn people off with all their arguing.

Besides, like all information, it changes with time. There's an entire team of scientists behind us doing research and development and studies that cost millions-of-dollars...that's *their* job. And we don't need to do their job. Our job is to *move product* to increase our personal product points, so we get paid a decent bonus and attract other business-expanders, which creates more money to do more research and develop more first-class products, which lead the market.

If potential customers have questions, by all means, get the information for them in order to facilitate a product order and a customer, but if each question turns into another question and no order, you may very well have an info-addict on your hands. The point of the *HealthPrint*™ program is to make the website the streamlined, predictable, re-producible expert. As time goes on you'll learn more and more about the intricacies of the products. There's a product-call that you can phone into every Tuesday evening that is free and has been going on for about 20 years, where all the details of products are discussed. Just don't mistake being a product expert for being a business-expander…they're two different animals.

Focus your customers on the benefits and use features (e.g. organic, GMO-Free, food-concentrates, pesticide-free, etc., etc.), as follow up information to support, validate and affirm their *purchase decisions*. In other words, explain why what they chose to purchase is so much better. All the product talks are archived and you can get the password from me and listen for free, on your own schedule. You can also refer your customers and potential customers to these recorded calls…again, know [where] to get the information and be able to link people to the information, but you don't have to be an expert, otherwise you give the impression you have to be an expert to do the business. In addition, that makes the information a 3rd party testimonial, which often seems more credible than coming from the person earning the money. If getting or providing information doesn't encourage product use by an expanding group or people or result in purchases or product use, there's no point to it.

Business-expanders, like me, who are coming from helping/health industries (e.g. massage therapists, personal trainers, physical therapists, doctors, nurses, etc.), tend to be used to needing a lot of clinical data or information to pass along to their patients and clients. In those careers its almost essential. But don't mistake knowing information for expanding your business. The time you set aside for launching and expanding your business, often 10-15 hours a week in the beginning, has to be used to locate the people who want what we offer, not memorizing data. When potential customers have specific questions, get the information for them. But, if they don't take the information to try the products, something may be off.

Statistically, when there's an exchange of $$$ for products or service, potential customers require, on average, 7 (seven) contacts or exposures to a product or service before they take action. So, just because they don't purchase the first time doesn't mean they won't, you can include them as part of your follow-up system. I am saying to develop your intuition and instincts whether a person is simply wanting to share information or actually looking to feel better. Remember, when I started in 1993, I had a long list of health problems and didn't feel good most of the time, but I was told, *"Take these products for 30 days and if you don't feel better, you can have your money back."* Does it get any more simple than that? Have potential customers fill out the *HealthPrint*™, help them pick out products for their first order based on what benefits they want and then encourage them that you guarantee they will feel better or they get their money back…*that's expansion of your customer base!* When you have cash-flow, you can continue to expand your business…its self-sustaining.

Bait and switch:

Offering big business to get people in the door as customers, with a promise of profit, followed by sabotage of any business activity that would lead to independence and success, because the sponsor wanted them to bring people to their house to learn about the products for their own customer base, but refuses to show them how to expand the business is about as bad as it gets in this industry.

Once your customers place their order, check back with them to make sure they got their order, and see if they have any further questions. Then follow up with them every couple-days to make sure they are using the products and that its going fine. If there are glitches, (lack of understanding how to use the products, etc.), you want to catch them early and clear them up. I generally follow up with my customers on a regular basis anyway, even if it's to send them a text message or an email, saying, *"Hey! How's it going"* If you don't keep in contact with your customers, someone else will!

Have to have income to do Step 1:

Some of your customers will ask you about expanding their own business. That's a good thing, but don't just give the business away, otherwise you'll watch your own profits drop, meaning have your requirements that you have, as a standard, of who you'll invest your time and energy with and don't compromise it. People sometimes think they can simply sign up as a business-expander, to get a discount on their products (which reduces your profit), but then don't get training participate in meetings, don't bring new people to the group nor do anything which contributes to the expansion of your business (giving your business away). With customers who express interest in having their own business, go through the same interview process you do with any potential business-expander. People often think if they become an expander, they'll get a discount, but not invest time, energy nor bring in other expanders and customers. If they want discounted products (more than their membership offers), offer to talk to people they refer you to and offer incentives/gifts for any customers that come from those referrals. That way they understand that perks and discounts come from expanding your business, not for the sake of using the products themselves…there's no shortage of Shaklee customers. Benefits have to be earned in order to establish value. Shaklee products are worth much more than the suggested retail price, as you'll notice once you've been using them. Especially when you compare quality with everything out on the market. If people want to become a business-expander, be sure to explain it requires minimum of 10-15 hours per week and what you're looking for is business partners, (not someone who wants a discount for signing a form).

Personally, once a person is a customer I don't talk about the business opportunity with them. There are people who combine product and opportunity, but I've seen this go astray many times. I've seen where a person who has no interest in the business stop purchasing products when pursued about the business. Some people are so afraid of rejection, sales, marketing, etc., that the slightest hint of business talk and they're gone, even if they would have otherwise been great customers.

Often, business-expanders mistake "high product use", by a customer, with an unspoken interest in the business. It works out sometimes to transition a person from customer to business-expander, but for the builders who promote this concept, I'm not sure how many customers they lose in the process and chalk it up as a cost of doing business in hopes of finding strong expanders. I'm really not sure. One thing is for sure, the people who start out as expanders and use the products, continue to use the products and refer other people, even when they don't follow through and build their business. The difference seems to be people who are business-minded or have minds that are open to opportunity. An exception to not approaching customers about the business is if they are talking to me about wanting or needing more money, a better job, etc. If they are saying these kinds of things, I consider it open game, since they are the ones bringing the topic up…they are stating a need or problem that the benefits I offer can solve. If you don't respond to their talk of needing more money, someone else will. But seriously, I've found many times that these people who complain about lack of money aren't motivated to "do" anything to improve their situations...they *want* more money...but, if they really wanted it, wouldn't they have already done something about it, even if it were a second job? If they are to expand a business, they're going to need some money to get started anyway, if for nothing else than their own products...not an impossible proposition, but think about it. We still have an obligation to offer and let them figure out how they'll get it done, if they so choose. Many times, people talk like they don't have any money, but they are actually wealthy. I knew a guy who lived on twenty-thousand dollars a year, but he was actually a millionaire and had a $6,500 monthly budget. How you get to the root of the situation is to talk "benefits"...*What does the person get for using the products?*...then leave it to them to decide which bank account they'll take the money out of. People who complain they don't have money are basically saying they haven't seen something they want enough to spend money on it. *It doesn't mean they don't have the money.*

You'll attract people based on your personal energy level:

I've seen people who want the benefits of the business, but think they can outsmart the system by *not* using the products. This never works. I, like many trainers, have found that you have to have a higher energy level than the people you're offering benefits to. If you aren't using the nutrition products you simply won't come across congruent...pushing the products but not using them yourself. You'll seem dishonest even if they can't put their finger on what is "off" about you.

Market to people who have money ! *Duh...*

Often, new business-expanders think it will be easier to approach people they know, but don't connect-the-dots that the people they know either don't value their health, don't want to do anything different to increase their wealth or don't have to money or motivation to buy their own products. Make it easy on yourself...find the people who have money, like to buy quality products and re-order when they run out of the first batch! The dietary supplement and weight loss markets are multi-billion-dollar markets that are growing all the time. People who use supplements are always looking for better product that produce better results and make them feel better.

Choose to change grow get better:

It should go without saying that, in order to get better results in life, you have to improve what you're doing…you can't expect to do the same thing, stay comfortable and make more money and have more free time…it doesn't work that way.

People who start new things, but bail out when they realize they have to exceed their comfort zone tend to struggle at everything they do because they're spending more energy avoiding self-improvement than they would if they simply did the work to reach their wildest goals. They'll struggle at everything they do because they retreat every time a project requires more of them than what they are used to investing, in themselves. I've noticed three categories of personality who are in every industry from personal training and being a medical patient to people who say they want more money, but behave as if it's going to drop in their lap.

Complainers: They [like to complain about what isn't working], and they'll take up others' time complaining, but they have no intention or inclination to take action to come up with solutions, since they get so much attention and sympathy for their complaining.

Visitors: They are seeking help or expertise because [someone has pressured them], not because they are motivated to change or improve their own life. They are simply there to be able to tell others they "tried" but it doesn't work…because they don't want to change.

Customers: Not just for products, but more in the sense of "customers-for-change" or improvement in whatever condition they seek relief from, whether it be poverty or poor working conditions. Think of Olympic Athletes with aspirations for a Gold Medal. They train for years, sacrifice most everything to attain their goal with no guarantee of success and get one chance very four years. Whatever their coach tells them to do they do with question or attitude or chip-on-the-shoulder. They set goals, follow through and maintain a positive attitude and leave all the emotional baggage behind…because it gets in the way. Instead of emphasizing their story, they emphasize taking and applying whatever advice or coaching they receive and they run with it without rationalizing lack of effort or making excuses. *They just do it!* They don't let anyone talk them out of their decision.

Learn to recognize whether a person is a complainer, visitor or customer.

So, in summary, pick three or four ways to offer products and get the information out there and three or four ways to offer the business and be consistent with those target markets. You'll still get requests and customers from outside these target groups, as people learn about you, but you need to have some focus and groups you master approaching and working with. For example, having been a personal trainer for 30 years and having worked in various gyms and studios and so on, I know the ins-and-outs of the personal training business thoroughly and other trainers recognize this. If you need help figuring out your target markets and approaches, ask. It should be part of your training.

Chapter Twenty-One

You don't need to know it all, *Part 2*

One guiding principle to expanding your business, is that, *"If it seems like hard work, it's probably not a match."* Meaning, You can lead a horse to water, but you can't make him drink,"…if you're working with a person on the business and it seems like it's going great, but then they don't follow through, you're essentially investing more energy than they are. This is a potential sign that it isn't going to work out, since they aren't doing their part. When the person isn't right it seems like hard work. When they are right, it seems easier than it should be. The time of your life. Often, new business-expanders think because a person seems excited and motived, they have found a good business partner. But, if they wait to take action until you tell them every single little step, something is off…more often than not, it has to do with motivation or inner-conflict. The bulk of your time has to be spent as messenger, showing people who you are and what you do…then training the ones who follow through…anything else will bog your system down.

It is NOT important if you hear, *"No's,"* or negative comments, but rather how well you keep yourself on track and how quickly you notice if you're off-track and how quickly you recover from surprises, disappointments and perceived barriers to success. This comes down to emotional-state control…*keeping yourself in a positive state of mind*…a powerful skill that can take time to develop.

Avoid information overload:

If at any time you feel like you're getting too much information [to make use of] (a feeling of being over-whelmed), simply go back to the very basic fundamentals and proceed from there (locating and training new business partners and customers). You should have only two to three sources of information you're receiving, in the beginning and two of these should be from the company itself, the person who helped you join and a couple sources outside the company (suggested by the person who helped you join), which provides general/generic training information, based on your particular goals and suggestions of the person who helped you join. The person who helped you join will point you in the right direction and demonstrate how to make use of the information, correctly. You have to have a pretty narrow focus during the first six-months, in order to develop a track record of success to build your instincts on. Do not attempt to do everything that you hear everyone else suggesting or doing in their businesses…it's for information only.

Think big picture and fill in the blanks depending on the situation with the individual you're working with. Avoid taking suggestion from people who constantly flip-flop, get distracted, change outcomes, etc.

Two ears, one mouth.

Case example:

Selene's main goal was to travel. She says, *"I do what I do for the travel."* Although she loves the added income, her main focus is earning points to take all the trips and take a friend or two with her, each time. In fact, six of the friends she brought with her over the last few years have all joined her as business partners and that pattern has seemed to hold truth to it.

Chapter Twenty-Two

Big Picture View

If people think they blew situations in the moment they aren't focused on the future. Those who have a long-term vision value the present and check out opportunities, that come to their attention. Keep your focus on doing the simple process of locating the people who want and value what you have to offer and have the means to acquire it, for themselves.

One very successful Shaklee business-expander drove hours to do a demo for Basic-H and afterward, she was so frustrated because she thought it didn't go well, it initially seemed to her. But ultimately, in the longer-term, she got 20 new business partners, a result of that one meeting she initially didn't think went well. We're our own worst critics.

Listen enough so that whatever comes out of your mouth in response is relevant to them!

When people ask you questions, answer the questions as to *how it relates to them* getting the benefits (for them). No extra, no idle chit-chat. No filler. How does it apply to them? What do they get from who you are wand what you do?

People who have trouble expanding their business talk about things that don't apply or provide a lot of information that doesn't apply to the person right in front of them. Prospective business-expanders and customers shouldn't have to work hard to sort out the answer they are looking for.

"I'm no good at sales."

In hindsight, we now know that when people say something like this, it reflects not on them, but whomever they were associated with or worked for in the past. An employer or potential team mate who 'pushes' a person to move product or service (without first training and preparing them) does a huge dis-service for the employee and their business, and potentially ruins a person's ability to make an amazing income that, if they were trained properly, could have been mutually beneficial.

In my personal experience, having done self-taught sales as well as receiving training here and there, I can take a person who doesn't believe they are good at sales or that they like sales and make an experience that is both fun and highly, financially beneficial. But my approach is way different.

Natural sales people have an advantage the same way a race car driver would have an advantage as a bus or taxi driver…they have a level of comfort in the vehicle itself…which indicates a level of self-confidence, self-worth, self-esteem and (a lack of) sensitivity to others' opinion, criticism, sarcasm and so forth. See the difference?

So, being a natural sales person isn't a requirement, as there are positions for trainers, teachers, educators, etc. Or people who are comfortable interviewing others. One way or another, as a person's confidence and competence increases, through any kind of experiences, that confidence carries over to other contexts.

We would rather have someone come in with no skill, than to assume they know everything, but be unable to adapt their skill to this environment.

People from all walks of life from stay-at-home parents, to teachers, to trainers, to massage therapists to police officers to doctors and everyone in between have reached the highest echelons, by sticking to the simple, fundamental 10-15 hours, per week, locating and training the people who want, value and afford themselves what we offer, you can have the income you want, the time-freedom you want, the tax advantages of a home-based business, free travel and free cars.

Ask me.

Chapter Twenty-Three

Become A Master At Making People Feel Genuinely Good

So, when you know a person isn't one of the 1% who are your 15 leaders, an unsophisticated, yet effective expander just turns the other direction and gets away from them, as soon as possible. The sophisticated network marketer notices it, doesn't react on the outside, but makes a calculated decision and builds a bridge conversationally and emotionally and extricates themselves, whilst making the prospect feel good. No harm no foul. If the person ever does grow or change enough to be a 1%-er *the bridge is already built*. No one feels offended, isolated nor alienated.

There aren't enough people in the world who focus on the positive and bring out the best in others, but when you are one of those people, you can write-your-own-ticket. That's because when you leave people feeling good and uplifted, they notice (even if they don't think about it in the moment) and want more of what you just gave them. No one ever feels like they got too many good vibes, compliments or lift-me-ups.

The point is not to manipulate others, but rather to make them feel good whether they are interested in what you want or not. Its in this way that you'll gain referrals from those who haven't personally joined you. When you make people feel good about themselves, it will carry over to whatever endeavor they choose.

People's temperament and sensibilities:

It's a good general rule of thumb, while you're expanding your business to avoid discussion about sex, politics or religion. It used to be that people could have open discussion and even if their viewpoint was different, it didn't affect business. Today, people are generally more sensitive and offended by others' opinion if it's different than their own.

An exception to this is if you definitely know you both agree on a topic...*but, never, never assume you know.*

I've heard business people openly express their opinions on these three hot topics, and say something like, *"Hey, this is who I am and if I can't be myself they shouldn't be around me,"* but often these are the same people trying to figure out why they aren't expanding their business and why people seem excited at first, then quit showing up or communicating, with them. If you're using your business as a platform to express your opinions, on non-related topics, you'll pretty soon have no business and be surrounded by people who want to debate today's news. Think about it. The people with the most money express their opinion by donating to the causes that are the most important to them, not by arguing every chance they get...they don't have time! They're busy doing business! The media would like us to think that we're supposed to have a day filled with debate. For the people who aren't using their time to expand their business, this is true.

Now, say you belong to a particular political party or religious organization and are attending a political event or religious event, where everyone is on the same page, then by all means mix business and topics. Just know, that if you are pushing your agenda and your audience doesn't agree, you've effectively eliminated at least 30% of your prospects, unnecessarily, before they even know what you do or what you offer. People can have different opinions and co-exist, it's just that most people have nothing else going on in their lives, have no goals and mistake arguing as having a life or a purpose, which is what the mainstream media wants us to do...be really busy accomplishing nothing. Consuming, but not producing anything of value to others. Don't make that mistake or you'll learn your lesson real-quick. This includes what kinds of posts you do on social media.

One of my helicopter instructors, Kenny Keller, of Online Ground School, put it this way: *"A Helicopter that decided to eat itself has already spit me out onto a concrete ramp! Life is too short for malcontents, haters, trolls, whiners and complainers, ok? We can part as friends and leave it at that."*

I've found the same thing. I crashed in a helicopter in August 2017. I was the only one on board. From the time I knew anything was wrong until the $300,000.00 helicopter was totaled was a split-second. It happened so fast that I'm not consciously aware of everything that happened. But, I do know that life goes by fast and can be gone in a split second. The dinosaurs know, too! What lasts is the value we create for those around us and all the people who are waiting to hear from us, whom we've yet to meet, get to know, help and travel the world with. If you want to supercharge a particular cause, make a wheelbarrow full of cash and give it to the cause.

Now, look at your weekly schedule and book time with yourself to tell people who you are and what you offer. Invest two hours each day, five to six times a week consistently, and in a year, you won't even recognize your life, as it is today. Until you're trained properly, during the first month of your business, some of these hours will be invested in training. Watching and hearing others successfully expand their own business…for the first month. After that, 10-15 hours per week is what it will take to expand your business as long as you're being efficient with your time.

Chapter Twenty-Four

Become A Rejection-Immune, Master-Locator

When I started in Shaklee, I was one of the most snow-flake mlm'ers you could imagine. I hung on every word anyone said, hoping they wouldn't say anything that might offend me or accuse me of poor intentions. [I literally believed that others' opinion of me had control over whether I would be successful or not.] Having grown up in a very *dys*-functional home and being overtly and chronically criticized, for the first 15 years of my life, I lacked a lot of the qualities I needed to attain the goals I aspired to achieve. In addition, I honestly thought that everyone would be as excited about Shaklee as I was. After all, I had been looking for a Shaklee distributor for 20 years! I couldn't fathom that anyone wouldn't be interested. Neither did it occur to me that the people who weren't interested would criticize, make fun of and go out of their way attempting to derail my efforts…but they did…and I kept going.

It was at this time that I began learning about this concept of rejection. Rejection simply means that because someone isn't interested in what we're offering, we get offended or have our feelings hurt to the point that we shut down a little (or a lot) emotionally, to feel safer When the emotions are locked, its near impossible to successfully carry out intentions, to work a plan of action toward the accomplishment of goals, since the visualization and accomplishment of goals are literally "charged" by the emotions. The people who aren't affected by others' opinions or really don't care what people think, won't be affected by the concept of rejection. If you already have a strong enough personality that you already don't care what people think of you or your intentions, then you're ahead of the game and the majority of the population. You'll simply work through the "numbers" and find your 15 leaders each year. 10 customers, 3 business partners and repeat.

If, on the other hand, you want to insulate yourself from the concept of rejection until you've develop a little more, there's a very easy way to do it that I wish I had back in 1993.

The concept is that instead of being as outright or forthright (bold), about what you're asking people if they have an interest in, you scale back and ask a series of preliminary/qualifying questions, which act as baby steps to the main question or offer you have, in a very casual, conversational manner. If at any point along the way they give a hint that they are happy and content here they are, you simply back out of the conversation and the person never knows what you were going to offer nor has the opportunity to shut you down, criticize, dismiss or *reject*.

I can't take credit for this example as it was designed by Rick Seymour, in Colorado. But, he used to offer a training system (*Action Academy©*), which included this formula which seems to be no longer available, although I have a copy, of the DVD training seminar and I've seen others reference it on the web. The process is a series of seven questions, each one gradually gathering more information which gives you hints as to whether you should proceed to the next level of questioning, to ultimately offer what you're offering to a person. Here's the general idea of the questions, which can be used in any context, whether for product or opportunity prospecting:

What do you do?

    1. How long have you been doing that? Or how long have you been there?

    2. What do you like about it?

    3. What don't you like about it? Is there a downside to it? Tell me about it.

    4. Where do you want to be in 5-10 years?

    5. What are you doing to get there? Or what are you doing to make that happen? Or is what you are currently doing going to get you to your goal?

    6. Have you found what you're looking for or are you keeping your options open?

As you can see and hear, they are simply conversational-type, preliminary (screening) questions and if a person isn't seeming conversational, you simply disengage from the attempted conversation. If the person is conversational and shares information, then you proceed to the next level of questions. At no time are you obligated to continue, or ask the final question of whether they are open to options. The point being that you can evaluate for yourself what their response will be like, to avoid getting into a conversation where you're providing more information than they are and giving them the opportunity "reject" your offer, before they actually know what it is.

If a person is happy and content where they are and don't have complaints (lack of money and lack of free time), then there's probably low odds they would be interested. Maybe they want more time with their family? Maybe they want more vacations? Maybe they want more spending money. How you know is to ask general questions to gather information that is *relevant to them*, so that whatever you offer applies *to them*. The reason being, we can't assume what a person's motivations are.

The same can be done with products. Take weight loss for example. You don't have to get real personal with people, simply ask them if they know anyone interested in weight loss options. If a person is open to conversation, ask progressively relevant questions to identify the people who are looking for good, healthy weight loss products.

1. Do you know anyone who wants to lose weight?

2. 80% of th population wants to lose weight.

3. How long have they been wanting to lose weight?

4. What have they tried?

5. Did that work?

6. What did they like or dislike about it?

7. Was there a downside to the program? Tell me about that?

8. There do you want your weight to be in a year?

9. Do you have a good plan?

10. Is what you're currently doing getting you to your goal?

11. Have you found what you're looking for or are you keeping your options open?

12. Are you open to looking at options?

13. Could I send you some information to see what you think?

The idea is to listen intently. To learn what you need about them to be able to help them the most. Listening implies learning. You're not asking questions, just so you can offer your information, but to learn about them so they can heal. Sometimes, its better to ask questions, gather information and make an offer at a more appropriate time.

Learn about people so what you offer is important to them. What you offer better include which benefits they get…what do they get out of it?

Chapter Twenty-Five

Making Full Use Of The Goal-Achieving Potential Of The Mind

American Novelist, Ernie Cline, born in 1972, has a DeLorean automobile parked in his garage, which he still drives. A *Ghostbusters*™ decal, on the doors and a full dashboard of futuristic electronics, bring his fantasy to life. You know, the car from the movie *Back To The Future*. Ernie and his brother grew up in a trailer-court in rural Ohio. Sound familiar? To him, the trailer-court is the most depressing place to grow up and I couldn't agree more. Ernie and his brother spent their time playing Atari. Ernie says, *"If I traveled back in time to talk to my younger self, he wouldn't believe any of this...I have a hard time believing it now"*

In 2011 Ernie's debut novel, *Ready Player One,* became a best seller. Now, he has just finished the movie version, alongside, none other than, movie director Steven Spielberg. When Ernie published *Ready Player One*, he had zero experience writing fiction...*his first piece of work.* The book is a sci-fi fantasy type book that envisions a future where most of the population is plugged into a virtual reality world, involving a high-stakes scavenger hunt. Cline says, *"I grew up in a trailer park and living in a trailer park feels...uh...not great. So, I imagined in the future, what would be worse than a trailer park?"* Playing video games and a love for StarWars™ fueled his fantasy of working in the movie, but for many years, the closest he came was working as a video store clerk. When writing screen plays didn't work, he started writing a novel. Nine years later, now with a baby daughter to support, he sent his work to publishers.

The very next day, he says, *"We had sold the rights to Ready Player One, for more money than anyone...you know, I , eh had ever imagined I would make or anyone in my family had ever made...my whole life had changed in that first 24 hours...and then they said, Oh, by the way, now there's a bidding war going on in Hollywood for the film rights.""* (1+1=8).

When asked why he thought it would make a great movie, director Steven Spielberg said, *"...well, because it was a great adventure...I wanted to make great movies...I hadn't made a movie like this...my God, for decades..."* When Spielberg signed on to direct the movie, Cline (the ultimate fan boy) became Spielberg's collaborator. Steven says, *"Cline is an ultimate authority on pop-culture and when we made the movie we kept going back to Ernie, just to pick his brain."*

Ernie says, *"Even now, just talking to him (Steven Spielberg), I'll hang up the phone from having a conversation with him ...just talked to Steven Spielberg...it never goes away, you know, because he was such a giant in my childhood."* When asked if he as Steven's phone number in his phone, he replies, *"No...he calls me...I don't ...I'm sure...I can get ahold of him if I need to..."*

Ernie still has the Atari video game console he got for Christmas 1978. The first virtual reality game he had was called *Adventure*™, where the designer of the game hid his own name, inside a secret, virtual room, within the game. This game was the inspiration for Ernie's book, about a virtual scavenger hunt.

Ernie says, *"I feel like I'm a testament to what happens if you be free about what you love and why you love it are not afraid or worried about what other people think about your love or your passions...just be bold and celebrate the things that you are passionate about...and amazing things can happen."*

Let it happen for you:

People who are successful in any area of endeavor, from business to competitive sports, entertainment and even relationships have a strategy they use, to do so. You can look at their strategy of a cycle of events or a routine that, in their mind and emotions they cycle through every day, week, month and year. Meaning they practice/do the things that get them their outcome and skip the things that would take them away from their outcome/goals. Below is a list of mental/emotional-activities that will help your cause, regardless of your goals. You apply them by beginning to add them to your mental/emotional-routine and little by little, let go of the ones that interfere in your success, replacing them with ones that have been shown to work, by re-wiring how the brain/mind works. For example, replacing resentment with forgiveness. Replacing worrying you won't succeed, with seeing your goal as accomplished. Let go of focusing on the problem, by focusing on the possible solutions. Looking for opportunity in things that most others see as disadvantages. And so on.

Releasing yourself from the past:

Forgive others: Anytime you remember someone who crossed you, let you down, disappointed you, hurt your feelings, etc., go through the forgiveness cycle.

   a. Forgive them,
   b. Forgive yourself,
   c. Ask for forgiveness,
   d. Work to forget the incident,
   e. Say something you're grateful for and
   f. State a thing you're looking forward to.

(Releases the reins on the resources of the mind, connected to past events that are not changeable, which permits you to attain a goal in the current time, releases energy being used in resentment, anger, judgement.)

A. **Forgive yourself:** (Releases the reins on the part of the mind that holds guilt, resentment, regret, and guilt attempting to fix the past, make up for past mistakes and so on, freeing up significant emotional-energy to come to creative solutions for your current goals. A lot of times, people feel [unconsciously] "bad", guilty, remorseful, regretful, or fearful that the past will be repeated…which recreates the past!). By forgiving yourself, it releases the reins on processes that we don't even know about or can name, because they are too deep. But, by practicing forgiveness of yourself, you free up creative resources that you didn't even know were being used to in attempt to deal with the past…which inhibits success in present time.

B. **Ask for forgiveness:** (Provides a sense of peace, tranquility and serenity, permitting more of the mind to utilize resources for creativity on current goals and expectations). By acknowledging that maybe, just maybe there's a higher power than yourself, you unconsciously let go of the sense of control, which inhibits spontaneous success. Everything has two sides. If we think we're the highest power, then that puts all responsibility on us, which engages control, which inhibits spontaneous success (1+1=8). That's not to say you aren't to be engaged in your own success progress…you have to tell the mind what it is you specifically want, then charge it with emotion and let it go. Asking your higher power for forgiveness permits yourself to make mistakes, knowing you'll succeed anyway.

EVERYONE makes mistakes, regrets things they said or did, wishes they had handled situations and people differently, had they known then what they know now. That's just a part of being human. We only do as well as we know to do at the time and quite often, we respond the way we learned to, before we even knew we were learning. Then, when things in present time don't work out how we thought they would, we often get into a downward cycle of beating up on ourselves, feeling guilty, feeling unworthy and so forth, which left unresolved attracts the same kind of situation, again. Quite often, people come into our life to teach us a lesson, then they move on. More often than not, we each teach one another different things. When the lesson is learned, some people move on. We're not supposed to be a permanent, lifetime-match for every single person…it just doesn't work that way. On the bright side, we do develop some lifetime friends and relationships. Just like the seasons, even what seems like the worst crisis doesn't last forever and we even meet new people who become part of our inner-circle…the ones we can count on and trust the most with our dreams and goals. When I look back at where I was and the kind of person I was 20 years ago, I barely recognize myself. If I work at it, I can cultivate feelings of guilt, shame, remorse and so on, but that doesn't solve or improve anything, let alone help anyone…rather it imprisons a person's spirit, preventing improvement.

So, in this context, forgiveness means do the best you can in every situation, treat others how you want to be treated (The Golden Rule), and be more gentle on yourself for mistakes, misunderstandings and times where what you thought was the right thing to do, got you the opposite of what you thought it would.

I knew a person who had been blamed by their father, for the feelings he was having. Every time he had an emotional feeling (on the inside, e.g. anxiety, fear, etc.) he didn't like, he blamed who was near him, who quite often was his daughter, who happened to be the person in the family who was attending to his emotional well-being the most. She became the convenient dumping-ground for his emotional-baggage, as she was striving to gain her father's approval, love and attention. She was trying to connect with her dad in a meaningful way. The mom sat by passively, neither nurturing her daughter, nor preventing or explaining how inappropriate her father's behavior was. In other words, the daughter couldn't understand where the problem started, why she was responsible or causing her father to feel bad nor clear guidelines how to gain respect, love and healthful affection. What does that kind of experience teach the daughter about her own worth and value, let alone how to cope with their own emotions, as they surface within relationship? One parent dumping their stuff on the daughter, the second parent behaving passive, helpless to affect change. Long story short, she learned to the same habit…to look to others, for the reason for the feelings she was having on the inside. Get that? Having feelings on the inside, but looking on the outside for the reason for the feelings…when both her father and she needed to go inside and examine the roots of the feelings. How does one un-learn emotional habits which they learned before they knew they were learning? The guide lines in this chapter, effectively free the person from this kind of history. Not overnight, although done with heart and intention, the unwinding process occurs by replacing unproductive, destructive strategies with ones that clear up the past.

The consequences of thinking that others were the cause of their internal state, made it very difficult to connect, relate and even simply be around other people, in any kind of meaningful way, let alone intimacy. Can you imagine of everyone blamed how they felt on the inside for whomever happened to be around them at the time?

Hint, hint…when you have feelings, go inside and ask what the root of the feelings are, instead of blaming those around you. No one can make you feel anything you don't already cultivate in yourself.

I had another friend, who had been told over and over by her father that he wanted a son. Her whole life she would spend her energy attempting to gain her father's approval, right to the end of her life, in her mid-thirties. She would attend to her fathers' disappointment of her, until her stomach problems and flu-like symptoms came back, then distance herself. Once she starting feeling good again, she would start pursuing her father's approval, love and affection. In relationships, she found herself in relationships with men who didn't seem to think she was good enough.

Her energy was all used up trying to please men who didn't think she was good enough. Mind you, she was beautiful, vibrant and fun to be around. We spent a lot of time together around 1997. When she insisted I tell her my thoughts on the situation, I explained that I thought she was expending more energy than she had, attempting to gain approval of people who would never approve of her (a mis-match). I suggested she save her energy and simply connect with the people who loved and approved of her how she was born. She was so angered that she insisted I take it back, so I did. A few weeks later I ran into her at the grocery store and she didn't recognize me. She had started taking increasingly higher amounts of Prozac. Within a couple months she had developed mouth cancer and died right after the surgery, having learned it went to her brain. That week, her mom, who had been healthy, died of stomach cancer. If you have ever seen the photo of me with really long hair and there's a beautiful blonde sitting behind me with a huge smile on her face, that's Shannon, who I met at hypnosis school in 1996. I miss her greatly.

C: Forget about it: (Eliminates energy going toward maintaining the past; allows creative energy to move toward gratitude and appreciation for present time and manifestation of current goals. Forgetting it comes after thoroughly and completely forgiving the thing.) If it's still being maintained in your memory, it's very likely you haven't fully forgiven. Remembering is an indication from your mind that it isn't forgiven. Have faith that you can handle whatever life throws at you without using your creativity to maintain old hurts. Often, people refuse to forget pain or let go of holding people accountable for past assaults, since they insist it will protect them from future pain. It doesn't. It simply gives a sense of perceived control, which isn't real. Often, the pains and lesson are to temper our spirit, so that we are then prepared for what we insist we want! If you insist on not having experiences, you miss out on the lessons which prepare you for the next level of growth. (That does not mean surrounding yourself with abusive people or participating in abusive relationships…there's easier ways to develop self-worth, self-esteem and confidence…like helping others, for example).

D: Practice gratitude: (Increases more of what you are grateful for. Gets the mind open to opportunities that you would have otherwise missed. Gets the mind's resources to focus on opportunity that presents itself in present time. Without gratitude, opportunities present themselves, land in our lap, but we miss them because energy is focused on what we "wish" we had (implies far off in the future) or all that we don't have.) The RAS requires a significant part of the mind be OPEN to opportunity, which is facilitated through the practice of gratitude. If you have two people who want the same things, in the same environment, the person who is more congruent in gratitude will receive opportunity that the "wishful" person doesn't even notice. It doesn't matter which thing you say you are grateful for, as the details/content don't matter as much as I've even said I was grateful for the dirt and grass...the details/content don't matter...it's the process and the context of using the mind to practice/activate the part of the mind that is habitually grateful. As the mind function improves, then you'll start recalling what your heart's desires for things you are grateful for, both tiny and huge.

E: Look forward to something: (Gets the mind off the past, into a positive state of mind). Positive expectation draws what we want to ourselves in the present moment. [It doesn't matter what you look forward to.] The point is to activate that part of the brain that looks forward to stuff. The thing you look forward to, has to have nothing to do with the thing you are forgiving or who you are forgiving, in any way...they aren't related, in any way except they are at opposite ends of the spectrum and that one inhibits being present and achieving goals and dreams and one enables dreams and goals to come to pass. The best example I know of, in relation to people looking forward to a bright future is when I visited the campus of the University of Washington, for the beginning of fall classes around 2005. My wife was doing her undergraduate studies in Microbiology and International Studies. I had never been to a big campus like this. We attended a get-together/orientation for all the freshman coming in, which my wife was an advisor for. The energy of "looking forward to a bright future" was as tangible as anything. Its not to say that everything will turn out how the freshman planned, its that "looking forward to a bright future" with anticipation, excitement and expectation is a tangible emotion that positively affects the physical well-being. It doesn't matter of you're looking forward to a big goal or your next sub-sandwich, the idea is to activate the latent part of the mind and deactivate a focus on sending energy to the past, attempting to fix the past. How you fix the past is by doing it differently next time. I've even said I was looking forward to finding a nice rock...the details/content (what you say you're looking forward to) don't matter...it's the process and the context of using the mind to see a bright future (faith). As the mind function improves, then you'll start recalling what your heart's desires for a bright future are.

F: Experience it, as done: (Frees up the creative resources you need your mind to use to reach your goals.) The person who is "wishing" or seeing what they want "off in the future" has effectively "locked up the combination" for the creative resources of the mind, which are required to achieve your goals. When you emotionally and sensorially (e.g. see, hear, feel, taste, smell), experience the goal as achieved (in the present moment), the mind effectively says, *"Oh, well if it's done, then you're going to need these resources to make that happen,"* and the resources you need get allocated to the thing getting done. As if the mind makes the thing "truth" by freeing up the resources for it to be truth. The opposite is to say, *"Eventually it will happen,"* in which case the mind says, *"Well, if we don't need those resources today, we'll keep them locked up until later,"* which keeps being put off into the future, since the person hasn't accepted it for themselves in the "now". Resentment, recycling past pain, control and attempting to hold others emotionally accountable also keeps resources locked up, since it takes you out of the present moment, effectively keeping your mental/emotional resources going to the past!

Beyond the six-step forgiveness process, there are a few other skills/techniques which amplify the goal accomplishment process.

1. **Future-pace**: (Unlocks the resources in the mind that are needed to bring about what you want in the current moment.) Future-pacing simply means seeing the thing as done, fully experiencing it from both first-person (looking out through your own eyes) and second-person (imagining yourself above yourself, watching you achieve your own goals). Include what you see, hear feel, taste and otherwise sense, everything in the environment, experiencing it as done.

2. **Practice faith:** No matter the facts, experience your goal as accomplished (faith; ("no weapon formed against you"). Remain in a positive state of mind. Acknowledging that others do not have a say, nor can they interfere, even if they insist they are going to.

3. **Leave room for exceptions:** First isn't last and last isn't first. Odds of success don't matter. When you're prepared to succeed,

chance takes over. Serendipity and providence step in. The person who is first can be last and the person who is in last place can switch to first, in the blink of an eye. What you focus on, regardless of the facts, expands. If there is only one "first-place" winner, there can be a "tie" where there are two, first-place winners.

You can see this in sports a lot. The more intense the competition, the more likely it is to happen. At the 2018 Winter Olympics, Norway's 24 year-old Simen Krueger, competing in the 30 kilometer (18.64 miles) Skiathlon, won gold by eight seconds after colliding with a Russian athlete, falling down and breaking one of his ski poles in the first 100 meters of the race. Krueger said, *"Its not how they start, but how they finish. I was completely last in the group, so I had to start the race again and switch focus to catch up with the guys…when I did, I was saying (to myself), "Ok take one lap, two laps, three laps and just get into it again"…I knew that my chance was to go early, try to surprise the group…when I got those meters, I had to go for it…I did not believe it when I turned and there was no one there…I just had to keep pushing forward until the final…Its an incredible feeling…it is an amazing day, but it started in the worst way with the fall after the first 100 meters and a broken pole…I was thinking this is over…it means a lot…it is something I have worked hard for, for many, many years and now I am here with an Olympic Gold medal."*

4. **Joke about/be sarcastic about having first-world problems:** (When you joke about or are sarcastic about a problem of having what you want, it engages the part of the mind which attracts what it fears (a double-negative, which is a positive). But, instead of attracting a thing you don't want, you attract what you really do want, by pretending you do not, thereby bypassing the part of the mind which normally tells itself it isn't capable of having, in the present moment.) For example:

"Oh bummer, I don't know if I should by the red Porche or the blue one."

"I don't know what to do, everyone found out I won the lottery for $400,000,000.00 and they all want some money."

I've got a big problem. I don't know if I should spend two weeks in Maui first, or on the Big Island, first."

People tend to attract what they fear. So, instead of fearing what you don't want, practice cultivating fear of what you do want. This permits the mind to accept, amplify and utilize (emotionally-charge) what you really want, with energy that normally is used to attract that which you don't want. Effectively, using the brain to attract what you want, using a system that often attracts what you don't want.

Richard Bandler, Founder of Neuro-linguistic™ programming (NLP), says about human excellence, *"When we have a sense of humor about it, those who adapt have a sense of humor....we just make better decisions...decide what you want to get out of it, loo ahead and work toward it."*

5. **Keep track of all the benefits you receive as well as other's testimonials:** (Positive comments your customers tell you about their experiences with the products build belief, inside you, which carries over to each interaction.) The more belief you have, the more confident you become. The more confident you are, the more effective leader you become. Keep a list of the positive testimonials you get. Keep a list of everything you wanted and got, no matter how big or small. What you focus on grows. Focus on what you are grateful for and you'll get more of it! Blame others and you'll get less of what you want and more to blame others for! This should include keeping track of all the benefits you personally receive from the products.

6. **When stressed, exhale longer than you inhale:** (Longer exhales signal the body to relax on the inside, regardless of what is happening on the outside. Navy Seals use this breathing technique to calm down during missions and to see the mission through, against all odds). When you combine longer exhales with seeing the thing as done, the emotional part of the brain charges your vision with the energy to accomplish what you want to experience. If you hold your breath, breath shallow or inhale longer than the exhale, you might possibly charge your anxiety and fear of what you don't want, thereby attracting what you don't want. The breath itself prevents/inhibits stress, anxiety, fear, depression, etc. from

attaching within the body tissues, whether one tends to store tress in the stomach or upper shoulders and back. When a person holds their breath, stress attaches within the body. When one consistently breathes and or combines with massage, exercise and nutrition density (B.N.B.B.s), this activates a state of "being present" and an unwinding of stress from the body. Stored stress can wreak havoc on the physical, mental and emotional well-being.

By building your own routine and cycling through these techniques each day, you effectively re-wire your brain/mind to disengage from/interrupt negativity and use much of the brain/mind toward positivity, so that the majority of the time, you're accumulating an unconscious habit of positive expectation, which effectively becomes a self-fulfilling prophecy. A clean start. The body follows the mind (mainly the unconscious), so by practicing these techniques/habits, you make it, so your body is doing the actions/behaviors that are in alignment with your stated goals, often outside your awareness. By focusing on blame, past pain, negativity, etc., your body will be doing the actions/habits which are the opposite of which you insist you want. You cannot insist you want a better life while focusing on all the world has done you wrong. Victim or Victor, *your choice,* but not both.

Remember, the RAS proves that whatever you believe, you are "right". You want to be proven you are correct, not that you're right, but actually wrong. In relationships, you can either be right or loved/loving. If you insist on being right all the time, having everything done your way, always having the last word, eventually you'll be all alone. The "right" person ends up very lonely. The person who is loving and loved is surrounded by people, purpose and mission without being concerned about who is "right".

Letting go of the past to create a new, brighter future can be a layered process. Meaning, each time you forgive, forget and let go of a past hurt, the next level that needs healing begins to surface. How you know the next thing that needs addressed (with the six-steps above), is when hurt pops into your mind again, you go through the process again, for that situation. If a particular situation or person/event repeats itself, that means there are multiple angles to it and the forgiveness process needs to be repeated for that particular incident.

You don't have to consciously think of things to work on, since what isn't resolved repeats itself! We keep attracting people and situations which reflect unconscious pain (hence, people who irritate us, make us angry, trigger pain, etc.). As unconscious pain surfaces, you address that particular incident that has surfaced. That's where you start and how you practice being present...in the present moment.

If you don't address the incident, then our outward behaviors will be based in unconscious pain...the hand grabs the cookie even though you consciously insist you want to burn fat. You have trouble increasing your income or finding the right job. You have trouble getting along with others. You do behaviors that are the opposite of what you insist you want as goals. The reason being that our habitual actions/habits (outside our awareness) are driven by un-acknowledged pain...until the mind is focused on where we want to go, rather than where we have been, past hurts guide current behavior, which usually ends up being what feels good in the moment, but interrupts/interferes with long-term, preferred, big goals

The trickiest phenomena, is when two or more people both have unresolved hurts, which are unconsciously driving their behaviors/habits and attracting people who are there to reflect themselves, or teach a lesson, but both people perceive the bad feelings or conflict are because of the other person's "stuff". In reality, if you don't have "stuff" that lines up with their "stuff" in some way, you wouldn't get "triggered" or "activated" by them...you wouldn't come into each-others' lives.

Say there is ten components to one person's painful experience (that they may or may not be conscious of) and ten components to the other person's painful experience (that they may or may not be conscious of) (e.g. disappointment, anger, frustrations, resentment, sadness, regret, guilt, etc.). Whichever ones you have in common with the other person, is what you'll unconsciously connect on, like a magnet, yet insist you resent about them (emotional self-trickery). Both people will be working out their own pain, but quite possibly unaware of the original stressor. Both people have different content/details, yet the emotional baggage is common to everyone. They can't make the other person be the person they want them to be, since they're unconsciously striving to resolve stuff from the past.

Until each person goes through the six-steps (at least) with their own pains, the other person will never meet their expectations, since they're trying to fix the past with present moment situations...which never works.

Remember my friend who was trying to find a man who didn't approve of her, yet she insisted she should be able to make a man love and approve of her? That is an example of using the emotions improperly. One hint to know if this is happening, is if you're doing behaviors that feel good or give a sense of satisfaction in the present but hurt you in the long run.

Another hint, is of someone isn't a match, but you're trying to make them be a match. A "match" isn't forced. It just happens and there are several healthy matches for everyone.

When a person is unconsciously attempting to fix the past (which you can only let it go), the person will find a person who isn't a match for them, creates havoc and disappointment in their life, but they insist on using their emotional-energy to "fix" the other person...make them good enough for them.

Finding your matches, both as friends, romantically and in business, is a sorting process. Meeting, talking, socializing and being around people that you have things in common with. From the masses comes a very few close matches and many more that you'll have a few other things in common with.

For the home-based business person, its as simple as letting everyone know you name, what benefits you offer and ask those who are not interested who they know that might be interested! What this does is create an amazing journey of discovering people who you had never met but might very well become best friends or soul mates with.

The opposite would be to find people who don't care who you are, don't value or want what you offer yet you send all your time trying to convince them to be on the prior group. Can you hear how exhausting, depleting and frustrating that would be? It sucks the life out you.

Often, if we hear ourselves blaming other for letting us down or disappointing us or not doing enough for us, it points to us not acknowledging the lesson about ourselves or the unresolved pains in ourselves, which drew them to us like a magnet. Chances are good that if they caused you pain, you caused or mirrored pain in them too. The exception to this, is the same as mentioned early on in this book about people being able to take care of themselves financially…if they have the mental/emotional capability to do so.

More often than not, when people say they were immediately attracted to someone or really was into their vibe, it points to having unconscious emotional patterns in common, without knowing it. Then, when their pains link up like puzzle pieces, conflict is the result, followed by anger, frustration and disappointment. In business, how you get around this phenomena, to avoid attracting people who seem like a match at first, but are the opposite in the long run, is to be around enough people that your thinking doesn't get clouded by the prospect of one person being your "everything". Bring in many people who are possible matches and then let the cream-of-the-crop rise up based on their latent strengths. The opposite would be to place all your hope as "the one" on one person, attempt to make them something they aren't and then go through the disappointment over and over again. The person who is constantly on the lookout for "the one" will often be clouded by false expectation, the fantasy of the person who doesn't actually exist, but whom would be the answer to all your problems if they did exist.

People quite often show us right away, in relatively short period of time, who they are and what they are really like, but out of a need to try to make the past the way we would have preferred it to be and in the absence of fulfilling our own emotional needs, we plug in people who we fantasize to be matches as friends, romantic partners and business partners. Its common, for people who lack this awareness to habitually (outside conscious awareness) repeat this process, then behave surprised that it turns out the way it always did. Then to fill the feeling of emptiness, go right back out and find another person who isn't a match, doesn't value what they offer or who they are, attempt to make them somebody they aren't and effectively use up the emotional-energy that would be required to actually attract the healthy matches, even in business. This relates to mis-use of emotional-energy…giving it in places where it isn't mutually valued and returned through trying to change or fix the past, rather than letting it go, forgiving, forgetting, being grateful and looking forward to a bright future (experiencing the emotions of being fulfilled and at-peace, rather than recycling dis-appointment, dis-satisfaction, anger and sadness, which attracts more of the same.). You attract the experiences and relationships which match/mirror the emotions you recycle and cultivate 51% or more of the time.

The people who didn't give you what you wanted and needed are gone. It done. It's over. Invest your time surrounding yourself with people who value, want and afford who you are and what you offer. Start fresh, right now. It's a sorting process, not a settling process. If there aren't people in your community or environment, move! Don't try to get people to be what they aren't! Move on! Explore! Discover! Travel! Experiment! Find new people! Its empowering instead of disempowering!

Instead of trying to get "a" person to be "the one", be around a lot of people and let the cream rise to the top. You might be surprised how different the people are that you attract in this way. Don't be in too much of a hurry to fill a spot with a person. Be around a lot of people and nature will fill those spots for you, with your best interest in mind.

Let it go.

Love soothes.

Chapter Twenty-Six

What Do You Get?
How Do You Benefit?
Why is this important to you?
How is this relevant to you?

Hi, my name is Sov.

I've got a crazy question for you, but would like a serious answer, fair enough?

If I could show you how to earn $20,000.-$50,000. per month and have complete time-freedom, would that be of interest to you?

If so, contact me at me via text, email or Facebook and we'll have a conversation to see if what you're looking for and what I'm looking for is a match. If so, I'll send you some a video to look over, via email.

Fair enough?

Chapter Twenty-Seven

Baker's Dozen: The 13th Worm

Also known as *B2 or 2B*

What you *don't* get might be better than getting what you do want...

Back in 1989 or so, I applied for and was accepted into a job training program at Lake Washington VocTech, in Kirkland, Washington, for Boeing on the B2 Stealth Program. It was an 8-week program, 6-8 hours/day/no pay, but high likelihood of being hired, if you perform well in class. I was working as a horse vet-tech at the time, so it was a full schedule and I was risking being laid off or let go, since it took away from the hours I was working at the veterinary clinic. I didn't plan on becoming a veterinarian, so I thought the risk was worth the potential reward. I attended all the classes, was on time every time and did really well.

Some students seemed to be "on probation" for one thing or another, the whole time. Some students wouldn't come back after lunch, some missed classes and so forth. The instructor had been a Department of Defense Instructor his whole career and this would be his last class, before retiring.

I was very quiet and introverted at that time and just did what I was shown. We were bonding titanium and a composite material. But through the whole class the instructor kept saying how we would be doing "different" stuff once hired...*using different materials.* So, what we were doing was very important to the training on such a hush-hush program, but we wouldn't be doing quite what we were doing in class?

The final day of the class the instructor was encouraging questions and I finally worked up the courage to ask, *"How come we're spending eight weeks using materials we won't use once hired?"*

The instructor sort of just grumbled and walked away. I went through the whole interview process and didn't hear anything back. Some weeks later I ran into a group of seven or eight guys from the class (there were about 40 in the class), at Gold's Gym Kirkland.

They asked, *"Where you been?...everyone was hired... Where ya' workin'?"* Apparently, everyone was hired except me. As the years went by, I interviewed with Boeing for a couple other jobs, but once they knew about me being in the B2 program, the communication would just drop off. Every four or five years, whenever I would run into someone who had worked at Boeing, I would tell them this story and they would say something like, *"Hmmm!"*

Occasionally, I would run into someone who had experience with that plane and they would tell me you can't touch that plane because it's so toxic...if you touch it you get cancer. I would think, *"Well that can't be right, I worked on that stuff and we had to handle the material... they probably just tell people that to prevent them from touching the plane."* I even knew guy who was an aviator in the Air Force and he said the same thing, *"The surface is so toxic that it will give you cancer."* It didn't make sense to me.

In 2013 (some 24 years later?) I ran into a Boeing engineer, while selling guns at a sporting goods store, in Seattle and told him the story.

For me, I was just curious, *"What happened?...did my question the last day of class really get me deleted from the program?"* In the years that past, since attending the class, I ran it through my head a thousand times. All my insecurities surfaced. What did I do wrong? How could I be the one that didn't get hired? What was so wrong with me? Ultimately, I went to massage school in 1991 and that started my career in health, healing and nutrition.

Well, this last time was different. This engineer who I met at the gun counter had been on that program and knew of the group I had gone to school with.

His reply?

He said, *"Oh, you can be glad you didn't get hired...all those guys died... the material they were working with were so toxic, they all got really weird cancer(s) and died... but, in order to be hired they had to sign a non-disclosure that they couldn't talk about any of it...you are probably the only guy from that class, who isn't dead."*

He said the materials were *SO* toxic, that each of the individual ingredients were so toxic that they pretty much start killing a person as soon as they come into contact with them. Each chemical was deadly toxic by themselves, but in combination the danger level was off the charts.

After two decades, I got the answer I was looking for... I did miss out on the crazy wages those guys earned, but I had been alive the whole time with really good health long after the program was over.

What you *don't* get might be better than getting what you do want.

And it might take a really long time to find out why you didn't get what you thought you wanted.

So, in the meantime,

someone is going to be the next five-figure, monthly earner…

why not you?

Final Words

Although there really are a ton of scams out there and it seems like for every legitimate business there's ten other scams and frauds, there are those of us who pride ourselves on truly helping people, and improve the lives of everyone we touch.

Nowadays, you have to do your due diligence, collect all your questions and get all your questions answered. That's not too much to ask and we offer that.

There is a company that offers so much, it's hard to believe, but we're in good standing and have a triple star rating with the Better Business Bureau, are owned by a conscientious billionaire, who has a track record of helping your everyday person become financially independent, while improving their personal health and all those involved.

You can join for a relatively small investment and on 10-15 hours each week, launch a home-based business that will provide a couple hundred to a couple-thousand-dollars each month, earn free travel, free cars and many other perks.

Or, you can use the same amount of time and energy to expand a into a multi-million-dollar business that provides a five-figure monthly income…it's up to you and what you want. At any time, you can give yourself a raise and you set your own schedule, working from home with your phone and lap top, or simply meet people at your local coffee shop. You Choose!

You can expect good training, an easy-to-follow training program and you can expect to make a lot of new friends and acquaintances while maintaining your current family, friends and relationships. The old style of doing business doesn't exist any more and the internet has made the entire world your neighborhood!

We work as teams, so you're never alone or by yourself. You don't have to do anything by yourself until you feel ready and excited to. Learn by watching and listening to the people who know how to build a successful, home-based business fairly quickly. Everything that works all together in one place.

And by all means, even if you aren't interested in earning great income and feeling better, share this information with the people who do want it!

We love referrals!

If there's anything we can do to help you feel better, lose weight, have more energy or improve your health, reach out to us ! We're happy to help and have hoards of testimonials from our satisfied customers! All of our products are 100% guaranteed, so there's no risk.

Pre-application Questionnaire

Do you want more income?   Yes____ No____

Do you want more free-time?   Yes____ No____

Would you like a free company car to drive every two years?
                                                              Yes____ No____

Would you like to travel the world, *first-class*.
and take your family with you, for free?   Yes____ No____

Have you found what you're looking for, or
are you keeping your options open?   Yes____ No____

Do you have 10-15 hours each week to make
this happen?   Yes____ No____

Are you open to looking at some information via
email, videos, etc.?   Yes____ No____

Would you or someone you know be interested in
healthy weight loss?   Yes____ No____

Are you interested in sports performance?   Yes____ No____

Would you like to have more energy?   Yes____ No____

Does anyone you know want help with digestive
problems or allergies?   Yes____ No____

Would you like to decrease how often you catch
colds and are sick?   Yes____ No____

Do you or someone you know want to feel better,
this month?   Yes____ No____

Does someone you know want support with children's health?
                                                              Yes____ No____

*Feel free to email or text your answers
to me, to the email address posted in the appendix.

Appendix

Sovereign Valentine

E-mail: sovereignmv@gmail.com

Business Overview Websites:

http://3steps.createmyfuture.com

http://3steps.brilliantmoney.com

Fat-loss Products:

http://fatlossresults.180yourfuture.com

Annual Shaklee Trips 2018:

https://www.shaklee.tv/2018-shaklee-dream-trip

Shaklee trips 2019:

http://www.shaklee.tv/shaklee-dream-trip

https://images.shaklee.com/u/how-to-earn-the-dream-trip/story_html5.html

Shaklee Car Program:

https://www.youtube.com/watch?v=5fnkc3D-bH4